MP3
POWER!
WITH WINAMP

WRITTEN BY
JUSTIN FRANKEL,
DAVE GREELY, AND
BEN SAWYER

MP3 Power! with Winamp

Library of Congress Catalog Card Number: 99-62265

ISBN: 0-9662889-3-9

5   4   3   2   1

Educational facilities, companies, and organizations interested in multiple copies of this book should contact the publisher for quantity discount information. Training manuals, CD-ROMs, electronic versions, and portions of this book are also available individually or can be tailored for specific needs.

MUSKA & LIPMAN

Muska & Lipman Publishing
2645 Erie Avenue, Suite 41
Cincinnati, Ohio 45208
www.muskalipman.com
publisher@muskalipman.com

This book is composed in Melior, Columbia, Caflisch Script, Muzak, and Courier typefaces using QuarkXpress 4.0.4, Adobe PhotoShop 5.0, and Adobe Illustrator 8.0.

Credits

Publisher
Andy Shafran

Editorial Services Manager
Elizabeth A. Bruns

Development Editor
Benjamin Milstead

Copy Editor
Tonya Maddox

Technical Editor
Stephanie George

Proofreader
Audrey Grant

Production Manager
Cathie Tibbetts

Cover Designers
Dave Abney
Michael Williams

Production Team
DOV Graphics
Dave Abney
Stephanie Archbold
Michael Williams
Linda Worthington

Indexer
Cary Sherman

About the Authors

Justin Frankel

Justin Frankel founded Nullsoft, Inc. after leaving the University of Utah in 1997. As the primary development and creative force behind Winamp, Frankel helped revolutionize the high-fidelity digital audio field on the Internet. Winamp is in use on an estimated 15 million computers, making it one of the most popular shareware programs ever. Frankel also drove the development of SHOUTcast, Nullsoft's innovative distributed streaming system. SHOUTcast has spawned hundreds of small Internet radio stations, with thousands of listeners worldwide. He is recognized by millions of Winamp users on digital audio, MP3, and streaming audio development. He also likes fast Audis.

Dave Greely

After graduating from the University of Maine in 1989, Dave Greely worked as a sportswriter for eight years at the *Kennebec Journal,* where he won numerous national, state, and regional awards. In 1996 and 1997, Greely worked with Sawyer on a number of projects, including the *Microsoft Internet Strategy Report* for Jupiter Communications, before founding Digitalmill.

Greely is the co-author of *Creating Stores on the Web* and *Creating GeoCities Websites.* He lives in South Portland, Maine with his wife Liz and his 2-year-old son Cameron.

Ben Sawyer

After graduating from New York's Bronx High School of Science, Ben Sawyer attended the City University of New York-Baruch. In 1992 he worked on the campaign staff for Clinton/Gore '92. He later worked on political projects for several major campaigns, as well as a Legislative Reapportionment and on the news analysis staff for then-President Elect Bill Clinton. In 1995, he returned to his home state of Maine and began a career as a high-tech freelance writer for a number of magazines and newsletters.

In 1995, Sawyer wrote his first book—the *Ultimate Game Developer's Sourcebook*—which was published in early 1996. In June 1997, Sawyer and co-founder Greely started Digitalmill, which performs book, research, and periodical work in the computer industry. Sawyer also founded Next Big Thing, which handles public relations, media relations, and Internet marketing for small software companies.

Sawyer has authored or co-authored several books including *Creating Stores on the Web* and *Creating GeoCities Websites.*

Dedications

To Mom
        —Justin Frankel

This book is for Beth, and Martha, both of whom make me smile by laughing with me, and at me.
        —Ben Sawyer

To Barbara, who will always be my little sister no matter how old and gray.
        —Dave Greely

Acknowledgements

Thanks to my parents for letting me live my life the way I have. APC (I think, it was so long ago) for my first MP3. Dmitry Boldyrev for getting me to start Winamp. Tom Pepper for keeping a constant interjection of Llama humor (oh, and for all that network crap) Robert Lord for helping me pick those low-hanging fruit and start planting more. Rex Manz for the Zen. Jennifer Spencer for putting up with long nights of coding SHOUTcast. Jake Stine for getting out of his basement once in awhile. Steve Gedikian for showing me how great cutting off Seal in a Sentra is. Brennan Underwood for his "it isn't done yet" religion. Cody Oliver for the bandwidth and the ride in the back of his RX-7. Ben Sawyer and Dave Greely for putting up with my busy schedule and writing this book.
                                        —Justin Frankel

Documenting a technology as hot as MP3 and a product like Winamp is not as easy as it seems. Thank you to the legion of fans and musicians who have made MP3, Winamp and SHOUTcast the successes they are. This book wouldn't exist if so many people hadn't been drawn to the power of music on the Internet in a form that is open and powerful.

This book also wouldn't exist without the hard work of the many developers who have made the products discussed here come to fruition. This includes the staff at Nullsoft: Tom Pepper, Rob Lord, Jennifer Spencer, Dana Dahlstrom, and Charles Frankel. It also includes the people behind the products at Xing Technologies, MPEGtv, Virtual Turntables, JJ McKay Productions, and MusicTicker. A special thanks to Mark Surfas at GameSpy Industries for keeping us up to date with MP3Spy.

We also need to thank the legions of programmers and artists who have created technologies that extend the power of the Winamp system. We thank all the developers who created plug-ins, as well as the skins and plug-ins contained on the CD-ROM that comes with this book. We'd also like to thank the folks at GoodNoise, especially Steve Grady for providing us with some great music to share with you, and for Lincolnville and The Piners for adding a few additional songs to the mix.

We want to heavily thank Justine Clegg of Digitalmill who kept us on track, and Matt Barker, our hardcore helper who added immense value to this book.

We can't forget the people at Muska & Lipman Publishing. A very special thanks (and congratulations on her engagement) to Elizabeth Bruns for not going crazy with what we put her through. In the midst of it all, she managed to make sure this book got done—and done right. Thanks to Dave Abney for his help with Toast. We'd also like to thank Ben Milstead who developed the book and gave us great suggestions to make the book better. Thanks to Andy Shafran, our publisher, who stuck through this project with the enthusiasm that was nothing short of amazing.
                                        —Ben Sawyer and Dave Greely

Contents

Part II Advanced Winamp

Part III Digitizing Audio

Part IV MP3 Radio and More

Introduction

Introduction

The following are several important concepts that you will learn in reading this book:

▶ Why MP3 technology is so popular

▶ Detailed technical info on both Winamp and MP3

▶ How to set up your own Internet Radio Station

▶ The basics behind digital audio

Readable and Friendly Text

As you read this book, you'll find we don't gloss over difficult subjects nor do we assume you understand all sorts of new terminology. Instead, we give you complete explanations, step-by-step techniques, and comprehensive coverage of all the features found within MP3 and Winamp.

By the end of this book you will feel comfortable and knowledgeable about MP3 technology, and have a solid reference for future use.

Conventions Used in This Book

As you read, you will find several different conventions that highlight specific types of information that you'll want to keep an eye out for:

TIP
Text formatted in this manner offers extra information related to the issue being discussed. You'll find personal anecdotes and experiences, specific design techniques, and general information extras in "Tip" boxes.

CAUTION

Actions and commands that could make irreversible changes to your files or potentially cause problems in the future are displayed in this manner, as "Caution" material. Also included are possible security concerns. Make sure you read this text carefully as it could contain important information that directly affects your files, software or hardware.

NOTE

Notes present interesting or useful information that aren't necessarily essential to the discussion, but provide additional material to help you avoid problems. Notes also offer advice relating to a specific topic.

Keeping the Book's Content Current

You made a long-term investment when you purchased this book. To keep your investment paying off, we've developed a companion Website for you. The site contains:

▶ Up-to-date information on the world of MP3

▶ Corrections or clarifications to the book's text and images

▶ New resources you can use to stay on the cutting edge

▶ A free electronic newsletter with new and unique articles delivered monthly

Essentially, this up-to-date Web site is your one-stop shop for this book, so take advantage of it!

Stop by at:

http://www.mp3power.com

Or, if you'd like to send e-mail to the production staff or authors directly, we'd love to hear from you. Your input and comments are critical to making sure this book covers all the right information in an easy-to-use manner.

Part I

The MP3 Experience

1

The History of MP3

The media has most often been the catalyst that moved recorded music from the studio to the listener's ears. This process has undergone a radical transformation. There was a day when vinyl—those big, black discs—dominated music. As recording technology progressed, everyone realized that vinyl albums had a number of drawbacks. To skip a song, you had to walk over to the turntable, pick up the needle, and drop it gently into the desired groove. If you weren't careful, you could scratch the record and ruin its performance. Vinyl records were fragile: drop them and they broke, leave them near heat and they warped, scratch them and they skipped. Heck, just jumping around the living room to your favorite Elvis tune might cause the needle to jump from "You ain't nothing ..." to "...all the time!"

Then there were tapes—the eight-track variety (which quickly became a retro collectors item) and cassettes, which began to dominate the market because of their size (you could put Deep Purple in one pocket and Led Zeppelin in the other), playability (you could pound your fist on the wall to the tune of "Iron Man" with nary a skip), and recordability (why listen to the weak songs on a record when you can make a mixed tape?).

For the past few years, compact discs (CD) have been the dominant medium. Nearly indestructible and offering pristine (too pristine for some ears) sound, one of a compact disc's few drawbacks is that it has not been a recordable medium at a mass-market level. Since the debut of the CD, several other new mediums have been introduced. This includes DAT (Digital Audio Tape), which was originally held up due to concerns about copying. DAT has grown slowly in popularity but has been very popular among tapers of concerts and musicians. The mini-disc had a horrible beginning when it was originally positioned as a new medium for pre-recorded music. Sony was the only major producer of mini-discs and thus the other music companies didn't support the format and it faltered. However, it has been somewhat successfully repositioned as a good format for recording concerts or making mix tapes of music for personal portable playback. Despite their gains, none of the post-CD formats has caught the world by fire...until MP3 came along.

So where does that leave us? With MP3, a way to encode, distribute, and listen to music that has revolutionary ramifications.

What Is MP3?

MP3—short for MPEG Layer 3—allows you to store music or other audio files on a computer disk so that the file size is small, but the quality is near that of a compact disc. Without the compression of MP3, a one-minute CD-quality recording would take up more than 10MB of disk space. MP3 compresses most sound files 10 times or more.

In other words, you can download music files from the Internet and listen to them while taking up a fraction of the space otherwise required with little or no injury to the sound quality. Playing MP3 files requires a player such as Winamp (**www.winamp.com**) or MacAMP (**www.macamp.com**).

NOTE

Although very basic and lacking in features and flexibility compared with Winamp, the Windows Media Player (starting with Internet Explorer 5 and Windows 2000) also plays MP3 files, in addition to other audio file formats including .WAV, .AIFF, and RealAudio.

MP3 was created as an extension to the MPEG format, an openly developed standard for compressing and transmitting video and audio content over networks—be it satellite, phone, wireless or even the Internet. The MP3 technology was primarily developed by engineers at the Fraunhofer Institute in Germany. MP3 is an ISO (International Organization for Standardization) standard, which means it is not controlled by any single private organization, but is defined very clearly and cannot change without ISO's approval. Fraunhofer and Thompson Consumer Electronics, however, do hold certain patents and commercial rights on the MP3 technology. For more on the creation of this format, see Chapter 2, "Inside the MP3 Format and Players."

MP3 as a format is useless in and of itself unless a device or program is created that allows people to use the format. MP3 also requires fairly fast, powerful PCs to enable the compression (called **encoding**) and decompression making the format usable. As fast Pentium chips became prevalent alongside the Internet, MP3, a format that had existed in design for some time, began drawing interest. Two enterprising people—Dmitry Boldyrev and Justin Frankel—began creating players that helped the format explode on the scene. MP3's wide support and ease of use, coupled with free, yet quality playback software, quickly caused a swell of support. That support exploded in the summer of 1998, and by the fall of that year, MP3 was becoming ubiquitous in digital music and garnering headlines in every trade journal, computer magazine, and eventually every mainstream paper and magazine in the country.

Winamp

Winamp was born in April 1997, shortly after Justin Frankel left the University of Utah (although the seeds of the idea were planted during his stint at the university). After Macintosh aficionado Dmitry Boldyrev began working on a MP3 player for the Macintosh, his friend Frankel decided that writing Winamp would be a good way to learn Windows programming.

In his senior year in high school and early in college, Frankel had worked extensively with 3-D graphics, primarily in DOS and Linux.

"In March of 1997, Dmitry told me he had an MP3 player he made on the Mac," Frankel said. "A couple weeks [later] I quit school." At the time, Frankel hadn't officially started work on Winamp—but having been opened to the world of MP3 through Boldyrev's player, Frankel's future was set in motion.

Boldyrev's MP3 player, the MacAMP, used a **ported** (re-coding from one computing platform to another) version of amp (a freely available decoder) as a decoding engine, so Frankel decided to do the same for DOS (which was the programming environment he was used to at the time). He created DOSamp. Since most people were using Windows 95 at the time, nothing much came of DOSamp and Frankel didn't pursue anything for it, as well.

The first version of Winamp was simply a floating title bar with a menu that allowed users to have basic playback functionality. That was Frankel's "sixth or seventh" Windows program and, he says, "it just kind of grew from there."

That first basic Winamp (version 0.20) took Frankel about a week to create as he grew accustomed to programming on a Windows platform.

Initially, there wasn't much special about Winamp. It wasn't the fastest player and didn't have the most features. The competition was Winplay3 (the fastest) and MuseArc (the most features). People began to catch the Winamp bug around the time of Winamp 0.97, which pioneered all of the standard features of today's MP3 players. Winamp 0.97 had a nice, non-Windows user interface, a graphical equalizer, a modeless playlist editor that allowed users to edit the current playlist, a little spectrum analyzer, and a number of options. It also coupled these unprecedented new features with a fast decoder and a good performing, skip-resistant output system. Other MP3 players lacked this.

Although Frankel didn't know much about the Windows Application Programming Interface (API) at the time, he had a solid background in C and x86 assembly, as well as 3-D graphics and sound hardware programming. He constantly phased out old code throughout the 1.x series of Winamp as he found more elegant solutions.

Winamp's evolution was primarily fueled by a growing user base—thousands of music lovers who just *had* to get their two cents in—that requested specific features. Things such as Visualization plug-ins were triggered by constant requests for full-screen visualization from users. The ability to customize the Winamp user interface and graphics (known as "skins") was created because people were doing it anyway (by modifying the images in Winamp). As people came up with good ideas, the ideas eventually found their way back to Frankel and into the next Winamp release.

The Legal Issues of MP3

MP3 is a file format that can be used legally or illegally. This analogy explains it best: Cars are legal but using one to run someone over is illegal. MP3 is legal when used to encode music from your own CDs—*if* you keep that music to yourself; much like making your own cassette copy of a CD or another tape or record. It is illegal to encode MP3s and trade or sell them to others unless you have the permission of the music's copyright holder. In other words, if a record company or band makes MP3 files available for download, they are yours for the taking (but not to give or sell to others). However, converting your new Hole CD to MP3 and then offering that as a way for people to get the music without buying the actual CD is illegal.

Another way that MP3 has been used legally and with growing popularity is to post live concert recordings on the Internet for free download. Bands such as the Grateful Dead (before Jerry Garcia's death), Blues Traveler, Phish, Pearl Jam, Primus, and many others allow fans to make audio tapes of their concerts. The fans quickly built tape-trading communities. However, many of these tapes were being turned into CDs and sold for enormous profit by unscrupulous bootleggers—bands are cracking down on this practice. Today, tape trading is moving to MP3s, but bands are trying to maintain the altruistic underpinnings that allow these types of recordings to occur in the first place.

With MP3 becoming more popular and more widely available, many Web sites are now dedicated to posting live songs or even entire concerts in MP3 format. In fact, sites such as **MP3.com** and **goodnoise.com** are quickly becoming the Web equivalents of major record labels. Artists who publish their music on the Web via MP3 files have exact control over what is published. The cost to a listener willing to pay for Web-delivered MP3s is typically much lower than buying a CD in a retail store.

Everyone wins in this instance. The fans get to hear the music they want (and might otherwise never hear) and the artists get the exposure that the concerts offer while undercutting the bootleg CD market.

A Look at the News

1998 was a tumultuous one for MP3. The format, already gaining popularity with music fans and musicians, received some coverage when three high-profile artists saw previously unreleased songs posted in MP3 format on the Internet. The following sections cover some of the more important news and separate the fact from the hype.

Leaks Everywhere

Web sites everywhere posted songs by artists large and small for some time, but in December 1997, the term MP3 became well-known—not just to those versed in technology but to readers of the mainstream music media. Four of the most popular artists in the world—Pearl Jam, Madonna, U2, and Alanis Morissette—had unreleased songs leaked to the public on the Internet through MP3. Publicity generated through released MP3s could become a dominant form of publicity that major labels may eventually garner from the MP3 format on the Internet.

A radio station in Syracuse, NY began playing cuts from Pearl Jam's unreleased album *Yield* nearly three months before the album's release. A number of Web sites posted the songs. Long after the band's loyal fans had ample opportunity to download the songs, Epic Records searched for MP3s of *Yield* and had as many of the songs pulled as possible. While the record label and the Recording Industry Association of America quickly hopped on the anti-MP3 bandwagon, none other than Pearl Jam guitarist Stone Gossard told online music news source *Addicted to Noise* that he was flattered so many people cared about hearing new music from his band.

By the time a Los Angeles radio station played an unreleased Morissette song in March 1998, she was just the latest superstar act to have a song leaked to radio and eventually released worldwide thanks to the Internet. As *Addicted to Noise's* Chris Nelson wrote, "It's a scenario that has become almost as commonplace as mosh pits at rock shows: A song is recorded, it's leaked to radio, and hours—or even minutes—later, it's broadcast to the world via the Internet by enterprising fans..."

Here Comes the RIAA

Not surprisingly, the RIAA (the Recording Industry Association of America), a group that represents record labels, began a crusade against MP3 in the spring of 1998. The group said it would go to whatever lengths necessary to stop copyright infringement. On May 5, the RIAA filed lawsuits against a pair of Web pages, feeling that the previous cease and desist letters sent did not deter Web page creators from posting illegal MP3 files.

That summer, yet another star act found themselves with a hit song on the Internet. "Intergalactic," the first single from the long-awaited new Beastie Boys record, was available in MP3 format for free download. There were no cease and desist orders and no RIAA lawsuits this time. The Beastie Boys had posted a remix of "Intergalactic" on their official Web site, thus taking advantage of the immediate worldwide distribution and promotional capabilities of MP3, giving the format a boost in the process.

Feeling that stopping people who posted illegal MP3s wasn't enough, the RIAA attacked the entire format in October 1998—including listeners of completely legal MP3s, artists who wanted to distribute their music through the format, and Diamond Multimedia. The RIAA filed an injunction to prevent the sale or distribution of Diamond Multimedia's **Rio**, which is a Walkman-like device that allows users to listen to MP3 files without being anchored to their computer.

It was part of a lawsuit filed by the RIAA on the grounds that the Rio violates the 1992 Audio Home Recording Act, which says that manufacturers and distributors of digital recording devices must pay a royalty to help offset lost revenues from the illegal copying of music. Diamond maintained that the Rio is a player, not a recording device, meaning that it would not be subject to the Audio Home Recording Act.

A California judge granted a 10-day restraining order but then declined to issue a temporary restraining order that would have prohibited the sale of the Rio. The judge ruled that the Rio was a recording device but said that the RIAA failed to establish that the Rio would not satisfy the requirements of the AHRA. In December 1998, Diamond filed a countersuit against the RIAA, claiming anti-trust and unfair business practices. As of April 1999, no further actions have taken place.

Here Comes the Rio...and More

Despite the recording industry's objections, and with the restraining order gone, Diamond began shipping the Rio, producing 10,000 of the players a week. According to *Addicted to Noise*, the early reception was good; many retail stores quickly sold their initial shipments. As of April 1999, Diamond said it had shipped 200,000 units to various retail and distribution partners.

NOTE

The Rio, which has no moving parts and is about the size of a deck of cards, was the first commercially available portable MP3 player. Initially sold for $199.95, the Rio is capable of storing up to 32 minutes of digital-quality music and up to four hours of voice-quality audio downloaded from the Internet. A single AA battery powers the Rio for up to 12 hours of continuous playback. An add-on flash memory card is also available in a 16-minute configuration (16MB) for $49.95 and a half-hour configuration (32MB) is available for $99.95. A Serial Copyright Management System (SCMS) was incorporated into the Rio to address the concerns of the RIAA over copyright protection.

In December 1998, Diamond announced that it intends to participate in the Secure Digital Music Initiative that is charged with developing a music technology aimed at becoming an industry standard. Diamond joined record labels and technology and consumer electronics companies in the initiative.

Instead of sitting idle and watching Diamond own the portable MP3 player market, a number of companies moved in. Among them are Creative, Varo Vision, and Koreu Media. In late January 1999, word began to leak that software giant Microsoft was preparing to enter the fray as well.

Winamp: The Future Stereo Platform Is Software

Perhaps what MP3 and Winamp show us most of all is where we are headed with music playback. Until recently, people used a specialized piece of audio hardware when they went to play a piece of music. That hardware was analog based; digital hardware eventually took over. Now we have the ultimate in digital audio—high-end computer processing power that lets us create a software-based audio listening platform.

At the center of this platform will be software (such as Winamp) that is so malleable that it acts almost like an audio operating system. Once loaded into Winamp, songs are simply played back. The file, however, allows you to do much more than just play it. With a program such as Winamp and the power of your computer, you can mix that audio with other audio bytes or make the music sound as if it were being played in a stadium or concert hall. You can store it and have the player learn the songs you most often want to hear, or perhaps strip out any one specific sound. Music will become a living application.

As you can see, the computer will become the next stereo. In fact, some people are going out and purchasing low-priced PCs, installing huge hard drives on them, and then setting up gigantic Winamp playlists. By networking it to their other computer and then connecting this system to their own speaker system, these intrepid users are completely ditching their stereo systems and replacing them with the future, where software is the stereo. The CD for this new stereo system is MP3.

To do this effectively, sound cards in PCs will have to get better and better. Creative's Sound Blaster Live, a great lower-end card, is becoming quite popular. For the true audiophile, higher-end sound cards from companies like Antex (**www.antex.com**) and Turtle Beach (**www.voyetra.com**) are becoming increasingly popular as people begin to turn to their PCs for true audio enjoyment.

The Future of MP3 Power

The future of MP3 is not just about changing the way individuals listen to music; it's also changing the way we think about selling music, discovering new bands, and packaging music. This doesn't just have to do with headlines about people who are trading **ripped** CD tracks (tracks taken directly from a CD and encoded in the MP3 format) of their favorite artists.

As in many other industries, the amount of product and content has been artificially controlled by the means that get it to market. There weren't millions of self-published writers prior to the Web. Previous to the WWW, you needed thousands of dollars in order to distribute your own newsletter, magazine, or book. When the Web came along, the cost of publishing your own work plummeted. MP3 brings the same power and promise to how we digest music, or any form of audio-like spoken word.

With the power of an open format and the Web, any artist can freely post high-quality tracks of his or her own creation. Once posted, either for free or sale, anyone in the world can show up to purchase it—all without having to incur the extra costs that come with distributors, packaging, and publishers. The result is a wider variety of music, better opportunity for lower prices, and the chance for the artists to eliminate the people and system that stand between them and their audience.

Will MP3 destroy the world of music as we know it? Will products such as Winamp change the way we listen to music? Yes and no. There will remain a need for record companies to help pick out and nurture the best of the best musical artists, and we'll still need hardware to produce the sounds, store the files, and run Winamp. In the end, however, MP3 brings computer users a system that allows us to quickly access and support the music we care about in ways never before possible.

With MP3, an open format, and players such as Winamp (which enhance the fun and capabilities of the MP3 format), the power in music will not solely shift from one particular group to another. This isn't about flipping the power structure on its head, as some would lead you to believe. MP3 allows—much like the Web has—for the power of a medium to spread itself more evenly among everyone who has a stake in it. Instead of the power being strictly with radio, record stores, top-tier acts, and record companies, MP3 puts the center of power more evenly among those groups and the listeners, new acts, and other stakeholders as to where the world of music and audio will go.

This is the promise that MP3 gives us as a community of music listeners, producers, and lovers. As you'll see in this book, those who have embraced the concept of an open musical format—Nullsoft, the makers of Winamp, MP3.com, Chuck D, GoodNoise, Diamond Multimedia—are reaping the benefits. They are embracing not just the format, but the community and the shift to a community-based system of music development.

As the Web has proven in other mediums, a strong sense of communal development can cause an extremely healthy explosion of alternative ideas, progress, and individual empowerment that everyone can benefit from. Call it an audio or musical renaissance of sorts; we will see a revival of artistic progress and achievement. The power to join this renaissance is right here.

Fighting with MP3 Power
An Interview with
Chuck D of Public Enemy

The leader and co-founder of Public Enemy, **Chuck D** is known as much for his outspoken personality, political activism, and willingness to discuss a wide range of societal issues as he is for his powerful, distinctive vocals. Public Enemy allowed Chuck to voice his opinions through a medium—rap music—that has become an increasingly important force in American culture. Chuck once dubbed rap, "black America's CNN." If that's true, then Chuck has certainly been the respected anchorman.

In addition to his music, Chuck recently released his first book, *Fight the Power: Chuck D on Rap, Race and Reality* and is in the process of developing the Internet's first 24-hour rap site, Rapp Station—Hip Hop Nation. His social involvement includes "Rock the Vote," the National Urban League, the National Alliance of African American Athletes, the campaign for National Peace, and the Partnership for a Drug Free America. Most recently he has become a leading proponent of MP3.

Born Carlton Ridenhour, Chuck D was introduced to MP3 by the Webmaster of Public Enemy's Web site (**www.public-enemy.com**). "We definitely wanted to embrace MP3 because we're down with changing the way the whole music business operates."

We were fortunate enough to get Chuck on the phone for a discussion on MP3.

Q *Tell me about Bring Tha Noize 2000.*

A: Bring Tha Noize 2000 was actually a finished CD as of around March of 1998 and eventually we [decided that] we wanted to put it out because it has been around since March of 1998 and Polygram didn't release it and Def Jam didn't claim it. We thought it was a perfect situation to release on MP3. We released two cuts a week. There was an industrial megamix of past Public Enemy hits with three unreleased songs on it. The first two songs on it were "There Were More Hype Believers Than Ever in '97" and the "Welcome to the Terrordome X-Games Remix," and it kind of alerted people that we had some fresh product out there. We looked at it as no different than a record company putting out 10,000 promotional albums. Let's alert the world that this exists and embrace this technology that we're going to use in other areas.

Q *The record label wasn't too keen on it.*

A: Yeah, they don't know what's going on and they're paranoid. Usually this comes from the legal department or the executives. When you don't know a lot about something there's a fear of that process. They look at the five-year fear. Right now MP3 can work as a perfect promotional system but legal teams and executives look at it as making them eventually obsolete . . . it has that possibility. I don't think that potential will ever be reached, but I think a large part of it will change the way the industry will have to think on giving the music to the people.

Q *So they're going to have to change the way they work.*

A: Everybody will have to change the way they work. For example, the day of the demo as we know it now can be eradicated. If you have a studio guy making demos in Cleveland, why send them to LA and New York looking for the major record deal? Put them up and he has his record company...and maybe that buzz can be built that way.

Especially if that person in the past would have to get $5,000 to get his CDs made up and send them out to all the affiliates and make that hard software [software distributed via CD or tape] and depend on someone else to build that buzz for them in the industry. Now you don't even have to go to the point of making hard software until it's time. It's something where they have a studio, they can cut [record] an artist, and the artist can be out for the public in the next week. Like back in the days of the 45 when distribution was wide open. But now with so many artists, it's cluttered, retail is cluttered, and there have to be new avenues opening to the public and why not? I think the public has been ripped off because the majors [labels] have mastered the…CD technology where they can make it for as little as 80-something cents.

Q *And look who owns the CD plants—Sony.*

A: Right [laughs]. So retail buys it for $10.50 and sells it to the public for $14.00–$17.00; what constituted that? The lawyers and the executives constituted that so they can make 300%–400% profit, seven-figure salaries and even eight-figure severance pay. The day of the green is gone and that's what makes these guys paranoid.

Q *How does MP3 allow you to go around radio stations that weren't in your favor to begin with?*

A: Radio is the middle person to get to the public. We're setting up **bringthanoise.com** and **slamjam.com**, which is an inactive label, as well as **public-enemy.com**, which is the hub to check everybody into these zones. MP3 and the Web is heaven-sent for a situation like Public Enemy. . .the majors are caught now, "If we have an artist, we have to spend money to promote and market the artist," and with the glut that exists out there now, their problem is that, "Do they keep the artists and keep investing money in their name or do they let the artist go and they've invested the money in their name but they automatically become a competitor in this new field?" So they have all kinds of dilemmas, but understand that they're a whole different animal. This works perfect for PE.

Q *What about Slam Jam?*

A: Slam Jam—I moved it out of Sony. I run some studios in Long Island and Atlanta. We're an inactive label but when we cut and something's hot, believe me it's going to be out to the world the next week [via MP3]. Maybe the first two years we won't sell things, but the artists understand that it's accomplishing something getting the artist out to the public. Eventually it might be a zone where people go in and pay a membership fee of $5.00 or maybe $10.00 or $15.00 or $20.00, depending on how strong the label is and what you have is a modern version of record clubs, which is why the majors will probably look at MP4 in the future because they won't be able to stop it. They have to take whatever comes. If the majors are smart, they will look at it as a perfect piece. It will change the way they think, but look at video. Videos have been money losers for companies, but if people are able to go up into the zones and program themselves with the video and get into the art, that's the best of a lot of people's worlds.

The singles will probably have to be given away and maybe people will really work hard to have their album promoted through all kinds of means and people will pay for the albums.

Q *Haven't singles been money losers for the record companies? At least that's what they say.*

A: Singles are money losers because they don't really do well over the course—that's what they say. Retail can't stock singles, that's the problem. So the singles are pretty much given to retail so they can continue to buy albums from the particular company. Retail can't build more space and Moms and Pops are being ripped off because they have to buy the CDs for a higher price. In layman's terms, if the public can get into a zone through a computer and get an album at up to $5.00, why in the hell would they spend $12.00 for it? That's just common sense.

Or better yet, if you're putting 25 of your favorite cuts on there for $5.00, the day of the $5.00 album is going to come back and right now the majors are trying to figure out a way to adjust to that.

Q *What about the line in typical contracts that deals with universal rights? Do universal rights include cyberspace rights? What kind of advice do you have for up-and-coming artists with MP3 possibly giving them more power?*

A: The thing about it is, don't give your Internet rights away, make 'em pay for 'em and don't let them have them for life. Get your rights back and also make them understand that that's a change in environment.

Q *Where do you see yourself and MP3, MP4, or MP5 five years from now?*

A: I see MP—whatever it is—being influential and instrumental as much as 20%–30% of the market. I see 300,000 independent labels out there. I see the majors having their super sites with people going up there with credit cards and . . .[with] $30.00 or whatever and being able to get all the product that is available to them. Futuristic record clubs. I see the demo as we know it eradicated. A&R people [the staff who find and sign bands for labels] will definitely have to change the way they operate.

2

Inside the MP3 Format and Players

Is MP3 a file format or a movement? In many ways it is both. What started as a simple compression scheme for sound has, in fewer than two years, become a movement to create and distribute music electronically in a quality form. This chapter examines the MP3 format itself, discusses some of the major players (including Winamp), and examines how this previously obscure format has rapidly become one of Internet's hottest phenomena.

Inside the Format

MP3 as a format was born in Germany, where the Fraunhofer Institute for Integrated Circuits IIS-A created it as part of an advanced audio and video signals compression development scheme. Fraunhofer scientist Dr. Karlheinz Brandenburg, who had worked on audio coding techniques for 15 years at Fraunhofer, developed the coding method for MPEG Layer 3. MPEG Layer 3 follows previous efforts dubbed Layer 1 and Layer 2, respectively. While both compressed audio, they didn't do so as greatly as Layer 3 does.

MP3 is the first widespread, high-quality audio file format small enough to be comfortably sent and received via the limited speed of a typical 33.6kpbs modem. Other formats (such as RealAudio) significantly decrease the sound quality to achieve their small file size and real-time streaming capabilities. .WAV and .AU files offer excellent sound but are too large to transfer effectively. MP3 answers the quality vs. file size conundrum by attempting to compress the file size with no discernable difference in the sound.

Perceptual Audio Encoding

As a format, MP3 is known as a **Perceptual Noise Shaping** or **Perceptual Subband/Transform Coding scheme**. To get technical for a second, according to Fraunhofer, the scheme analyzes "the spectral components of the audio signal by calculating a filterbank (transform) and applies a psychoacoustic model to estimate the just noticeable noise-level." In simpler terms, it analyzes the audio files for only those sounds that are within the hearing range of human ears.

Human hearing can't discern sounds below 20Hz (**Hz** is cycles per second) or above 20,000Hz. Even within that range, the capabilities of normal human hearing aren't equal. Loud sounds that take up more frequency tend to mask out quieter, similar sounds. The people at Fraunhofer who commented on the Layer 3 specification knew this and therefore sought to incorporate these physical aspects into their work. Understanding this and other issues concerning human hearing, the Fraunhofer folks knew they could remove much of the information in a sound recording without destroying much of the range to which human hearing responded. The first thing the format does is throw out sounds beyond the frequency range of human hearing. This however isn't a completely great move. While humans can't hear these frequencies, they still stimulate the eardrum and can help the ear hear other discernable frequencies. Still, the overall removal is a great technique for compression without nearly any loss in audio quality.

More redundancy in the audio is created by eliminating the other sound frequencies which are masked by louder more important ones in the audio file. These frequencies, while for the most part inaudible, can help create a fuller sense of sound. This lets you use compression and makes the file size smaller. The encoding scheme then rearranges the sound file in order to meet the actual playback needs. In some audio cases, it may be better to drop the sound quality in order for the file to be smaller, thus have quicker playback over low-bandwidth systems (such as slow CD-ROM drives, satellite communications, phone lines, or the Internet). This appreciation for the needs of lower bandwidth playback is the reason MP3, as a technology, is focused on strong compression and has been so successful in the Internet age.

In short, rather than actually compress the specific bits of audio that make up a sound wave, the scheme evaluates the audio signal and tries to create a facsimile of the sound wave that "tricks" the ear into thinking it is listening to the original sound. By encoding audio in this manner rather than through other compression methods, MP3 is able to produce an incredible 12:1 compression ratio on near-CD-quality music. The MP3 format tries to maintain the original sound quality as much as possible, but it does so in a way that also lets it sacrifice minute enhancements in exchange for the compression that keeps the file size small.

Crash Course in Bit Rates, Sampling Rates, and Frequency Rates

To understand the MP3 format more—or any audio format for that matter—it pays to understand the relationship between bit rate, sampling rate, frequency/bandwidth, and file size.

MP3 becomes especially important to the MPEG (Motion Pictures Engineering Group) system in that it is engineered to work well at extremely low bit rates. The **bit rate** is how many bits of information are transferred per second from the file. As you increase the bit rate of a file, that file should be bigger because the ability for the file to send more information at any one second is greater as you increase the bit rate; thus, more information is needed. Think of it as widening a water pipe. The bigger the pipe, the more water it can transfer, the larger the amount of water in the pipe. The more water in the pipe, the closer the sound quality comes to that of the original sound. It is possible to transfer more information when a file has a larger bit rate setting, which really means you can offer recordings that have playback sound quality closer to that of the original sound.

Sound quality for any digital recording is based on several factors, all of which affect the file size. One factor is whether the sound is recorded in stereo or mono; **Stereo** sound records two separate waveforms for each channel (left and right), while **mono** combines both the left and right channels into one single stream of information. Thus, stereo requires twice as much information in a sound file than mono does. Another factor is whether you record the file using 8-bit or 16-bit sampling range. The higher the sampling size, the lower the background noise can be. CDs are recorded at 16-bit sampling. Dropping the sample size to 8 bits per sample while compressing 2:1 will noticeably add nasty background noise.

TIP

The MP3 format doesn't concern itself with issues related to sampling rate size. This is because MP3 files are created by converting raw sampled files. Thus, MP3 files rely on what the original sound file source used for a sampling range size. Most MP3 decoders, however, are optimized for 16-bit output. For more on this information see Chapters 8, "Digital Audio," and 9, "Creating Your Own MP3 Files."

The third issue is the frequency at which the sound is sampled. The higher the sampling rate, the higher the frequencies that can be reproduced. CDs use a 44100Hz sampling rate. For example, dropping the sampling rate to 11025Hz (for 4:1 compression) reduces the ability to reproduce high frequencies such as cymbal hits.

MP3 steps into the picture because the better the compression, the more information you can squeeze through at smaller bit rates. **Table 2.1** shows this dramatically. Notice how, as the compression level of each layer improves, it takes increasingly lower bit rates to actually transfer through music of the same stereo quality.

Table 2.1–
Compression levels
for MPEG Layers

MPEG Layer Version	Compression Ratio	Bit Rate Needed for CD Stereo Delivery
1	4:1	384kbps
2	8-6:1	256–192kbps
3	14-10:1	128–112kbps

Source: Fraunhofer Specs

Without the compression of MP3, we couldn't have small enough files to transfer over the Internet and still maintain the near-perfect quality of the original recording.

Table 2.1 however, tells only half of the story. The same compression level of the Layer 3 scheme can also help create incredible compression levels on sound files with lower-than-CD quality characteristics. **Table 2.2** shows how encoding sound files in the MP3 format at a lower frequency quality and with or without stereo, will result in even higher reduction ratios.

This is what enables Winamp's SHOUTcast Radio (**www.shoutcast.com**) system (see Chapter 12, "Creating Your Own MP3 Radio Station: SHOUTcast and Beyond"). That system lets users broadcast lower-quality audio over the Internet in real time. While the sound is lower quality, the technology of the Layer 3 format lets you stream higher-quality audio at lower bit rate than many other compression schemes.

Table 2.2–MP3-encoded sound files with and without stereo option

Sound Style	Frequency	Stereo (Y/N)	Bit Rate	Compression Ratio
Phone	2.5KHz	No	8kbps	96:1
Better Than Shortwave Radio	4.5KHz	No	16kbps	48:1
Better Than AM Radio	7.5KHz	No	32kbps	24:1
FM Radio	11KHz	Yes	56kbps	26–24:1
Near CD	15KHz	Yes	96kbps	16:1
CD	>15KHz	Yes	112–128kbps	14–10:1

Source: *Fraunhofer Specs*

Table 2.2 shows that Layer 3 can squeeze any level of sound quality down tremendously and that, for a given bit rate, you get a very high-quality sound due to the compression.

More Details

For the real bit heads who are interested in the format, here are some additional points to understand:

▶ **Same Encoding Approach Is Used by All Layer Types**—All versions of the Layer format (1, 2, and 3) use the same basic analysis approach and perceptual noise-shaping scheme to achieve their compression. This is what allows all files encoded in earlier layer formats to be decoded by players conforming to the MP3 spec. Of the three layers, MP3 is the one that provides both the highest compression and quality.

▶ **Header and Embedded File Information**—All Layers (1, 2, and 3) have header information embedded in the file format to explain specific file characteristics such as the bit rate and recording level. The formats, including MP3, also support insertion of associated **metadata** (data that describes what the associated data is) or other useful information. In the case of MP3, this includes the commonly found ID3v2 tags that describe song title, artist name, and so on. See the "The ID3v1 and ID3v2 Formats" sidebar for more information on this aspect of the MP3 file format.

THE ID3V1 AND ID3V2 FORMATS

Layer 3 as an MPEG specification does very little to describe how information about the characteristics of a file should be defined. This is mostly because the Layer 3 designers really decided to leave that work up to others. This is because they focused only on the compression and not necessarily the application of the format. In terms of MP3 files, the format has been extended in this area by some enterprising developers and has resulted in what are commonly referred to as ID3 tags. ID3 tags are an important part of the MP3 file format because the MP3 community has more or less adopted them.

Currently, there are several versions (successive formats actually) that have emerged from the original work of one developer, Eric Kemp, who created a simple information structure that lets users attach information to an .MP3 file. Kemp's original idea was to append an 128-byte tag to the end of an MP3 file. This 128-byte tag is divided as shown in Table 14.2 to identify the name of the song, album, the year it came out, the genre, and a comment field.

As with any good idea, someone came along and made it better. Noticing that a track listing was missing, Michael Mutschler, the author of MP3Ext, created an extended version of the original ID3 specification that included a way to insert track listing information. This derivative of ID3 was named v1.1 and is the main variant used until recently.

The biggest problem with the ID3v1 formats is that they're constrained by the 128-byte limit. The comment field alone is no bigger than 30 characters, which isn't much if you want to include information such as lyrics, album covers, and more in the file. We needed a much more dynamic format—one that could be much more conducive to where digital music and MP3 are headed. This is where Martin Nilsson stepped in and, with the help of others, has developed the ID3v2 spec.

ID3v2 takes over where ID3v1 leaves off—and it's quite an ambitious offering that will allow MP3's or any digital music format that commits to it to include a heavy dosage of information such as Web links, album photos, lyrics, artist notes, and more. Aside from size and scope, ID3v2's dramatic difference is that rather than be placed at the end of the MP3 file, it is placed at the beginning of the stream. This means it is a true header-style format. The theory here is that the ID3v2 tag can work better as a header in streaming MP3 situations (such as SHOUTcast).

Not every player is fully supporting the ID3v2 specification at this time. For the moment, Winamp is in the preliminary stages of offering support. As you'll see if you look at the field structure for ID3v2 (available on **http://www.id3.org**), there is a lot of programming needed in order to support much of the data an ID3v2 tag can offer. It is also suggested that there will be an alternative to the ID3v2 proposal, although it is likely that much of the original intent of the tag system will be kept while the technology implementation itself will be changed. In order to create ID3 tags you'll need an editor and know how to use it. This is explained in detail in Chapter 9.

As it stands, ID3 tags are a major part of the MP3 file format. The support exists mostly for ID3v1.1 and in the future it may be ID3v2 or a similar higher-end tag scheme.

Fraunhofer Extensions "MPEG2.5"

While the original Fraunhofer MP3 format is the ISO standard, there is a little-known derivative usually referred to as MPEG 2.5 (or MP2.5). Fraunhofer developed it as an extension to the MP3 format and named this as extension MPEG 2.5. It is a specialized implementation of the MP3 file format that supports low bit rate encoding of audio files.

While MP2.5 is not part of the ISO specification for MP3, it is supported in whole or in part by some of the popular players, such as Winamp. Why is this extension useful? If you want to encode audio at 8KHz, 11.025KHz, or 12KHz, at bit rates of less than 16kbps, you would use an encoder and player that supported these extensions. These bit rates are useful for speech and other recordings that don't need the fidelity of a musical recording.

Format Quality?

An important issue that has been widely debated but is not very well understood is the quality of the MP3 format and music files stored as that format. Experienced MP3 users will certainly understand that by the very nature of its design, MP3 files aren't as good as other storage means for music (such as CDs, .WAV files, or even highly tuned vinyl). Understanding some of the reasons for this will give you further insight into the format itself. In Chapter 8, you will learn even more about digital audio in general, which sheds further light on the raging quality debate that pervades not just digital formats but all forms and styles of music.

As great as it is, MP3 does have some limits. By using a perceptual encoding scheme, MP3 is what is known in compression speak as a **lossy** format. As stated earlier, MP3 as a format throws out a lot of the high and low frequencies in a sound file. It also throws out a lot of duplicate frequencies found in an original format. This is done to achieve better compression. Formats that don't do this are known as **lossless**. However, as has been pointed out, lossless formats such as .WAV files are huge compared to MP3 files.

MP3's foremost limit is that the sound quality, while excellent, isn't perfect. Anyone who has made or listened to MP3s and then listened to the original uncompressed digital recording can certainly hear some differences in the tonal quality and fidelity. However, these are very acute differences that, for most purposes, are negligible.

A number of other things can affect the quality of an MP3 file. This includes the process used to digitize the original sound/music file, the quality of the encoding program, the quality of your sound card, and the specific settings under which the MP3 is saved. In Chapters 8 and 9 you will find much more direct information about how to tweak the quality of your MP3s as it relates to these issues.

Not all computer sound cards are created equal. The same can be said for the speakers you use. Many audiophiles run their computer's stereo out to their home stereo system for peak performance. Others may purchase high-end computer speakers.

How do you overcome the quality issues of the MP3 format? You can learn from Chapters 8 and 9 how to make the best MP3 recordings possible. You can also purchase a good pair of speakers and headphones.

TIP

Winamp provides a built-in feature that can help improve the quality of MP3s—the graphic equalizer. Many sound cards (and other issues surrounding digital audio) tend to flatten out certain frequency ranges. This can give an MP3 a thin, tinny sound. You can improve the sound by adjusting and balancing these frequencies with the graphic equalizer in Winamp. For more details on these issues, see Chapter 6, "Advanced Winamp Configuration Guide."

Sorting Through the Format Confusion

For even the semi-serious MP3 fan there is some confusion as to exactly where MP3 falls among the many iterations of the overall MPEG architecture. MPEG is an acronym for the Moving Picture Experts Group, an industry standards group working in conjunction with the International Standards Organization (ISO) and the International Electro-Technical Commission (IEC). They develop open standards for the coding and moving of pictures and audio over communications networks (including the Internet) and recordable media (such as CD-ROM). The group sets the goals for what each version of MPEG should contain and then, having evaluated proposals and schemes submitted by other companies, works to create an endorsed standard for that specification. Every so often it announces a new version of the standard, which comes about mainly as newer technology allows for improved versions of MPEG.

The first version of MPEG (MPEG-1) was approved in 1992. It was followed by MPEG-2, which was first approved in 1994 with subsequent additions and modifications coming onboard in later years. The MPEG-4 spec was first approved in 1998 and will eventually become the new standard in multimedia audio and video encoding. What happened to MPEG-3? Isn't that what MP3 files are?

MPEG-3 is not the same as MP3. MPEG-3 was supposed to be the successor to MPEG-2 and define the specification used for HDTV (High Definition Television). However, that effort was eventually dropped as MPEG-2 proved sufficient.

What we call MPEG-3 or MP3 is actually a subset of the original MPEG-2 specification. Technically speaking, MPEG-3 files are actually Layer 3 files, which are part of the original MPEG-1 and MPEG-2 file formats. Layer 3 is the third version of a group of three audio coding systems that has accompanied the MPEG standards. As developed, each layer is increasingly more capable of producing higher-quality sound and higher compression ratios. Also as developed, each format is compatible with the versions before it. An MP3 Decoder can also decode files stored as Layer 2 or Layer 1 files.

The Layer 3 file format also includes more advanced feature improvements over the previous Layer 2 version. The frequency resolution is 18 times higher, which allows a Layer 3 encoder to suppress noise (pops and hisses) that can come from the encoding method. In addition, Layer 3 has improved stereo sound coding methods.

MP4, AAC, VQF? What's After MP3 and Is It Better?

As good as MP3 is, and as much as it is improved over Layers 2 and 1 technologies, it certainly isn't the be-all, end-all format for music on the Internet—or is it? Competing and superior technologies are quickly coming to market; these include the next-generation MPEG audio or MP4. Newer compression systems such as AAC (which is actually a similar, improved MP3 that performs about twice as well) and VQF are also out there. Many of these formats are indeed superior to MP3 in terms of any number of characteristics. However, by the nature of how much software supports it and the number of files bands have been releasing in the MP3 format, the issue will be this: Are these new formats so superior that they might dislodge the MP3 format from its lofty position? Right now most people don't think that will happen as quickly as backers of other technologies think (or hope) it might.

The good thing is that great players such as Winamp, while primarily known as MP3 players, utilize a decoding engine plug-in system that lets them swap in and out multiple decoding engines so they will support formats above and beyond MP3. Chapter 13, "Alternative Formats to MP3," covers a number of alternative formats to MP3 and how to use your Winamp player to play those and other common multimedia audio formats (such as .WAV and .MIDI). **.WAV files**, of course, are uncompressed audio files. **MIDI files,** on the other hand, are a string of notes and other descriptive information that allow the sound card to reproduce music using its internal synthesizer capabilities. Think of this file format as digital sheet music as opposed to a digital recording.

The Players

At last count there were more than 100 different players for MP3 files. They can be found across every major computing platform, including BeOS, Linux, and even Windows CE. Of course, not all players are created equal. While there are many choices available, it pays to identify the leading players on each platform and know a bit more about them.

Winamp

www.winamp.com

As the title of this book suggests, Winamp is the leading MP3 player. It is the king of all players because it does so much more than just play back MP3 files. It is important to know how Winamp compares to other leading MP3 players available for Windows or other platforms.

Winamp is a Windows-only product. There are two versions of Winamp. One version supports Windows 95, 98, NT for Intel processors. The other version exists specifically for Windows NT for Alpha processors. In terms of Windows players, none comes close to the level of support, add-ons, and features of Winamp. While there are several other notable players, such as Sonique from Night55 (**www.night55.com**) and MusicMatch from MusicMatch (**www.musicmatch.com**), Winamp remains the favorite player of nearly any respectable MP3 fanatic with a Windows-based computer.

Windows Media Player

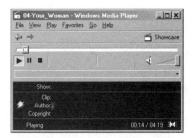

www.microsoft.com

While the true fans use Winamp, Microsoft gave MP3 files a huge boost when it released the latest version of the Windows Media Player. This is because the newest version included support for MP3 files. While other media-playing giants, most notably Real Networks, just added support MP3 files, Microsoft charged forward and added it to its player. The Microsoft Media Player is fairly basic, so it's not much of an alternative to Winamp. It does mean that if you're producing your own MP3s, you will find that any basic user with the Media Player installed will be able to listen to them.

MacAMP

www.macamp.com

MacAMP was actually created by Dmitry Boldyrev at about the same time as Winamp and supports Layers 2 and 3 formats. As it has grown, the player now also supports CD Audio and MOD Q formats. The software is now developed by a company called @Soft, which is the official developer of MacAMP. The product is sold as shareware and there are two versions—MacAMP 1.0 and a new version—MacAMP Lite.

MacAmp supports skins and plug-ins as well. If you own a Macintosh, this is the player to get.

FreeAmp (Linux)

www.freeamp.org

FreeAmp is an MP3 player being developed as an open source project by three developers. **Open source projects** are programs created and offered for free, including access to the program's source code. Developers can then modify the source code in any way they want as long as they donate their improved code back to the community of programmers developing the program. While a version of FreeAmp exists for the Windows platform, it is overshadowed by Winamp. It also exists for the Linux platform where it is a leading player.

If you own a Linux-based system, FreeAmp is an excellent player. For Windows users who have Winamp, FreeAmp is useful only if you want to learn about programming MP3 decoding systems.

Xaudio (Various Unix)

www.xaudio.com

Xaudio is an MPEG3 audio decoding engine developed by MpegTV (**www.mpegtv.com**), a leading developer of MPEG tools. The company was founded in 1997 and the founders, Tristan Savatier and Gilles Boccon Gibod, have worked on various MPEG-related software. The company has developed an MP3 decoding program that is available for a wide range of platforms. Unlike some of the other players mentioned, Xaudio has versions of its software for a wide range of Unix operating systems.

The Xaudio MP3 Player for Unix is available for every flavor of Linux, Solaris, SGI Irix, AIX, Digital Unix, FreeBSD, and OpenServer.

Xaudio for Windows CE

www.xaudio.com

MpegTV has ported its Xaudio MP3 software to be used as a player for WinCE devices. WinCE is used to power palmtop computers such as the Philips Velo or Casio Cassiopia. Depending on the sound, RAM, and processor power of your WinCE device, you can use the Xaudio player for WinCE to create a portable MP3 player.

From Format to Movement

The beginning of this chapter posed the question of whether MP3 was more of a movement than a file format. What grew out of a project to create a new updated format for compressed audio has evolved from Fraunhofer's Layer 3 technology into a burgeoning industry and community that has rallied around and extended the entire idea of what an MP3 file is. In fact, what was once the moniker and file extension of a just another file format has grown to a technology used by millions of people and is on the verge of revolutionizing the entire music and audio industry. MP3 is now almost tossed around as a phrase more than the file name, and as players such as Winamp spread and people create add-on technologies such as ID3 tags and streaming radio systems, the term is being used to brand a whole industry of pioneering digital audio technology.

MP3 is a format, but to think of it strictly as just a format is truly missing the point of what it has actually become.

3

Your First MP3 Experiences

While many of you are experienced MP3 listeners and Winamp users, some of you may need some help getting started. This chapter is for you. This chapter discusses several things to help you through…read on to:

▶ Discuss the hardware you need for playback

▶ Find out where to locate and how to install Winamp (the top MP3 player for Windows) and MacAMP (the top MP3 player for the Mac)

▶ Find an MP3 file at MP3.com, save it to your desktop, and play the song

▶ Cover the basics of listening to a Winamp SHOUTcast

▶ Discuss the Rio player

Before Beginning: Hardware Issues

MP3 players exist for nearly every platform, including Windows, Macintosh, Linux, and more. (See Chapter 2 for a complete listing of the available players.) Regardless of which player you choose, you'll need a relatively powerful computer to play MP3 files with ease.

For Winamp, you need a computer running Windows 95 or later that is at least a 486/100MHz machine, although it is recommended you have at least a Pentium processor. You need at least 8MB of RAM and a 16-bit Windows-compatible sound card. Various plug-ins for Winamp may have their own separate requirements, including MMX or a 3DFX card. See Chapter 7, "All About Winamp Plug-Ins: How to Configure the Leading Plug-Ins," for more details.

For MacAMP, its developer, @Soft, recommends a Power PC Macintosh computer running at least System 7.5, with at least 16MB of RAM and preferably 32MB or more. If you have a non-Power Mac, one with less than 100MHz or less RAM, consider the newly released MacAMP Lite at **http://www.macamp.com/lite/**, which requires less CPU power.

You should also have a good set of audio speakers or route your sound through your stereo; if you're going to build up a sizable collection, make sure you have a decent amount of hard drive space.

TIP

If you plan on putting together a large archive of MP3 music, consider purchasing a CD-R (CD-ROM recorder). Once almost exclusively the domain of businesses that could afford it, CD-Rs (and blank CD-ROM media) have evolved to be both affordable and relatively easy to use.

NOTE

MP3 decoding—which is essentially what all MP3 players do—needs so much computational power that if you use an older processor (first-generation Pentium and earlier) and minimum RAM (16MB or less), you will find it difficult to run other processes while playing MP3 files. You may experience skipping or erratic playback and your other applications may run slowly. Upgrading is the only solution for this; currently a Pentium 200 or better machine (or a Power Mac) is more than capable of playing back MP3s while allowing you to simultaneously run additional software.

Downloading Winamp

If you are a Windows user, you'll want to dive into the world of MP3 by downloading and installing Winamp. The following steps show you how:

1. Go to Winamp's home page at **http://www.winamp.com (Figure 3.1)** and click on the Download button to get the latest version of Winamp.

Figure 3.1
The Winamp home page.

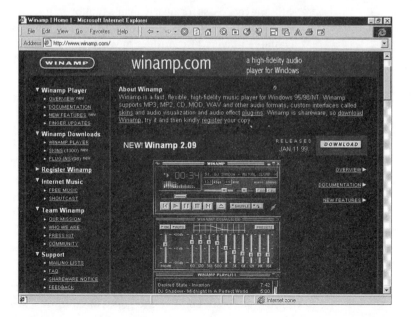

2. The Winamp Download page (**Figure 3.2**) asks that you read the shareware license by clicking on the corresponding link. After you have read and agreed to the license, you can begin downloading Winamp.

Figure 3.2
The Winamp
Download page.

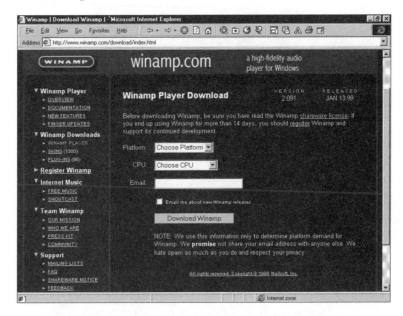

3. Using the drop-down menu, choose the correct platform (Windows 95, Windows 98, Windows NT) and CPU (Intel Pentium, Intel Pentium II, AMD K6, AMD K6-2, Cyrix, DEC Alpha, Don't Know/Other). Enter your email address and click on the Download Winamp button.

NOTE
According to Winamp, the information you supply is used only to determine platform demand for Winamp and your email address will not be shared with any other parties.

4. You are presented with a number of Winamp download locations. Choose one that pertains to your location and click Download.

5. The File Download window (**Figure 3.3**) appears. Choose Save This Program to Disk and click OK.

Part I   The MP3 Experience

Figure 3.3
The File Download
window allows you to
save Winamp to disk.

6. The Save As window allows you to save Winamp on your computer.
    The file will download when you click Save. You receive a
    Download Complete message when Winamp is finished
    downloading. Click OK.

You saved Winamp to your desktop (**Figure 3.4**). There it is!

Figure 3.4
The Winamp icon on
your desktop.

Installing Winamp

Now that you have downloaded the latest version of Winamp, you must
install it on your computer:

1. If you have downloaded Winamp to your desktop, which makes it
    easy to find, double-click on the Winamp icon to begin the
    installation process. If you have downloaded Winamp to another
    location, open it as you would any other application with Windows
    Explorer.

2. The Winamp Installer window opens. It includes a message that
    Winamp is shareware and that it is your responsibility to register it
    after 14 days of evaluation use. You can set the suggested folder to
    install it in. Click Browse to choose a new directory. Click Next to
    continue with the install. Next the installer presents five major
    configuration questions (**Figure 3.5**) concerning how Winamp installs:

Figure 3.5
During the Winamp
installation, you are
presented with a screen
of installation options.

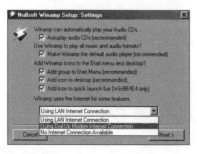

—Check the **Autoplay Audio CDs** if you want CDs inserted into your player to automatically play once the CD drive has cleared.

—Check **Make Winamp the Default Audio Player** option if you want Winamp (upon installation) to play many of the major computer audio formats (including .WAV, .MID, and formats other than .MP3). You can individually select the file types to play once the program is installed (see Chapter 4 for more information).

—The next three options deal with where startup icons appear to launch Winamp. You can choose to have icons for launching Winamp setup in your Start Menu, Desktop and the IE4/W98 Quicklaunch bar. Just check off the options you want.

—Finally tell Winamp your Internet connection type, LAN, or Dial-up modem.

—Click Next once you've answered everything.

3.   The final install screen concerns personal information you can send to Nullsoft. Nullsoft uses this information to inform you of updates and other Winamp news as well as for statistical information used to fuel advertising sales for its site (which helps Nullsoft fund further development of the player). You can fill out this as you wish and check whether you want information sent to you or not and never to be asked for this information again. Click Next when done and Winamp will finish installing and launch.

Finding and Playing an MP3 File

So you have your Winamp player—what else do you need? Some music would be nice. Chapter 5, "Where to Get MP3 Files," offers a number of places where you can find MP3 files.

NOTE

When Winamp installs, it will load up its demo.mp3 file that you can play to test the program and make sure it's working correctly. This four-second demo was recorded by voice over star JJ McKay (**www.jjmckay.com**) and proclaims how great Winamp is.

MP3 is one of the most searched-for phrases on the Internet and there are countless sites offering MP3 files—some legal, some not—for download. One of the best is GoodNoise (**www.goodnoise.com**). The GoodNoise home page is shown in **Figure 3.6**. There are several free GoodNoise tracks included on the CD-ROM with this book. You can easily browse and play the MP3 songs found there.

Figure 3.6
The GoodNoise
home page.

GoodNoise, which is covered in more detail in Chapter 5, offers a number of musical options, including downloading entire albums or individual tracks by participating musicians (for a price far less than buying a full CD or a single). While, like many Web sites, GoodNoise may change its procedure for downloading music, many of the emerging legitimate MP3 music sites are using a similar method for distributing MP3 files. While this exercise is specific, it provides a good illustration how GoodNoise and other sites will generally operate. Like GoodNoise, most sites will have both free and for sale tracks. As a first experience however, choose a free sample track:

1. Click on the Free Tracks link (on the left side of the page) or find an album that offers a free sample track.

2. Here you can choose a full listing of tracks or look at new releases by clicking on the corresponding link. Full Listing has been clicked; the offerings have been perused, and for this demonstration Frank Black was selected by clicking on the artist's name.

3. The artist page of GoodNoise includes review snippets, links to related stories and, of course, the opportunity to buy or sample music. **Figure 3.7** shows Frank Black tracks available through GoodNoise. A former member of the band called "The Pixies," you can find a complete Frank Black track on this book's CD-ROM

Figure 3.7
The Frank Black
track list.

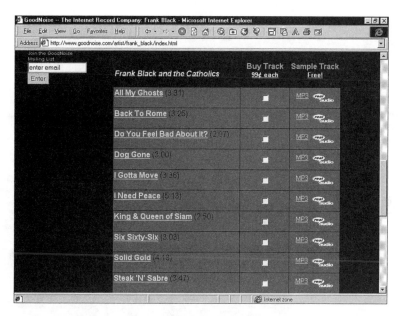

4. As the screenshot illustrates, on GoodNoise you can purchase a track for 99 cents or sample a track as an MP3 or in Real Audio. Choose to listen to the free sample track of "I Need Peace" or some other track by clicking on the corresponding MP3 link.

5. On GoodNoise, the "I Need Peace" lyrics appear with links to sample and to purchase the song. Click on the corresponding link to sample the song. Choosing Sample will give you a sample of 30 or so seconds.

6. If you like the song, you can go back and buy it. To buy the song, click on Buy and follow the procedure.

7. Either create an account or log in if you have already created an account.

8. Follow GoodNoise's instructions and the track is yours!

You can also save your free sample track or other free MP3s by right-clicking on them. Save the sample of "I Need Peace:"

1. Right-click on Sample.

2. Choose Save Target As.

3. The Save As window opens, allowing you to save the file as you would any other.

Finding and Installing MacAMP

So you have a Macintosh, not a PC. Not a problem! In fact, one of the first MP3 players was MacAMP. Downloading MacAMP from the MacAMP home page (**Figure 3.8**) is easy.

Figure 3.8
The MacAMP
home page.

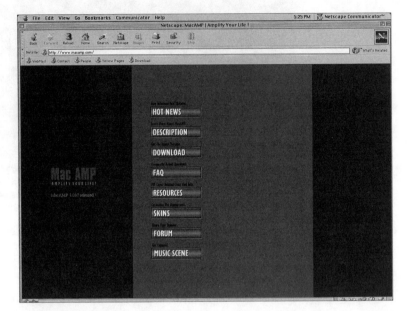

1. Go to **www.macamp.com**.

2. Click on the Download button.

3. The site offers several ways to download it, depending on your connection and Mac computer type. Choose the method you wish to use to download the software. **Figure 3.9** shows that MacAMP 10b7; MacBinary (720k); Mirror has been clicked. Depending on your Internet connection speed, it could take a few minutes to download and expand the application.

4. Double click on the MacAMP application icon to launch it.

Figure 3.9
Downloading MacAMP.

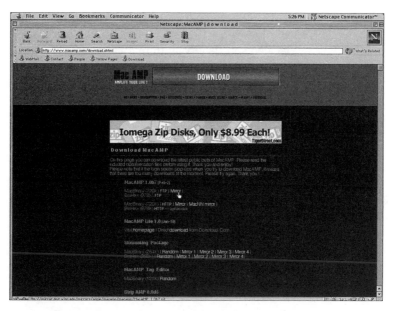

Playing an MP3 with MacAMP

As we noted above, MP3 files are all over the Internet. For this exercise, we went to MP3.com (**Figure 3.10**) to find some music. Before moving forward ensure that your browser is properly configured to use MacAMP to play MP3 files. By default Netscape Navigator doesn't necessarily know which helper application to use to play back an MP3 file.

Figure 3.10
The MP3.com
home page.

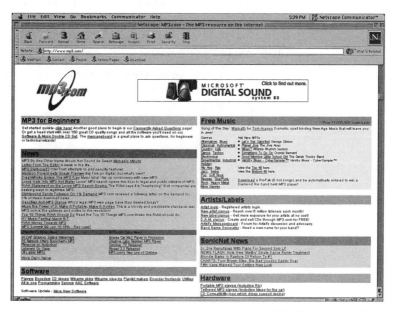

Go to MP3.com's, MP3 for Beginners-FAQ page (**http://www.mp3.com/faq/**) and follow the Netscape configuration instructions. The instructions are located specifically at: (**http://www.mp3.com/faq/mndefault.html**). **Figure 3.11** shows the preferences screen in Netscape Navigator that you will need to go to to set or change the MP3 default player. Essentially you are telling your browser to launch MacAMP whenever you encounter an MP3 file on the Internet.

Figure 3.11
MP3 is the default player.

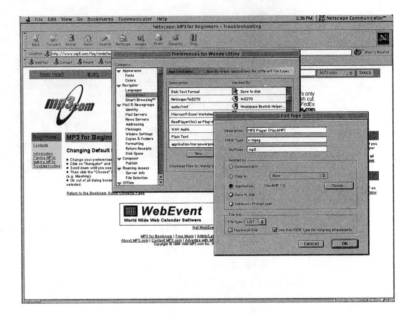

Follow these instructions to change your preferences. Note also that in the preferences screen of your Netscape Navigator browser, you may also choose where you want your downloads to go by clicking choose and navigating to the folder you want to specify.

1. To find a song, go to **www.mp3.com** and start browsing. Check out the Online Top 40 chart or browse through your favorite genre (**Figure 3.12**).

Figure 3.12
Browsing through
MP3.com.

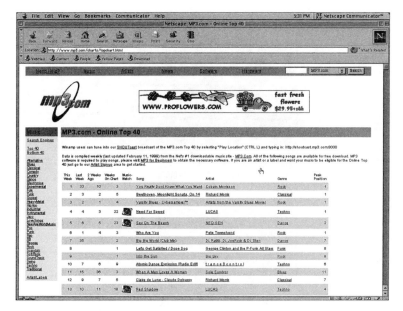

2. Choose the Get MP3 option; the song downloads to your chosen location. (You may at some point be prompted to download RealPlayer. If so, simply follow the on-screen directions if you do not already have it.)

3. Download to your chosen location several samples of songs you might like to hear.

4. To play a song, launch MacAMP. Upon launching, you are prompted to accept the terms of the MacAMP unsupported public beta preview; do so by clicking on Accept. Under the Window menu, check Player, Playlist, and Eqs. This includes MacAMP's built-in equalizer.

5. Drag your selected songs to the Playlist box (**Figure 3.13**).

Figure 3.13
The Winamp playlist.

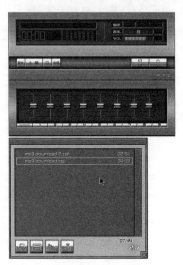

6. Highlight the song you want to play, place your cursor on the Play button, and click! You will hear your selection and experience the beauty of MP3.

Downloading and Listening to MP3s on the Rio PMP300

Diamond's Rio PMP300 is the first portable MP3 music player for under $200 that stores up to 30 minutes of digital-quality sound (and more if you purchase optional memory boosting cards). It's smaller than an audio-cassette and has no moving parts, so it never skips. Powered by a single AA battery, Rio provides up to 12 hours of continuous music playback. As of this writing, the Rio currently works with Windows-based PCs because it requires a parallel port to communicate with the device. In the future as new versions of the product ship, and as other companies get involved with creating portable MP3 players, a USB version compatible with the Mac is expected to debut.

Installing the Rio Software

The Rio player comes with a CD-ROM that contains the PMP300 management software. A menu should automatically come up if you have an AutoStart CD-ROM player. If that's not the case, open the Windows Explorer and tune it to your CD-ROM drive. The software will install when you double-click on the Setup.exe program.

The software also offers you the option to set up the MusicMatch JukeBox MP3 software. This software includes both an encoder and a player so you can convert your CD collections to MP3 for downloading into the Rio. While the encoder is decent, there are other encoders out there— such as Xing's—and the Winamp player offers a lot more functionality.

> **TIP**
>
> You can download the Rio management software from **www.diamondmm.com/products/drivers/rio.html.**

One common complaint about the Rio is that it doesn't come with software that works for platforms other than Windows 95/98. At the time of this writing, however, Diamond had released software APIs and development tools for other companies to create software for the Rio hardware. A number of intrepid software developers has already created utilities for Linux Systems, Windows NT, and more. Many of these programs offer increased functionality over the software included with the Rio. For the more advanced user try RioShell (**http://www.w3.to/RioShell/**). You can also try RioExplorer from 2B Systems (**www.2bsys.com**). Both are also available from C|Net's Download.com site.

Downloading MP3s to the Rio

You are not far from being able to listen to MP3 files on your Rio player. Just a while longer in front of the computer and you will be walking down the street to your favorite MP3 music.

1. Now that you have installed the Rio software and you put it on our desktop for easy access, double-click to open it.
2. Double-click on RioPMP to open the Rio software player.
3. To view the Rio player's memory (**Figure 3.14**), click on the MEM button (on the right side of the Rio software player). If you have no songs on your Rio, the playlist will be empty and you are told that you have more than 32,000K of memory remaining.

Figure 3.14
The Rio software player and memory.

4. There are buttons marked Open, Download, Refresh, Delete, and Initialize on the left side of the Rio's Internal Memory. Click Open to place an MP3 file on the Rio for listening.

5. The Open window appears and at this point you are simply opening a file. Find an MP3 that you have saved on your machine and open it.

6. An image of a disc sailing from a computer to a Rio player (**Figure 3.15**) indicates that you are downloading a song from your computer to the Rio. The name and size of the file will appear on the playlist. Within a minute you will have a song ready to listen to on your Rio.

7. Now that you've done it once, fill that Rio up, disconnect it from your computer, and crank those tunes! It's as simple as hitting the Play button.

Figure 3.15
An MP3 file is transferred from the computer to the Rio.

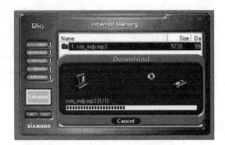

Where to Now?

With Winamp or MacAMP installed, and perhaps a Rio for the power user, you're well on your way to enjoying the world of MP3 music. However, we know you want more—much more. After all, the MP3 revolution and Winamp offer much more than sitting back and pressing Play; there is so much more—from learning the ins and outs of the Winamp player to understanding how to create and market your own MP3s. MP3 power also extends beyond your computer and the Rio. People are already building MP3 systems for cars and as standalone jukeboxes for their corporate networks—or even for their living rooms.

If you're a beginner, you've learned the most important part of your MP3 experience: the software and hardware you need in order to begin enjoying MP3 files from all over the world. Now it's time to move on and find out how to make the most of this powerful new technology.

4

Winamp:
The MP3 Player

What Is Winamp?

When people think of MP3 files and how to listen to them, Winamp is
the answer. But to call Winamp an MP3 player is misunderstanding
exactly what Winamp is. The player's original purpose was to provide
great playback of MP3 files, but the program is much more.

At its core, Winamp is a total cross-audio playback system. What started
as a Windows version of a free MP3 decoding engine has now become a
digital audio playback system that accepts any compatible audio stream,
decodes it, runs it through a special effect filtering process, interprets it
for graphical display, and then plays the final audio via several playback
outlets.

The Shareware System

As for marketing, Winamp is sold via the tried-and-true shareware
method of software marketing. Nullsoft makes the product available for
free download and use but asks that after a 14-day trial period, users
register the software. Essentially you're on the honor system. By using
shareware, Nullsoft has provided millions of users with a player while
letting those who use it most and want to support its continued
development, register the software.

Winamp costs $10.00 (U.S. dollars) per computer for personal use and
$25.00 for commercial use. Registration is available online by secure
credit card transaction or by mail.

The Winamp Screen

The main screen in Winamp is a small console that displays critical data about the song it is playing and lets you control some of the most critical elements of song playback. **Figure 4.1** shows the main Winamp screen and identifies the major elements. Winamp has a very simple look; it's a cross between a car radio and a CD player. The interface is very simple, but there are features that are not immediately obvious, some that even seem hidden. Since the main Winamp screen offers so much, it pays to really understand each specific element to the fullest possible detail.

Figure 4.1
The Winamp faceplate.

Upper Corner Box Menu

There is a small symbol that resembles an audio waveform in the upper-left corner. If you click on this little symbol, a menu that allows the user to change almost every aspect of the Winamp player appears. This same menu can also be pulled up by right-clicking anywhere on the interface (except on the areas that display song information, such as the time or title scrolling areas). Those pull up menus are related to the functions they perform.

This menu is designed to allow new users to easily find features and change the Winamp player's configuration. You compare the features on the Winamp faceplate with each menu function later, when you explore all of this menu's functions (**Figure 4.2**).

Many things that you can do on this menu can be either done through buttons on the Winamp interface or through the use of quick keys. **Quick keys** are combinations of keys such as Alt+L (which pulls up a load song menu). Many quick key functions are listed next to what they do on the main menu for quick reference, or you can check out Appendix D for a complete listing.

Figure 4.2
Winamp's main menu.

Visual Song Display

The visual display in the upper-left corner shows either the time remaining or the length of a song, as well as several interesting graphic depictions of whatever sounds Winamp is playing. This graphical display is often referred to as the **Vis** display (**Figure 4.3**). Right-clicking on the time display pulls up a small menu that allows you to change whether the time display shows the time remaining in the song or the time elapsed.

Figure 4.3
Winamp's Vis display.

The Clutterbar

The Clutterbar runs down the left side of the Vis display. It's a little tough to see depending on the interface colors and skin (especially in the default interface). The Clutterbar displays the letters *O*, *A*, *I*, *D*, and *V* running vertically down the left side—right next to the time display.

All of these functions can be selected from the main menu, but the Clutterbar makes it easy to access the functions from the faceplate.

If you click on the *O*, it brings up the Options menu.

The *A* button makes the Winamp player automatically stay on the top of your desktop, overlaying anything else displayed.

The *I* button pulls up all the information on the current song playing. The MP3 format used to only compress songs now allows a good deal of information to be embedded into the song, including the title, artist, year, genre, and more! Clicking *I* allows you to view and change this information very easily.

The *D* button changes the display size of the Winamp player. For users who run very large desktop resolutions of 1,024×768 and greater, this makes the Winamp interface much more readable.

Finally, the *V* button pulls up the Visualization menu, which allows the user to select plug-ins and other graphics capabilities.

Song Title Display

Winamp has several displays and some buttons that tell about the file playing (**Figure 4.4**) and allows you to pull up some excellent features; these displays and buttons are to the right of the visual display. The top display lists the name of the file and any other information embedded in the file. Right-clicking on this display pulls up a menu allowing you to change file information, jump to another file in the playlist, jump to a specific time in the current song, and turn on and off the autoscrolling of the song name.

Figure 4.4
Winamp's song title display, which includes information on the quality of the recording in the MP3 file.

Recording Quality Information

Under that display, Winamp displays the recording quality of the .MP3. The kbps display shows **kilobits per second** (the rate at which MP3 files are measured); the kHz (kilohertz) display shows the frequency at which the MP3 is being played back. These two items have a reciprocal relationship: The higher the recording quality, the more kbps the file takes to play.

Another factor that can affect how much information is being decoded is whether the recording was made in stereo or mono. A **stereo** recording usually takes twice as much processor power as a **mono** recording simply because the Winamp player has to decode both left and right channels instead of one channel. A lower-quality recording can be recorded at 11kHz or 22kHz, but most are recorded at 44kHz, which (at 128kbps and up) produces near-CD quality.

In Figure 4.4, you can see two displays that are lit up to denote if the file is a Mono or Stereo recording.

Volume and Balance Sliders

There are two slider bars and two buttons under the Mono and Stereo displays. The left slider bar controls the volume of your music, directly changing the wave audio volume in the Volume Control utility on every Windows-based machine. Any change you make in the Volume Control panel will show on the Winamp slider, and vice versa (actually, a lot of sound cards don't update this properly and Winamp will maintain its own independent volume). The second slider bar controls the balance between left and right speakers. This also affects the balance control in the Volume Control utility, making it easy to change or undo any changes right from Winamp.

Equalizer and Playlist Buttons

Two buttons—EQ and PL—sit to the right of the sliders. The first button pulls up Winamp's graphic equalizer, and the other pulls up Winamp's Playlist Editor, which we discuss in depth in Chapter 6.

Play Controls

The most often used controls on the Winamp player are located at the bottom of the Winamp faceplate (**Figure 4.5**).

SONG POSITION BAR

The main play controls and the rest of the Winamp console are divided by the song position bar. This bar indicates the position within the song that is currently playing. Sliding the position indicator allows you to immediately skip ahead or back to a specific point in the song.

Back to track	Skip back to previous song in playlist
Play	Play current song in playlist or resume from pause
Pause	Stop playing but hold current position in current song
Stop	Stop playing current song
Skip to next track	Skip ahead to next song in playlist
Open file	Click to open a new file
Shuffle	Set Play mode: play songs in random order
Repeat	Constantly loop current playlist

Figure 4.5
File play controls.

TIP

One of Winamp's best features is that you can change the program's graphics appearance by using skins, which let you redo the interface graphics. Don't worry: Even though skins change the appearance of the Winamp player, they don't change how the player works. Despite different layouts, every button will work the same. All the interface parts remain constant from skin to skin. Later on in this chapter, we cover how to create or edit your own Winamp skins.

The Graphic Equalizer

Sometimes an .MP3 file, just like any audio recording, might sound better if various parts of the sound spectrum in the file were amplified more. This can help a file add more bass, or treble depending on the frequency range you punch up. Just as on other audio equipment, Winamp provides a graphic equalizer to help you tweak the playback to just what you want.

Making Your Sound System Sound Better

Anyone who has ever used a graphic equalizer knows what an improvement it can make to a stereo's sound. It can do the same thing for your computer. Since not all sound systems are built equally, nor are all listening areas or ears the same, Winamp offers an excellent graphic equalizer (**Figure 4.6**) that allows users to make their computer sound the way they want it to.

Figure 4.6
Winamp's graphic equalizer.

You can access the graphic equalizer by clicking the button on the faceplate that has EQ on it; you can also do so by right-clicking on the faceplate to pull up the main menu. Notice that this equalizer offers a 10-band graphic equalizer with frequency controls ranging from 60Hz to 16KHz.

NOTE

Most human ears can hear sound ranging from the low rumble of a 20Hz wave to the crisp highs at 20,000Hz. Volume of those frequencies can be moved up or down by 20db (decibels), more than most home equalizers, which usually allow users to adjust frequencies up or down by 12db.

The first thing that you need to do is turn the equalizer on. Click the On button in the upper-left corner. Note that the little light on the button is now green, indicating that the equalizer is working.

Load a song and try out the equalizer. The slider can be dragged up or down by clicking on any of the vertical sliders and holding the mouse button down. Note how the line at the top of the equalizer changes to conform to the peaks and valleys of the equalizer sliders.

You will then notice that it takes a couple seconds for changes made on the EQ interface to be audible in the song. That is designed to keep the song playing smoothly as the software adjusts the changed frequencies. The equalizer is an excellent utility to keep running even if you have a slower computer; it doesn't take much CPU power to run.

The first slider on the left of the equalizer faceplate is designed to increase or decrease the preamplification of the equalizer. **Preamplification** allows you to increase or decrease the overall volume adjustment for all of the frequencies of the equalizer from one single slider.

CAUTION

Turning the preamp setting way up will usually result in a distorted-sounding file.

If you like different equalizer settings for different types of music, Winamp's EQ allows you to save and load settings with the Presets button in the upper right. Clicking on the Presets button pulls up a menu allowing you to load, save, or delete an EQ setting. If you find an equalizer setting that you would like to have loaded each time you play a particular MP3 with Winamp, you can save it as an autoload preset. (Enable the Auto Equalizer option by clicking on the Auto button in the equalizer.)

TIP

The equalizer does not currently affect files other than MP3. CD Audio, MID, and other audio files won't sound any different.

The Playlist and Playlist Editor

The third major component of Winamp is the Winamp playlist (**Figure 4.7**). Turn on the playlist by clicking on the PL button, which is on the main Winamp screen; a green light always denotes when it is being displayed. The playlist consists of the Main List window and its own control console.

Figure 4.7
Playlist Editor.

Creating a Playlist

There are several ways to create a playlist. First, you can just open multiple files when loading new files into Winamp. The player automatically creates a new playlist upon opening multiple files. However, most people create a playlist file by file. To do that, you can use the controls at the bottom of the Playlist window.

There are four major buttons used to manage and create your playlist (at the bottom of the screen); another button lets you load and save existing lists (in the lower-right corner).

TIP
Each button is actually a menu that, when you click and hold down the mouse button, reveals several options. Right-clicking on the buttons will also bring up the menu.

Add File Menu (+ File)

This menu offers three choices: Add File(s), Add Directory, and Add Location. A single click on this button brings up the common Windows Open File dialog box, where you can select and add a file to the current playlist. The Add Directory button brings up the Open Directory dialog box (**Figure 4.8**), where you can work through a directory tree and locate an entire directory of MP3 files and add them to the playlist. The Add Location button brings up the Open Location dialog box, where you can input a specific location on the Web to retrieve either an .MP3 file or tune into a SHOUTcast Server stream. SHOUTcast is Winamp's answer to Real Audio and lets you listen to streamed MP3 files broadcasted over the Web. SHOUTcast is covered in much more detail in Chapter 5 "Where to Get MP3 Files," and Chapter 12, "Creating Your Own MP3 Radio Station: SHOUTcast and Beyond."

Part I   The MP3 Experience

Figure 4.8
Open Directory
dialog box.

Remove File Menu (– File)

This menu lets you remove files from the playlist. You can simply click it once to remove any currently highlighted file on the list; if you've selected multiple files, choose either from Remove Selected to remove all the selected files or Crop Selected to remove everything but the selected files. Clear Playlist clears the entire current playlist.

Select Menu (Sel All)

The Select All button contains three menu items: Select All, Select None, and Invert Selection. Select All chooses all the items in the list; Select None deselects all currently selected playlist items; Invert Selection deselects current selections and selects all unselected files.

Misc Opts Menus

This button houses a menu with three main selections—File Info, Sort, Misc—all with submenus. File Info lets you call up each selected file's ID3 tag information, and the playlist entry brings up the Playlist Name Editor (**Figure 4.9**). The Editor lets you edit the names of the files that appear in the playlist.

Figure 4.9
Playlist Name Editor.

The Sort submenu offers several choices to help arrange your playlist. The options include Sort by Title, Sort by Filename, and Sort List by Path and Filename. Also offered as choices are Reverse List, which reverses the order, and Randomize List, which lets you randomly rearrange your list order (sort of like Shuffle Play).

The Miscellaneous submenu offers two interesting options. First is Generate HTML Playlist, which generates an .HTML file of your playlist upon execution and displays it in your browser. You can use this playlist to publish to your Web site MP3s that you're listening to or have legitimately available for trading. The Read Extended Info On selection refreshes any additional information from the ID3 tag for the selected file(s).

Load List Menu

This menu lets you load, save, and clear playlists. There are two types of playlists: PLS and M3Us. The PLS format was originally part of the MuseArc program, an earlier player, while M3U was used by the Winplay3 player. The PLS format contains a bit more information, although neither contains a ton of track information.

To clear out and start a new playlist, hold the mouse over the Load List button; either that or right-click on the Load List button and choose New List from the menu.

To save a current playlist, either hold the mouse over the Load List button, or right-click on the Load List button and choose Save List from the menu. You get a standard Windows Save As dialog box and can choose to save in either the .M3U or .PLS format.

To load a current playlist, click on the Load List button. A standard Load File dialog box is displayed, allowing you to choose from any previously saved .M3U or .PLS files.

Playlist Mini Play Control Console

Note that the playlist also includes a miniature playing and time display console at the bottom of the screen. You can use this for when only the Playlist window is displayed. To display the playlist only, right-click on an empty area of the Playlist Editor and then click on the main window (Alt+W) option. You can also press Alt+W or simply hold down Shift and click on Winamp's Close button. The result is that only the Playlist window is displayed on the screen. To bring the main window back, simply hit Alt+W or select Main Window from Winamp's main menu (in the Playlist Editor or equalizer).

The Winamp Minibrowser

New in version 2.10 of Winamp is the addition of the Minibrowser (Figure 4.10). This is a miniature browser that brings up information and Web links relevant to various MP3 files you're playing.

Figure 4.10
The Minibrowser in Winamp offers features, like automatic linking to purchasing the album of a file you're listening to on Amazon.com.

The browser works simply. When active, it will open by default to the Amazon.com page showing a link to the artist named in the MP3's ID3 tag. At the bottom of the box are four icons and text showing the name of the content opened in the browser.

The first two arrows work to let you go back and forward through previous screens displayed in the browser. The red Stop button lets you stop a page from loading. The rounded arrow button is a page refresh button.

The up arrow displays a menu of additional browser options. Most of them are self-explanatory, letting you search for artist information on other sites like Rollingstone.com, and MP3.com. The Update Links menu item lets you update the linking information the browser uses. Choose this item if previous links don't seem to be working properly. The open Internet location lets you open a specific page from the Web in the Minibrowser.

Nullsoft plans to add many more features to the Minibrowser so stay tuned.

TIP
Looking for a cool SHOUTcast radio station? One of the best features of the Minibrowser is the Top 50 SHOUTcast Stations page.

Exploring the Main Winamp Menu

The Winamp main menu has many functions, and while some of it is self-explanatory, some functions require discussion. You can access the main menu for Winamp by right-clicking on the Winamp faceplate. Let's step through this menu item by item.

Nullsoft Winamp

The first menu selection pulls up the Nullsoft Winamp Information menu shown in **Figure 4.11**. If you click on this, a menu that describes Nullsoft and Winamp pops up. There is a series of tabs here that display different information areas.

The first tab, Winamp, has a funky moving Winamp logo, as well as information about Winamp and its copyrights, Web page, and version.

Figure 4.11
The Nullsoft Winamp
Information tab.

Credits is the second tab on the Nullsoft Winamp menu. It details who was involved in the development of Winamp, and it displays a little humorous poetic license toward the end of the scrolling credits.

The third tab is the one that Nullsoft hopes you will use once—when you have realized how great a program Winamp is. The Shareware tab tells you all about registering and allows you to enter the registration code to change Winamp from shareware to a registered version. The Shareware tab also lets you track the Winamp player's usage, allowing users to see how many times Winamp has been used, for how many minutes, how many songs, and how many days it has been used. (This is good if you're not sure if you want to register; it can be pretty scary how much you'll use it.)

The fourth tab is an excellent guide for all the keyboard assignments for Winamp controls. It has All Windows, Main Window Specific, Playlist Editor Specific, Graphical Equalizer Specific, and Minibrowser sections.

The fifth tab in the Nullsoft Winamp Information menu displays a complete guide to the Winamp Internet community. It offers links to all Winamp official pages, such as the Plug-Ins page, Skins page, Troubleshooting, Bug Reporting, FAQ, and others. It offers a complete guide to all the Winamp skin and plug-in sites such as Customize.org, MP3.com's Plug-In section, and Winamp Facelift. It also offers excellent links to sites for music and many MP3 sites.

NOTE
While promised in a future version, Winamp doesn't contain a Help file. There is a standard Help FAQ on the Winamp.com Web site located at **http://www.winamp.com/support/faq.html**.

Play File
The Play File command menu item brings up the Open File dialog box. Use this to load a new file or a group of MP3 files into Winamp.

Open Location
The Add Location button brings up the Open Location dialog box, where you can input a specific location on the Web to retrieve either a file or to tune to a SHOUTcast Server. See Chapter 5 for more on using SHOUTcast Server.

Viewing File Information

This menu item brings up the appropriate information dialog box for whatever file type you are playing. For .MP3 files, that information dialog box is the ID3 Tag Editor as seen in **Figure 4.12.** This dialog box gives you the ID3 information for the MP3 file, which includes song title, name of the artist(s), album, etc. You can add or edit this information and save it.

Figure 4.12
View File Info on an
.MP3 file brings up the
ID3 Tag Editor.

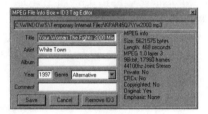

To edit the ID3 tag information, simply enter or edit the information in the fields and save it by pressing the Save button. To clear out and remove ID3 information, click the Remove ID3 Tag button.

Other file types will have their own View File dialog boxes. **Figure 4.13** shows the View File Info info box, which shows you the information that is coupled with any standard .MOD file. **Figure 4.14** shows the View Module File Info info box associated with .WAV files. Unlike the ID3 information associated with MP3 files, the information contained in these dialog boxes isn't editable.

Figure 4.13
The View Module File
Info info box.

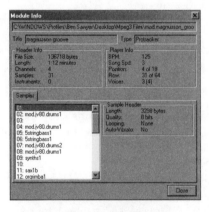

Figure 4.14
The View .WAV File
Info info box.

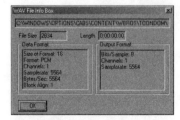

Main Window Flag

This menu item lets you switch between the Taskbar/Collapsed mode and Open Window view for the Winamp player.

Playlist Editor

This option opens and closes the Playlist Editor window.

Graphic Equalizer

This menu item opens and closes the Graphic Equalizer window.

Mini Browser

This menu item opens and closes the Minibrowser window.

Options

This menu item brings up the Options menu, which is explained in depth in Chapter 6, "Advanced Winamp Configuration Guide."

Playback

Playback displays the Playback menu, which features a number of specific menu items, some of which mimic the function of many of the main screen buttons (Previous, Play, Pause, Stop, and Next) as well as some newer options. Most of these are self-explanatory: Stop w/Fadeout, for instance, lets you stop the current song but not in an abrupt fashion. You can use the Back 5 Seconds and Fwd 5 Seconds to precisely skip around a particular song while using 10 Tracks Back and 10 Tracks Fwd to rapidly navigate large playlists. Jump to Time brings up the Jump to Time dialog box (**Figure 4.15**), which lets you jump to a specific time in any .MP3 file; the Jump to File menu item brings up the associated dialog box (**Figure 4.16**), with which you can quickly jump to any file in the current playlist.

Figure 4.15
The Jump to Time dialog box lets you jump to any specific time point in a file.

Figure 4.16
The Jump to File dialog box lets you jump to any specific song in the playlist.

Visualization

This menu item brings up the Visualization submenu, which controls the shape and characteristics of Winamp's built-in scope display. You have a number of ways to customize your scope display.

First in the menu is the Vis mode, where you can choose Analyzer, Scope, or Off.

Next is the Mode menu, which lets you define the type scope to run. You can choose from Normal, a Fire-Styled display, Vertical Lines, Plain Lines, Bars, or Peaks.

The Scope menu defines the style of the scope. The style can be Dot, Line, or Solid Shape.

The Window Shade VU menu defines how the VU display will look when you run Winamp in the Windowshade mode. Choose from Normal and Smooth.

The Refresh Rate submenu defines how fast the scope's refresh will be. Choose from Full, Half, Quarter, and Eighth.

Analyzer falloff can run at various speeds for different tastes. You have five choices: Slowest, Slower, Medium, Faster, and Fastest. Slower falloffs make for smoother movement, faster falloffs provide a more accurate experience.

The Peaks Falloff submenu sets how fast your scope items fall back to 0 after hitting their peak level. You have five choices, ranging from Slowest to Fastest.

Plug-In Menu Items

There are three other menu elements below the main Visualization menu: Start/Stop Plug-In, Configure Plug-In, and Select Plug-In. These menu items control the status of the current visualization plug-in you have selected from Winamp's Preferences section.

NOTE
Plug-ins are covered in much more detail in Chapters 6 and 7 of this book. For now, understand that if you want to start or stop the currently selected plug-in, configure it or select a new one to run these menu choices.

Skins

Skins are the types of features that show why Winamp is simply ahead of most other MP3 players. You can completely change the appearance of your Winamp playing system with **skins**. They don't change the arrangement of key interface items but the graphical look of each element can be customized, as you can see from **Figures 4.17** through **4.19**. There are literally thousands of Winamp skins out there to use with your player.

Figures 4.17–19
Various Winamp skins let you change the appearance of the player to suit your own taste.

Getting a skin is a fairly easy process. There are several sites that lead in archiving skins or you can always create your own. Follow these steps to download and use a skin:

1. Locate a great skin archive like the one on Winamp.com (**www.winamp.com/skins/index.html**) or the 1001 Winamp skins site (**www.1001winampskins.com**).

2. Download a skin upon finding the one you like. Most skins are stored as .ZIP files; save the file to your hard drive.

    Locate the stored .ZIP file and copy it to the Skins directory of your Winamp directory (usually C:\Program Files\Winamp\Skins or similar).

TIP

You can rename the .ZIP file whatever you want, as long as it maintains the .ZIP extension (PureSkin.ZIP would be called PureSkin, for example).

You need to call up the Skin Browser to display a new skin. The Skin Browser is located in the main Winamp menu under the Option menu; you can also get to it by pressing Alt+S. The Skin Browser displays (**Figure 4.20**) a list of loaded skins.

Figure 4.20
The Winamp Skin Browser.

1. Chose a skin from the list; the Winamp screen(s) automatically changes. Choose Close or double-click on a skin listing. Either action will allow you to exit Skin Browser.

2. The Skin Browser window also offers you the option to Select Random Skin on Play, that when checked forces Winamp to load a new random skin each time it is brought up. The Download Skins button opens your browser to Winamp.com's Skin directory; the Set Skins Directory button lets you set the specific directory you want to store and retrieve your skins from. (The default directory upon installation is the Winamp\Skins directory.)

Editing Cursors

To customize all the Winamp cursors/mouse pointers, you need a program that lets you create cursor files. Nullsoft recommends Microangelo (**Figure 4.21**) from Impact Software (**www.impactsoft.com**). This program is fairly straightforward; simply draw the cursor you want and then save it.

Figure 4.21
Microangelo is Nullsoft's recommended custom cursor editor.

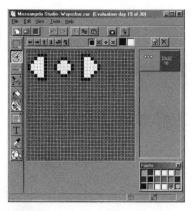

Each cursor is saved as a specific file name as shown in **Table 4.1**.

Table 4.1–The file names for Winamp cursor types

Cursor Type	File name
Close Box Icon	Close.cur
Equalizer Close Box Icon	Eqclose.cur
Equalizer Normal Icon	Eqnormal.cur
Equalizer Slide Icon	Eqslid.cur
Main Menu Icon	Mainmenu.cur
Minimize Winamp Icon	Min.cur
Normal	Normal.cur
Playlist Close	Pclose.cur
Playlist Normal	Pnormal.cur
Position Bar	Posbar.cur
Playlist Size	Psize.cur
Playlist Title Bar	Ptbar.cur
Playlist Vertical Scroll Bar	Pvscroll.cur
Playlist Windows Size Normal	Pwsnorm.cur
Song Name	Songname.cur
Winamp Title Bar	Titlebar.cur
Volume Balance	Volbal.cur
Volume Bar	Volbar.cur
Winamp Button	Winbut.cur
Winamp Close	Wsclose.cur
Winamp Minimize	Wsmin.cur
Winamp Normalize	Wsnormal.cur
Winamp Position Bar	Wsposbar.cur
Winamp Button	Wswinbut.cur

TIP

Cursor changes happen immediately. There's no need to reload the current skin in Winamp to see them.

Editing Winamp GUI Graphic Files

All of the graphical elements aside from cursors are stored in the .BMP format. There are 15 specific files you can edit, although you needn't edit each one to make changes. In fact, you can pick and choose which ones to change; if one file is missing, Winamp loads the default graphic for that element.

Table 4.2 outlines each file and what element(s) it specifically stores.

Table 4.2–The file names associated with each Winamp GUI element

GUI Elements	File Name
Main Winamp SCREEN BACKGROUND	Main.bmp
Control buttons (Normal and Depressed)	Cbuttons.bmp
Main title bar, WinShade mode graphics, Close and Menu boxes, and Clutterbar menu elements	Titlebar.bmp
Shuffle, Repeat, Equalizer On, Playlist On buttons (Normal and Depressed)	Shufrep.bmp
Position bar and slider (Pressed and Depressed)	Posbar.bmp
Volume slider and background	Volbar.bmp
Balance slider and background	Balance.bmp
Mono and stereo indicators (On and Off modes)	Monster.bmp
Scope elements	Spec.bmp
Time indicator numbers	Nums ex.bmp
All Playlist Editor elements	Playedit.bmp
Play/Pause elements shown in Timer area	Playpaus.bmp
Winamp text	Text.bmp
Playlist fonts	Font.bmp
All equalizer elements	Eqmain.bmp

You'll need a graphic editor in order to edit each graphic element. We recommend Paint Shop Pro (**Figure 4.22**), which is available as shareware from JASC (**www.jasc.com**).

Figure 4.22
JASC's Paint Shop Pro is great for editing Winamp skins.

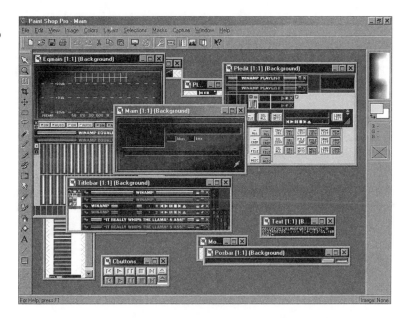

You can edit skins after saving them to your Winamp/Skins directory (each skin should be in its own folder). Create new folders to create completely new skins. When you are working on a skin set Winamp to that as the active skin using the Skin Browser (ALT+S). As you are editing a skin and saving changes to the appropriate elements hit F5 in Winamp to reload the images and see how things are turning out.

Final Skin Editing Issues

When editing your own Winamp skin, there are three .TXT files that can affect a final few elements. Pledit.txt lets you change the font and color of the playlist text. The format is:

```
[Text]
Normal=#00FF00
Current=#FFFFFF
NormalBG=#000000
SelectedBG=#000080
Font=Arial
```

The first [Text] line indicates to the player that the following lines apply to changing the text. The next four lines specify the colors for the text. The colors are specified in standard hexadecimal format, which is what you also use to define colors in HTML markup.

TIP

Paint Shop Pro will actually tell you the hexadecimal text for any color you identify in its palette bar.

The last line, Font=Arial, specifies the Windows font for use with the Playlist Editor. Be sure to either use a font everybody has standard with his system (such as Arial or Times New Roman) or include the font with the skin, which the user will have to install in order for it to work.

The viscolor.txt file has 24 lines, and each line consists of an RGB triplet and a comment. For example:

24,33,41, // comment

These 24 lines define the colors used in Winamp's built-in visualization scope (which displays below the Timer area). The default viscolor.txt is documented as to what lines change what color. Each color is defined by the RGB elements.

TIP

Using the standard palette in Paint Shop Pro you can easily see what RGB combinations produce which colors.

The region.txt file lets you specify a subregion of Winamp's main and EQ windows to show. This lets you carve out the parts you want to show and make the rest transparent. The file essentially contains a number of points, which define a polygon shape. Elements within that shape are drawn, while elements outside the shape remain transparent. For specific instructions on how to use this file, look at the region.txt file itself; thanks to Adam Kennedy, it is very well documented. You can find the directions in the region.txt file in the base Winamp skin for more information.

5

Where to Get MP3 Files

As MP3 has grown from underground format to widespread phenomenon, a number of legitimate sites that allow you to access great MP3-based content have been born. This includes some of the Internet's best-designed and most heavily trafficked sites—**goodnoise.com** and **mp3.com**. It also includes archives of bands that allow fans to tape their live performances (such as the Grateful Dead, Phish, Primus, and Pearl Jam), and the new SHOUTcast Radio scene, which features hundreds of radio stations broadcasting many different genres around the world.

This chapter gives you all the information you need on where to go and how to get the best, legal MP3 content available on the Web. If you crave music that is cutting edge, legitimate, and fun, then read on. This chapter covers four key aspects of MP3 content:

1. Sites that are supporting new artists using MP3 to break through the stifling record industry distribution model.
2. Major artists like the Beastie Boys and Public Enemy, who are distributing singles and live versions of their work using MP3.
3. Fan sites of bands that allow concert taping and non-profit trading.
4. Sites using Nullsoft's SHOUTcast streaming audio to create personal radio stations.

We won't pretend that no one has ever posted illegal, pirated MP3s or that this isn't still happening. However, it can be argued that the most exciting MP3 content isn't of the pirated variety. Instead, it is the music of new artists trying to break through, communities of fans trading tapes of past concerts, the hundreds of personal radio stations being created with SHOUTcast, and the many established artists, such as the Beastie Boys, who are using MP3 as a promotional tool.

The Tools Necessary for Accessing Content

When it comes to accessing great MP3-based content, you'll want to use tools such as the previously mentioned **Winamp** player (or any of the alternative players highlighted in Chapter 2), **MP3Spy** from GameSpy Industries, and of course, your favorite Web browser. Other tools to consider are **GetRight,** a program that makes it easy to manage multiple file downloads from the Web, and **TweakDUN 2.2** or **MTUSpeed,** both of which let you enhance the settings on your modem for faster download times. (This is always a plus because a single MP3 file for a normal length song is still usually between 3MB–5MB, even with compression.)

Finding and Downloading MP3s from the Web

To download files from the Web, you can use your Web browser, and when you find an MP3 on any of the sites mentioned here, you can just click on it to download. However, there are a few ways to enhance your download capabilities.

Making Downloads Easier with GetRight

For many modem users, downloading even a single MP3 file can take a good deal of time. At 3K–4K per second, a 4MB file can take as long as 20–25 minutes to download. Because of this, many users like to schedule MP3 downloading for the middle of the night. With a program such as GetRight (which is Windows only), you can set up several MP3 files to download, one after the other while you're away. In fact, if you began using GetRight at 9 p.m., you could probably download 100MB of MP3 files by the next morning.

GetRight, which is a popular download scheduler/manager from Headlight Software, is available on the Web for download at **www.getright.com.** This program is shareware that is free to download but carries a $17.50 registration fee.

Figure 5.1
Using a tool such as
GetRight, you can set up
multiple downloads for
overnight or during
other long periods of
modem inactivity.

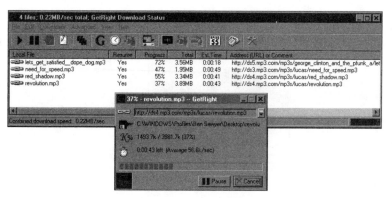

Part I   The MP3 Experience

Speeding Downloads with TweakDUN or MTU Speed

Mulder and Scully probably won't investigate this conspiracy, but your
modem might not be running as fast as possible because of the way it was
preconfigured. Deep within the Registry of your Windows operating
system are some variables that, when changed, allow you to set your
modem up for optimal maximum transmission speeds. What does this
mean to you? Well, even with 12:1 compression, it can take a while to
download an MP3 file—but you can get a 20% increase in transfer speed
by tweaking your dial-up connection (Dial-Up Networking or DUN). You
can then shave minutes off the time it takes to download an MP3 file.

To do this, you need a program such as TweakDUN (**Figure 5.2**) or MTU
Speed, which will step you as safely as possible through the process of
making changes to your system Registry for three modem variables: the
Max-MTU, RWIN, and TTL values. (You don't have to know what these
are to change them.) By optimizing these values, you can improve
download time by as much as 30%.

All of this is especially useful for Windows 95 because it was the worst
culprit in having poor Max-MTU settings. Windows 98 is set to a more
optimal value. However, with TweakDUN or MTU Speed, you may find
you have to do some experimentation. No matter what the setting is,
some tweaking might improve the performance of your modem's
download speed. Experimentation is the key.

Figure 5.2
You can potentially speed MP3 downloading in Windows with a product such as TweakDUN.

To use either program (MTU Speed is easier, but TweakDUN is a little more robust), download them from their respective Web sites:

TweakDUN:
http://www.pattersondesigns.com/tweakdun/
MTU Speed:
http://www.mjs.u-net.com/

Once you have them downloaded and installed, run the programs and work with the on-screen help to identify the optimal settings. Have those settings applied to the Registry. Once you are done, you should notice an increase in your modem's throughput. The improvement will vary from system to system and site to site.

Sites Supporting New Artists

As rapper Chuck D says, "The day of the demo as we know it is dead." Today, with the MP3 format, artists good and bad around the world can create music and post it on the Internet for all the world to find—hoping to gather a following or land a recording deal. Finding these artists used to take some effort, but then sites such as **mp3.com**, the Unsigned Artist Coalition, and Dimension Music have come about and now act as hubs.

Some sites, **mp3.com** and **goodnoise.com**, for instance, are actually helping bands promote, sell, and distribute their albums over their sites.

GoodNoise:
www.goodnoise.com (www.emusic.com)

GoodNoise (**Figure 5.3**) is one of the pioneers of downloadable music and has fully embraced the MP3 format. Recently renamed EMusic, GoodNoise calls itself the Internet Record Company and is working with artists like Frank Black (formerly Black Francis of the Pixies) and major independent record labels to develop a leading Web site for sampling and purchasing high-quality music in MP3 format. One of its most important moves came in the fall of 1998, when it acquired Nordic Entertainment and Creative Fulfillment, Inc., two other independent sites devoted to selling digitally downloadable music. The acquisitions brought together the largest catalog of downloadable music for sale on the Internet.

On GoodNoise, you can browse all the albums available for sale. As you'll see on almost every album, some selected tracks are available for free download in the MP3 format.

Figure 5.3
This is GoodNoise.

MP3.COM:
www.mp3.com

MP3.com (**Figure 5.4**), founded in 1997 by programmer Michael Robertson, has become a center point in the MP3 scene. Initially a source of utilities and news, the site is now setting its sights on becoming the place to download legitimate MP3 files from artists big and small. The site even created its own record label: DAM (Digital Automatic Music).

With DAM, artists sign up on MP3.com and upload their music. Users can download various tracks and those who want to purchase the full CD can order a DAM CD for $8. Many of the CDs include both the audio and MP3 versions of the tracks. Also, because nearly any artist can sign up for free, there is a wide range of music available. However, as critics point out, there is also a wide range of bad music. Although critics like to harp on its open publishing method, some of the music on MP3 isn't bad; in fact, some artists have gotten recording contracts. The company is branching out to partner with major independent labels.

Finding music on MP3.com isn't difficult. You can't miss the Free Music section on the home page. There is also a list of the top 40 downloaded songs—and the infamous "Bottom 40." If you want to explore a certain genre, MP3.com offers more than 20 different indexed genres of music.

Figure 5.4
This is MP3.com.

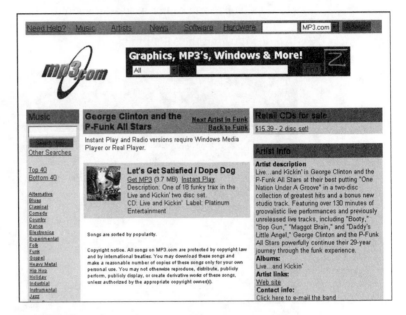

Ultimate Band List:
www.ubl.com

The Ultimate Band List (**Figure 5.5**) is one of the most popular music sites on the Web. While the site is devoted to far more than MP3s, it has also become an excellent place to find limited-release MP3 songs by major recording artists. It is a must see for the loyal MP3 listener.

Figure 5.5
The Ultimate Band List.

Part I   The MP3 Experience

MP3Now:
www.mp3now.com

Similar to MP3.com, MP3now (**Figure 5.6**) is sort of a portal to tons of MP3 information and links on the Web. As the site has grown, it has begun posting legal MP3s or linking to band sites in an effort to help bands and MP3 fans promote and listen to legitimate MP3 files.

Audible, Inc.:
www.audible.com

Audible (**Figure 5.7**) specializes in audio books that are stored in a downloadable format. Originally, it used the RealAudio format but recently announced it would begin supporting the MP3 format and Rio portable player.

Figure 5.6
This is MP3now.com.

Figure 5.7
This is Audible.

Platinum Entertainment:
www.platinumcd.com

Platinum Entertainment is one of the largest independent record labels around, with artists like Taylor Dane and Roger Daltry among its offerings. You can find on its site MP3 singles from all their major acts; the company has jumped on the MP3 format as a means of promoting its artists.

Winamp:
www.winamp.com

On the Winamp home page, Nullsoft hasn't forgotten that the point of Winamp is to listen to music. You can find a number of sites in its Free Music section (**Figure 5.8**) for either independent labels or artists that offer free and legitimate downloads of Winamp-compatible music, most of which are MP3 files.

Figure 5.8
On Winamp.com there is a special section devoted to finding legitimate MP3 music.

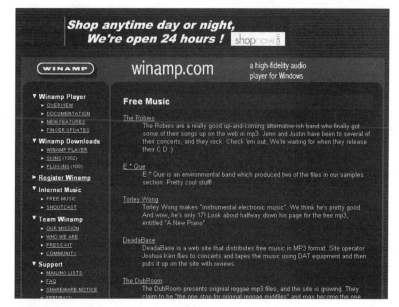

CityMusic:
www.citymusic.com

CityMusic is an electronically distributed music label started by Audiosoft, a leading creator of audio software for computers.

Music Global Network:
www.musicglobalnetwork.com

The Music Global Network was started by Michael David Butterfield in an effort to create a site where, as a free service to music makers, they could post MP3s to help independent artists and bands promote themselves on the Internet. You can find files available in a variety of genres.

music4free.com
www.music4free.com

music4free (**Figure 5.9**) explains its mission as "to promote 'new' good bands/singers (for Free) and give people the opportunity of finding new favorite artists."

To do that, the site is telling artists to put their music in the MP3 format and give the site permission to have the music placed on music4free for advertising purposes. The site is well organized and its collection is growing. The site currently has ten categories of music and offers reviews and good explanations of each song featured on its site.

Figure 5.9
This is music4free.com.

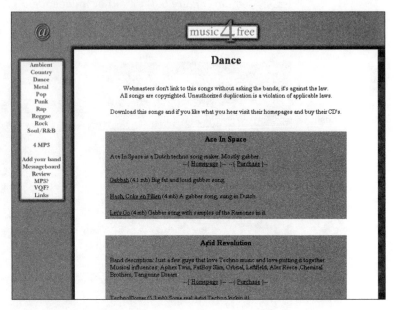

The Free Music Archive:
www.free-music.com

The Free Music Archive grew out of the work that established an electronic label for free house and garage bands' music. From that record label (known as Buttmunch Records) came **free-music.com**, which links to and posts hundreds of free MP3 and other music files from any band that submits their work.

The archive currently features hundreds of songs from bands with names like Chicken Fried Funk, The Offramps, and Frantic Dogpaddle. If you enjoy the local band at your favorite bar, this is the place for you.

ModArchive:
www.modarchive.com

Since Winamp includes support for the classic Mod-type formats, we thought it would be fun to include a great resource from which to download Mod-style music. The best place to go is the ModArchive, which contains hundreds of originally composed MOD files—many from some of the top Mod composers in the world. Songs are searchable, and many songs are reviewed to sort the good from the bad.

SITES THAT REVIEW LEGIT MP3S

One problem with MP3 is that it allows anyone who can encode their recorded music to become a published artist. In addition, there are no middlemen or record labels to give reviews (as if they themselves did it any better); it's hard to separate the good music from the bad. While beauty may always be in the eye—or ear—of the beholder, there are a couple of sites worth checking out. They're working to review all these unknown MP3 artists and help you skim the cream of the crop.

MP3critic:
www.mp3critic.com

MP3critic (**Figure 5.10**) bills itself as the Internet's Independent Music Guide. You can find reviews of the latest MP3 releases by various artists, all in their own categories; new reviews are added constantly. Incidentally, if you're interested in reviewing MP3s for the site, you should write a review in Microsoft Word and submit it. Once you mail it in, your submission will become the property of MP3critic.com, and you will most likely see your review posted shortly.

Figure 5.10
MP3critic.com is one of two leading review sites for new and legitimate MP3 songs.

The Rambo Report:
http://www.breakingartists.com/

You have to love a reviewer's site that says it features "The Good, The Bad, and The Ugly... Down and Dirty MP3 Music Reviews & News." The Rambo Report site may not look as polished as MP3critic's, but it too has active reviewers of the latest independently released MP3s. With both Rambo and MP3critic you can find diamonds in the rough.

Major Artists

While the RIAA (Recording Industry Association of America) seems to be trying to prevent the use and spread of MP3 files by major recording artists, some of those very same artists are trying hard to embrace the MP3 scene in ways that may benefit more than harm them. There is nothing like finding a legitimate MP3 by your favorite band that you can download and listen to without worrying that you've ripped them off.

In many cases, artists are using MP3 to distribute non-album tracks. This can range from live or alternative versions of hit radio singles to b-sides or special covers.

Public Enemy:
www.public-enemy.com

Public Enemy is perhaps one of the most famous rap groups of all time. Always on the cutting edge, the band is embracing the Web with their **www.public-enemy.com** site. In addition to being a great online community, the group is also releasing MP3s of some of their latest work. While this originally caused a disagreement between them and their record label, the group is now committed to MP3 and newer digital formats.

Beastie Boys:
www.beastieboys.com

The Beastie Boys are one of the biggest acts going today and made major waves when they posted some MP3s of live versions of their songs on their site. This didn't necessarily surprise many Beastie watchers, as their site has been one of the most cutting edge of all Web sites, and the group has regularly used new technology to promote their work.

Soul Coughing
www.soulcoughing.com

New York-based Soul Coughing is an alternative band with a strong following. They regularly post an "MP3 of the month" on their official site **soulcoughing.com**.

Fan Taping Sites

Many bands that allow taping of their concerts are also allowing those tapes to be translated into MP3s. As long as fans don't resell the recordings, they're free to tape, encode, and trade tracks with other fans in support of the band. When it comes to knowing where to find some of the best free and legitimate MP3 files, part of the strategy is knowing which bands are embracing the format and which ones are letting fans tape live concerts.

Bands That Allow Taping FAQ:
http://www.eklektix.com/dat-heads/recordable_bands.html

This URL leads you to the FAQ that people use to find bands that allow taping of their shows. Put together by Kurt Andrew Kemp, the FAQ lists many major and regional bands and the circumstances that come with each group (such as board access, venue issues, and who to check with on-site).

Astrojams:
www.astrojams.com

Astrojams (**Figure 5.11**) is a free music Web site that is dedicated to providing free music in the MP3 format for users to download. Many of the songs are from known bands that allow taping of shows. Users submit MP3s of shows they've legitimately taped and the site organizes and posts them including bands like Phish, Widespread Panic and the Dave Matthews Band.

The company used to be called The Deadabase and featured an amazing archive of Dead Concerts in the MP3 file format. That was until the Grateful Dead's attorneys decided that MP3 versions of taped shows were something they didn't want to see so much. Still, the site's founders are pressing on hoping to build on their excellent following. If a band allows taping and MP3s to be made from those tapes Astrojams hopes to offer it.

Figure 5.11
Astrojams is a growing place for MP3s of live music from major bands that allow taping.

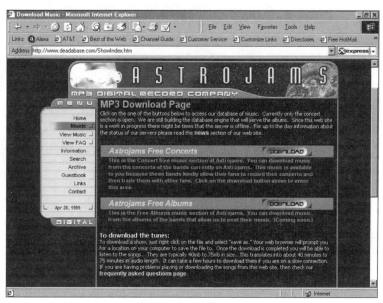

Josh Wardell's Pearl Jam Archive:
http://www.jwardell.com/pjmp3/

Josh Wardell started out simply, posting and collecting MP3s of live tracks from Pearl Jam shows. Little did he know his site would grow to become a bastion of the best live recordings from one of the biggest bands in music today. With over 500 tracks, all legit and live, his Pearl Jam Archive is downloading over 4GB of songs a day to hungry Pearl Jam fans worldwide.

Phish & Jambands Mp3s & Real Audio FTP List:
http://www.musicgods.com/phish/mp3phish/

Phish may be presented by some media as the heir apparent to the Grateful Dead, but while the band has some overlapping fan base, both bands are different in their own right. If you're into Phish and want to "Go Phishin" for some MP3s of taped shows, this is the place to find links.

Dave Matthews Band
http://www.musicfanclubs.org/davematthews/

Next to the Grateful Dead, Pearl Jam, and Phish, the Dave Matthews Band may be one of the leading bands on the Web that has fans trading MP3s of live shows and building archives. The band has an official taping policy and also asks for you to report people who are actually selling the tapes or bootleg CDs of live shows. Two of the better sites follow:

The DMB Explosion:
http://www.cyrizproductions.com/dmbexplosion/mp3s.html
Dig's Dave Matthews Band MP3 Archive:
http://www.cynosure.com/dmb/

SHOUTcast™ MP3 Streaming: Hi-fi Radio

With the release of Winamp 2.09 came one of the most important new features in Winamp's history and important new technology to MP3 fans worldwide.

SHOUTcast radio lets any Winamp listen to any SHOUTcast-enabled radio station. Users can create their own radio station by using Winamp with the SHOUTcast plug-in installed and running the SHOUTcast Server system. The broadcasts use the MP3 format to enable—even in a degraded form from the original recording—the best quality radio broadcast around.

Because it is so simple to operate and because many people want to broadcast their MP3 collections, SHOUTcast has already spawned hundreds of personal radio stations. Each of these stations is capable of supporting, on average, 20–30 simultaneous users.

Part I The MP3 Experience

NOTE

The **SHOUTcast Server** is a highly demanding program of both software processes and bandwidth. Make sure you have the consent of your ISP and sysadmin before running SHOUTcast Server. For more on creating your own radio station and SHOUTcast Server, see Chapter 12.

There are many niche-oriented stations, including comedy, techno, rock, metal, and country. With so many stations (and some closing as fast as new ones start), the trick to SHOUTcast is knowing where to find good stations and connecting to them.

You need Winamp (2.0 or greater) to listen to SHOUTcast radio. Once you have that downloaded, make sure that the .PLS file extension is registered to Winamp. To do so, open Winamp, go to the Preferences box, and choose the Setup option. There you can choose the file types associated with Winamp. Be sure PLS is selected in the listbox and then exit the Preferences menu.

You need to find a station once Winamp is configured. Finding stations is easy when you use **SHOUTcast.com**. The home site for SHOUTcast radio (**Figure 5.12**) lets you find many different and popular SHOUTcast stations. You can also use a new and popular product called MP3Spy, discussed in the next section.

Figure 5.12
On SHOUTcast.com you can tune into stations or find information about starting your own station.

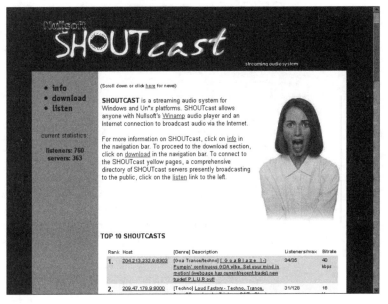

MP3Spy

GameSpy Industries:
www.mp3spy.com

For people who prefer multiplayer games such as Quake, Heretic II, or Half-life, an application called GameSpy (**www.gamespy.com**) is not just a program, it's a way of life. The program helps players locate game servers on the Internet, check various characteristics of the servers (like response time and number of players on each server), and then connect to them.

With SHOUTcast the company has created MP3Spy (**Figure 5.13**), a program that applies its GameSpy technology to the world of SHOUTcast radio. With MP3Spy you can easily find servers and connect to them. However, MP3Spy is much more than an interface into the world of operation SHOUTcast servers.

Figure 5.13
MP3Spy organizes and helps you listen to the hundreds of active SHOUTcast radio stations now on the Internet.

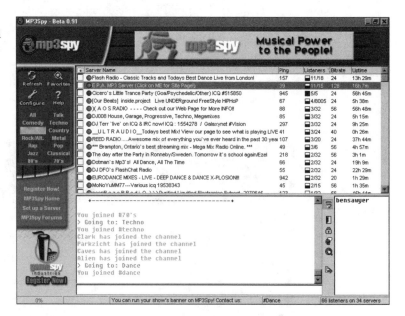

MP3Spy also includes integrated chat, including the DJ who is broadcasting what you are listening to, as well as other listeners. This makes it a great tool for sending in song requests and for generally interacting with people who may like the same type of music you do.

Future versions of MP3Spy will include more ways to interact with station operators, playlists, and other station information. If it catches on, it can be expected to become the central way to find and listen to SHOUTcast radio stations around the world.

NOTE

The full registered version of MP3Spy also lets you turn off ad banners, obtain free lifetime updates, and have special access to sneak previews of new product versions.

The MP3Spy Environment

The MP3Spy screen is divided into three major windows and one major menu. As seen in **Figure 5.14**, the three windows consist of:

▶ Main Menu

▶ The Server List window

▶ A chat area

Each chat area is directly related to the same station you are listening to and may include the actual station DJ himself.

Figure 5.14
MP3Spy enables you to quickly find stations you want to listen to.

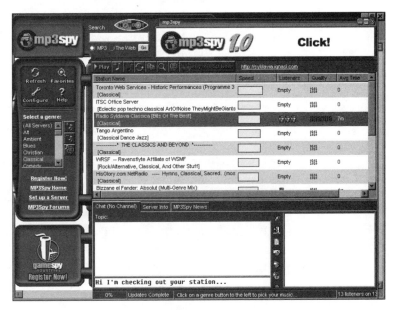

The main menu is on the left side of the screen, where you can refresh the server list, look at favorite stations, change configurations, or tune into different channels of music. At the bottom of the screen is the status bar, where you can see update messages, followed by the address of the server you're currently listening to and the total number of listeners and servers active for that musical genre.

Configuring MP3Spy

When you first install MP3Spy, you can configure your MP3Spy settings. These settings are also available to you within the program itself as well. Pressing Configure on the menu brings up the Configuration dialog box (**Figure 5.15**). You have a number of configuration options separated by four tabs: General, Chat, Firewall/Proxy, and Skins.

Figure 5.15
The MP3Spy Configuration dialog box.

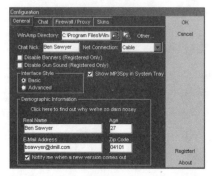

General Settings

The options in the MP3Spy Configuration dialog box control most of the major settings for MP3Spy:

▶ **Winamp Directory.** Place the directory where you installed Winamp. Pressing the Find button next to the field causes MP3Spy to attempt to automatically locate your Winamp directory. Clicking Other lets you locate Winamp manually in case Find doesn't work, or you have another SHOUTcast-compatible player to use.

▶ **Chat Nickname.** Set the name you will display to others in MP3Spy chat rooms.

▶ **Net Connection.** Set your connection speed so MP3Spy will help you only connect to servers your speed will support.

▶ **Disable Banners (Registered Users Only).** Turn off the banner ads associated with MP3Spy.

▶ **Disable Gun Sound (Registered Users Only).** Turn off the gun animation and sound associated with the GameSpy Industries Logo button in MP3Spy.

▶ **Interface Style.** Toggle the information that displays in the Server Listing window from Basic Display to Advanced Display.

▶ **Show MP3Spy in System Tray.** Adds MP3Spy to your Windows 95/98 system tray. A small MP3Spy button will be added that you can click on to launch MP3Spy.

▶ **Demographic Information.** The next set of options has to do with giving GameSpy Industries some basic personal information it can use to better sell ads (which in turn lets the company further develop this great product).

The company promises to not resell this info and only use it to "use The Man's cash to support further development and cover our costs for running servers and sucking down bandwidth." You can always register if you want to avoid ads. If not, just fill out your name, age, and zip code, and give them an email address where they can contact you. Clicking on the Notify Me When a New Version Comes Out checkbox causes the MP3Spy developers to email you right away when there is a new version or update.

Click the OK button when done or another tab to further configure MP3Spy.

Chat Settings

MP3Spy does more than help you find stations, it's also a communications tool that lets you talk with station DJs and others listening to your favorite SHOUTcast stations. You have the following options (**Figure 5.16**) to configure the Chat functions.

Figure 5.16
The Chat configuration options.

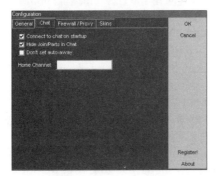

▶ **Connect to Chat on Startup.** If checked MP3Spy will automatically connect you to chat when you start the program.

▶ **Hide Join/Part Messages**. Click here to eliminate all messages pertaining to entering or leaving a chat room by yourself or other users.

▶ **Don't Set Auto Away.** Prevents you from appearing as having left a server chat room when you click on the MP3Spy News or Server info tabs.

▶ **Home Channel.** Type in the name of the genre channel you want your MP3Spy client set to when you start MP3Spy.

Firewall/Proxy Settings

If you are running behind a firewall or proxy server, you need to configure MP3Spy to work with your Internet connection. The Firewall/Proxy Settings tab (**Figure 5.17**) lets you configure MP3Spy to work from behind a corporate firewall/proxy server.

Figure 5.17
The Firewall/Proxy
settings configuration
options.

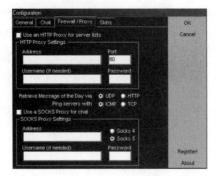

▶ **Use an HTTP Proxy for Server Lists.** Check this box to activate your Proxy Settings for accessory Server Lists.

▶ **HTTP Proxy Settings. Proxy Address, Port, Username, and Password.** If you're in a company and need help with this, you should contact your Webmaster or network help desk.

▶ **Retrieve Messages of the Day Via.** Sets your client to automatically retrieve the messages of the day via either UDP or HTTP protocol. UDP is faster but not supported by all proxy setups.

▶ **Ping Servers With.** This setting allows you to determine the method used to ping servers for their information when downloading station information with MP3Spy. ICMP (Internet Control Message Protocol) is faster but not supported by all proxy systems.

▶ **Uses a SOCKS Proxy for Chat.** This setting allows you to determine the method used to chat with when sitting behind a proxy. Check with your sysadmin for information on configuring a specialized SOCKS client to enable chatting with MP3Spy from behind a corporate firewall.

Skins

Like Winamp, MP3Spy supports interface skins that let you change the appearance of MP3Spy.

Here you can set the skin to any skin in the MP3Spy Directory.

To download a skin, go to **http://www.mp3spy.com/skins**. Skins are stored in .ZIP files. Unzip the file into your mp3spy/skins directory and then relaunch MP3Spy to make it available in the Skins configuration area.

TIP

Want to make your own MP3Spy skin? Full instruction is available at the bottom of the **http://www.mp3spy.com/skins** page.

The MP3Spy Screen

The MP3Spy Screen (**Figure 5.18**) has a lot of sections to it. So it pays to understand what each section is before explaining the specifics of the program any further.

Figure 5.18
The MP3Spy screen.

The top of the MP3Spy screen includes the MP3Spy logo (click here to go directly to mp3spy.com). Next to that is a simple search box. Type in anything, choose MP3 or The Web, click Go and MP3Spy will automatically launch your Web browser and search for the term on Hotbot (one of the best search engines). If you choose MP3, it automatically submits MP3 as the file type you're searching for on Hotbot. If a station is using the DJ plug-in to display the title of a song, MP3Spy will automatically place that song's title here for easy searching. Next to that section is the advertising banner space for MP3Spy. Advertising is how MP3Spy remains a free program to use (registered users can disable advertisements).

The next section to focus on is the toolbar down the left side of MP3Spy. Here you see four main buttons: Refresh, Favorites, Configure, and Help:

Refresh will refresh any server list (good for updating critical server information).

Favorites lists your favorite stations (which you must define).

Configure brings up the Configuration dialog box (covered just earlier in this chapter).

Help brings up the MP3 Spy Tips dialog box.

TIP

Uncheck the Show MP3Spy Tips at Startup checkbox to prevent this box from showing every time you launch MP3Spy.

Below the four main buttons is a list of station genres you can use when trying to find a server. Next to this list are three icons, three musical notes, one with a minus(–) sign the other with a plus(+) sign and one with a chat balloon. These icons are used to add, remove, and join the chat area for specific genres of music in the genre list.

Below the list are four Web links that take you to information on MP3Spy.com for registering the program, checking out the home page, setting up your own SHOUTcast server, and the MP3Spy message forums.

The final item on the left side of the screen is the GameSpy Industries logo, which when clicked on will take you to the registration page for MP3Spy.

Moving back to the main screen you see the main server information window. Above that is a second set of toolbar icons that you can click on:

Play will play the currently selected station in the station list.

The Add to Favorites button will add the selected station to your Favorites list.

This is followed by the Delete from Favorites button, which will delete a favorite from the Favorites list.

The Refresh Station tool, unlike the Refresh button, only refreshes the selected station on the server list.

 The Copy Server to Clipboard button will copy the selected station's IP address to the clipboard for pasting into your playlist or any other application.

 The Find button will let you search for stations in the server list. Simply type in any word and it will help you locate that server.

 The Chat button lets you join the chat channel for the highlighted server.

 Whenever you have chosen a server that displays a song title in its listing, you can click the Buy this CD Now! button to be taken to CDnow.com to purchase the album that song is from.

TIP

Right-click on any server in the Server Listing window to bring up a menu with the same choices offered on the toolbar.

Next to the toolbar is a Web URL. Click this link to be taken to the home page of the highlighted server.

Below the toolbar is the Server Listing window. This is where the server listing is displayed for whatever genre you have selected from the server list on the left. See Connecting to a Server below for more information on this window.

Below the Server Listing Window is the Chat, MP3Spy News, and Server Info windows. This series of windows lets you rapidly switch around to different pieces of information and chat rooms provided by MP3Spy. The MP3Spy News tab displays the latest information on the program, such as news about upcoming updates to the program, interesting MP3 news and events and more. The Server Info tab, when clicked, will display information about the currently selected server. Most of this is the same as displayed in the Server Listing window. Any tab with a number sign (#) followed by a genre (such as #FUNK) or a server number (such as #129.255.255.255:8000) is a tab that brings up that station's or genre's chat room. See "Chatting with MP3Spy," for more information on this section of MP3Spy.

NOTE

It's possible to have many Chat tabs when switching around to different genres.

The final piece of the MP3Spy screen is the status bar at the very bottom of the MP3Spy screen. From left to right are four pieces of text information.

▶ First is the download status bar. When you select a genre to retrieve station listings from, this bar represents how much of the total station information for that genre has been downloaded thus far.

▶ Next to the download status bar is a textual reference to the download status.

▶ A scrolling informational bar that includes information about registering MP3Spy and other announcements follows this.

▶ Finally, there is the genre status information. This text box shows the overall amount of listeners and servers for this genre area.

Connecting to a Server

To connect to a server you first must connect to the Internet and then start MP3Spy. Once it has started, simply click one of the 30 predefined music categories (on the left side). MP3Spy will build a new server list.

TIP

If the server name column or any column isn't wide enough for you to read all the information, you can widen it by dragging the right side of the column header farther to the right. Place the mouse directly on the border line; the cursor will change shape to denote that you are in position to widen or contract the column size.

Each server list is divided into six columns that provide critical information on each SHOUTcast Server.

NOTE

As discussed in the MP3Spy configuration section earlier, the program has two modes for displaying information about each station.

▶ In Basic mode, the information for each station is shown mostly as bar graphs.
▶ In Advanced mode, you can view precise numerical values for these graphs.

To switch between modes, do the following:

1. Click on the Configure button on the left-hand side of the MP3Spy screen.
2. Click on the General tab of the Configuration dialog box to switch the interface mode.

The first column is Server Name and denotes the name of the SHOUTcast radio station. You may want to look at the name closely because many stations put their ICQ number or Web page address, which lets you contact the DJ for requests or to view their playlists and station info. This section also may include the current song being played if the station is using the MP3Spy plug-in for Winamp (See Chapter 11 for more information about using this plug-in for your SHOUTcast station.) This song information is shown on the second line of the Server Name section in bold. Also shown in brackets is the main genre(s) of music the station plays.

Next is the ping rate (which in Basic mode is shown as Speed). Ping rates will vary from server to server. Low rates mean that data is traveling fairly fast to you from that server, while long ping rates may indicate potential difficulty in listening to that server. Very long ping rates can even denote that the server is down. In Basic mode, fast ping rates are shown as large bright green bars; the closer to red in color and shorter the bar, the higher the ping rate, which means the server is slow.

To sort servers based on their ping rates, simply click on the Ping column header. MP3Spy will automatically rank all the servers in ascending or descending order.

TIP

In Advanced mode, a colored circle is used to denote the overall ping health of that SHOUTcast station. Stations with green circles should be ready to go with few listening problems. Stations with yellow circles are experiencing a high ping rate, which could indicate problems. Red stations are almost sure to have skipping problems and may even be down completely.

Next is the Listeners column. Here you can see whether a particular SHOUTcast station is full. Every SHOUTcast station has a maximum number of listeners it can support. MP3Spy lists the number of current listeners followed by the maximum number of listeners. In the Basic Interface mode, this information is displayed as a graph of people—the longer the graph, the more people are listening. The words full are shown for servers at maximum capacity. Clicking on the Listeners column header will let you quickly rank each station in the list by the number of listeners they currently have.

TIP

Remember to refresh every once in a while to ensure that you have the latest data when looking for stations with lots of listeners.

The Bitrate column is next. The **bitrate** denotes what the quality of the stream will be. The higher the bitrate, the higher the MP3 stream quality. Bitrates range between 16 and 128, with 128 being equal to most of the regular MP3 files you download from the Web. In the Basic Interface mode, the bitrate is shown as a graph of zeros and ones. The longer the graph, the higher the bitrate and, the higher the audio quality will be. To rank SHOUTcast stations by their bitrates, simply click on the Bitrate column header.

The next column (and final column when using the Basic Interface mode) is Avg Time. This denotes in hours and minutes how long the average listener is listening to this station. One might assume that a high average listening time denotes a station with a good playlist that is keeping listeners hooked.

The final column (found only in Advanced mode) is called Uptime, which lets you know how long the station has been broadcasting since it last was launched. It's not uncommon for DJs to take their SHOUTcast servers down from time to time to install new software; perhaps they're tired or there are bandwidth issues. Clicking on the column header to rank stations for uptime will let you find stations that have been running strong for several days or more.

To connect to any station simply double-click a listing or highlight a listing and click the Play button on the top toolbar. You can also right-click and select Play from the pop-up menu. MP3Spy will launch your Winamp player and tune you to the desired station any time you double-click on any station.

Chatting with MP3Spy

With MP3Spy, each station is also, in effect, its own chat room, where you can chat with other station listeners or the station staff.

All chat takes place on the lower half of the MP3Spy program window. The graphical icons displayed as a menu between the main chat window and the list of chat room occupants let you control all chat functions. The first icon—the Plug—controls whether you are connected to the chat network. If you aren't seeing any chat activity, press this icon to connect.

When you connect to any SHOUTcast station, you are automatically transferred to that station's associated chat room. If you want to just chat on another station's chat room but not listen to it, simply click once on any station in the list and then choose the Door icon to be connected to that station's chat room.

Pressing the Lock icon keeps you in any current active chat room, even when you change genres or tune to a different SHOUTcast station.

MP3Spy has its own specific chat channel, which you can get to by clicking the MP3Spy icon. The Globe icon lets you automatically connect to the associated Web page of any selected server.

Finally, the File Transfer icon lets you send files to anyone you've selected from the chat room occupant list. This can be a great way to transfer MP3 files you want to share with other listeners.

Seek and Ye Shall Find

Finding MP3 content used to be hard and most of what you found in the past were illegally pirated tracks. As the MP3 scene has grown and the tools have matured, many new bands and other musical artists have quickly come around to embrace MP3 as a de facto standard for Internet distribution of their music. This has been enhanced by the invention of SHOUTcast radio.

The trick is to know where to find all of this content and how to separate the truly good from the bad. With what you've learned in this chapter, you're well on your way to accessing a host of MP3-generated content that will supply your ears with listening pleasure for years to come.

So turn off your stereo, fire up your browser, Winamp, and MP3Spy, and go find the next new unknown band or radio station!

Interview:

Josh Wardell

The rock band Pearl Jam has developed a reputation for being an explosive live act while maintaining a fiercely loyal following. Before finally adopting an official pro-taping policy for its 1998 tour, the band had maintained a hands-off approach to taping. Singer Eddie Vedder had often talked about taping his favorite bands when he was growing up and Pearl Jam fans weren't discouraged from taping Pearl Jam. However, a well-publicized battle with TicketMaster contributed to a limited touring schedule for the band for several years. Before Pearl Jam launched its sold-out 1998 tour, fans hungry for live music by the band satisfied their appetite first through a network of tape traders and eventually through live MP3 archives.

One of the first and most popular Pearl Jam MP3 archives (**Figure 5.19**) is run by Josh Wardell, a Syracuse University student.

Figure 5.19
Fans like Josh Wardell are creating huge archives like this. This allows shows like Pearl Jam to be taped.

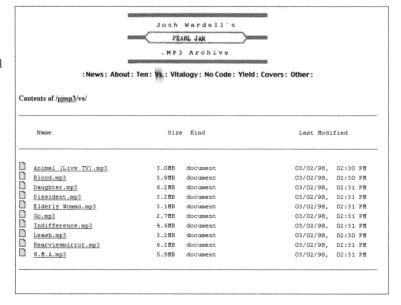

Q *When and how did you hear about and get started with MP3 and your archive?*

A: I started in late January 1997, when MP3s were just becoming popular. Back then, there were no specialized sites; every site just had a collection of usually a few hundred megs of random popular songs. I came across a few live and rare Pearl Jam songs—I think I had about eight when I first started—and because I was such a fan I figured it would be a great idea to set up a band-specific server. I thought this was a great idea because, first of all, it was legal, unlike every other MP3 site [at the time]. Plus, it would interest not just MP3 fans but fans of the band as well.

It provided a new alternative to the popular tape trading scene: There were no "generations," as each copy was always the same; things could be downloaded instantly instead of being mailed; and you didn't have to trade something to get something new.

Q *Tell us about the archive. How big it is, what it is composed of, and how it is built up?*

A: It resides on my computer at college, which is networked to the Internet. I run it on a Web server, unlike most others, which are FTP. As a Web server, I can be more personal with the browsers and post information that interests the fans. It is currently about 700 megs in size. It normally grows faster, but I have been so busy this semester I haven't added any songs since early spring (of 1998).

Q *How do you manage the archive?*

A: It is run on my own computer, so I have full control. Normally I am very involved with it, replying to every email and updating the front news page every few days, while actively controlling those who abuse the server.

Q *Why did you choose MP3?*

A: MP3 allows near-CD–quality sound at 1/11th the file size or smaller, allowing songs to be transferred easily and large amounts to be archived. There may be a few better quality/compression formats out now, but none has the availability and acceptance [that] MP3 does.

Q *Are there any tricks to transferring live shows from tape to the MP3 format? If somebody wanted to start a similar site, how difficult is the process and the upkeep?*

A: Well...I took everything from submissions, so I did not do much encoding myself. Encoding is relatively easy, although processor intensive. From CDs, you can "rip" or record the data of the songs into a sound program and then compress that into an MP3. From tape, you actually have to hook the tape player to your computer's microphone input and record the whole song—a bit more troublesome. Upkeep of the site depends on how devoted to it you want to be. You can just let it run in the background, or spend time responding to emails, looking for news and new songs, and making sure it runs optimally.

Q *How do you trade music via MP3? Where do you get the songs?*

A: In "the old days," MP3s were mostly traded in IRC [Internet Relay Chat]. You would join the #mpeg3 channel in effnet for example, and ask if someone had whatever song you were looking for, and they would send it to you. Some people had FTP sites and would advertise them in the channels. Now you can find MP3 servers almost anywhere, for anything. They are usually not traded much anymore; if anything, the only form of trading is those servers that require you to upload something new in order to get download access. In addition, much of that trading was for illegal music. Now with legit music and the Web, most of the trading is done via email.

Q *Do you think MP3s of live shows hurt or help bands?*

A: I think they are great. I don't see how [live] MP3s could hurt a band. How could they help them? Well, I guess [those bands that are good live performers] may acquire new fans after [fans] hear how well they perform. I get emails from Pearl Jam "newbies" that say they can't believe how good PJ sounds live and how great their covers are, all thanks to my site. I would like to think these people have come to appreciate the band more because of this.

Q *How many Pearl Jam MP3 sites are there out there? Do you all communicate/trade with each other?*

A: Mine was the first, and [the others] were slow to follow, but now there are several—much more than I can keep track of. I communicate and trade with a few. What I find interesting is the sites are becoming more detailed than just what artist they are for. Mine is excellent for the newcomer to live Pearl Jam, with classic recordings of many songs. Others are there to archive entire shows.

Q *How many visitors do you get? How many downloads?*

A: Too many! I have not done statistics this semester, but I notice I get about four gigabytes of downloads a day.

Q *You don't offer commercially available tracks, but you were involved in posting some tracks from Pearl Jam's 1998 studio album Yield after those songs were leaked by a radio station. How did that situation play out and how did the record company treat you?*

A: I *never* offered studio recordings off of albums; I did that in protest of the ways some people use MP3 to rip off artists of CD sales. I instead have always linked to online stores to buy them. When those songs from *Yield* appeared, I "bent" my self-made policy slightly, I will definitely admit. However, those recordings would in no way hurt the sales of the album. They were 30-second to one-minute clips of the songs, and the quality was terrible. All they could do was show what was to come, and get people excited to buy the album. With all the publicity it generated, we know it definitely generated more sales for the album.

Q *What did you think of the potential popularity of MP3 when you started the site and what do you now think its future is?*

A: I think it has pretty much followed what I have always expected it to. It revolutionized the way people can get music and, like downloading software on the Net, it explodes to everyone who has the capability to do it.

Part II
Advanced Winamp

6

Advanced Winamp Configuration Guide

You have installed Winamp, played some MP3s, downloaded skins, and learned a little about this excellent music player—but now you want more. One of Winamp's best features is its capability to be customized and modified from within the program. Visual and auditory effects can be easily added, setting icons to represent the Winamp program, playlists, or MP3s is a snap, and controlling almost every function of Winamp is possible.

Want to play two songs at a time? Winamp allows you to open a song multiple times, enabling them to be played simultaneously. Customizing icons for songs, playlists, and the Winamp program is a breeze. Do you have a slower computer? Winamp allows you to control many features that can improve playback performance. Do you have a faster machine? In addition to allowing users to add impressive sound and graphics capabilities, Winamp also allows users to smooth out playback. Many of the programs written today neglect older machines, but Nullsoft has gone the extra step to make sure that if users take a little time, Winamp can even work on a fast DX/4 computer.

To some it may sound a little complicated, so many people never use Winamp to do anything but play music. Some of the most impressive features, however, come into play in the form of plug-ins. **Plug-ins** are simply programs that Winamp runs along with the music. They allow a user to add visual components to music and to change the way the music sounds. There are currently over 100 plug-ins for Winamp, and most are freely distributed across the Internet.

Let's find out how to tune the Winamp player to the best of your computer's capability and your own personal tastes!

Part II Advanced Winamp

Configuring Your Way to Power Playing

No Winamp power user is truly powerful without mastering the Preferences menu. This menu allows the user to control almost every aspect of the Winamp player and all the files associated with it. You can control how much CPU consumption playback takes, what icons are assigned to files, how Winamp is displayed, how many players you can have open, and many other functions.

The first order of business is to open the Preferences menu (right-clicking on the faceplate to pull up the main menu) and select Options, Preferences. This pulls up a menu with five tabs running across the top: Setup, Audio I/O, Options, Visualization, and Misc. Plug-Ins. You take a look at the Setup tab first.

The Setup Menu

Winamp makes it easy for you to identify the types of files that you can play. The Setup section on the Preferences menu allows you to deal with settings that control what language is displayed, the connection type you're using, and where icons that launch the program can be installed. The File Types subsection lets you set what icons are associated with the Winamp program and the files it plays.

Figure 6.1 shows the first, and main Setup preferences you can configure. Click the Language Pack button to bring up an open file dialog box where you can locate *.LNG files that Winamp uses to add support for other languages. At this time other language packs aren't available, but when they are, they will be posted for download on Winamp.com.

Below the language pack are three buttons that when clicked will add a startup icon to either the Menu Group, Desktop Icon, or the QuickLaunch bar. Note that the QuickLaunch bar is only present on your system if you've installed Microsoft Internet Explorer 4.0 or higher or Windows 98.

The Internet Settings box lets you tell Winamp what kind of Internet connection you have: LAN, Dial-up/Modem, or No Internet Connection. Below the access choices is a box where you can type in Proxy Server information. If you are running a proxy server (many corporations do), then you may need to insert special information in this box for it to work. Everyone else can leave it blank. If you know you have a proxy but don't know the information to place here, talk to your company's IT/Webmaster/Sysadmin staff to find out.

Figure 6.1
Winamp's Preferences
menu at the Setup tab.

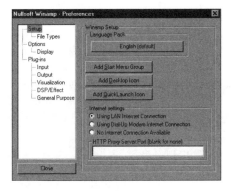

Setting File Types

Clicking on the File Types section of the Preferences tree will bring up
the File Type Preferences options (**Figure 6.2**).

Figure 6.2
The File Type
Preferences options.

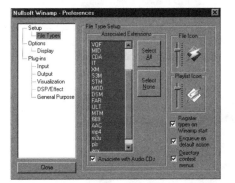

The menu on the left side of this options screen displays all of the file
types that Winamp is capable of playing. Winamp plays all the file types
you select in this box by default whenever you run a file associated with
one of these file types. The file types mp3 and mp2 should be selected,
but Winamp can also be selected to be the default player for your .WAV
files(instead of Windows sound recorder, for example). Simply click on
WAV to highlight it in the box in the upper right. At the bottom of the
menu box is a checkbox: select Associate with Audio CDs to make
Winamp the player that pops up when an Audio CD is placed in your
CD-ROM drive.

Controlling icon appearance and locations is a snap. Selecting an icon for
your playlists and .MP3 files is just as simple as using the slider bars on
the left of the Setup menu to find an icon that you like.

Below the icon appearance selection is a series of checkboxes that
control how Windows reacts to files that Winamp plays back when you
click on them:

▶ **Register Types on Winamp Start**—Triggers Winamp to take back file types that become unassociated with Winamp as the result of another program trying to steal them. It is checked by default and is the recommended setting.

▶ **Enqueue as Default Action**—When you attempt to launch a file that Winamp will play back, checking this option will merely add that file to the current playlist, instead of clearing out the current playlist and playing just that file.

▶ **Directory Context Menus**—Adds a feature to Windows Explorer so that when you right-click on a file that Winamp will play back, a menu pops up with the Play and Enqueue options.

The Options Menu

You just learned how to manipulate the icons associated with Winamp in the Setup menu. Not satisfied with that degree of control, Nullsoft added the Options tab (**Figure 6.3**) to the first of two Preferences screens.

Winamp can be customized even further from this tab, allowing you to micromanage many of the automatic player's features. Most people will never change some of the features, but some features can be reconfigured to be extremely useful. Here is what you can configure on the Options Preferences screen:

Figure 6.3
Winamp's Preferences menu at the Options tab.

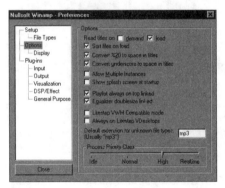

Read Titles on Demand or Load

Check these boxes to configure when Winamp reads any file or ID3 information to subsequently display. You can set it to read titles on demand (i.e., when the file is actually played) or upon load (i.e., when you load the file into the playlist).

Convert %20 to Space

Sometimes when you download a file from the Web, Web browsers replace spaces in the file name with %20, which is more Web-friendly. When this option is checked, Winamp automatically converts any %20 to a space.

Convert Underscore to Space

Many users will name .MP3 files using underscores instead of spaces in the name; for example, artist_title_date.mp3. Checking this box automatically converts those underscores into spaces between words when playing the song, and displays it on the Winamp player or playlist.

Allow Multiple Instances

If you click on this box, it allows Winamp to have more than one player functioning at a time. This is handy when editing, sampling, or even making songs. Some programs, such as Virtual Turntables—an .MP3—use two or even three consecutively running Winamp players to allow users to create their own scratches, remixes, and samples. On most systems, Winamp requires use of the DirectSound Output plug-in in order to play multiple MP3s at once. See the section on Nullsoft DirectSound Plug-In v.80b (x86) later in this chapter.

Show Splash Screen

The Winamp splash screen that displays when you first run Winamp can be disabled or enabled by this option.

Playlist Always on Top Linked

Checking this box keeps the playlist linked to the main Winamp faceplate. This causes the Winamp program to remain on your screen when you switch to another program.

Use this if you like keeping Winamp in view but don't want to crowd your entire screen with the Playlist Editor.

Equalizer Doublesize Linked

Checking this box keeps the equalizer linked in size to the main Winamp faceplate. This lets you prevent the equalizer from going into the screen-hogging Doublesize mode.

Litestep VWM Compatible Mode

When enabled, this box allows Winamp to stay offscreen, which is good for Litestep's Virtual Window Manager.

> **NOTE**
> Litestep is a shell replacement for Windows 9x/NT that is fast, stable, customizable, and recommended for advanced users and power users only. You can learn more about it at **http://www.litestep.net**, **http://floach.pimpin.net**, and **http://litestep.m1crosoft.com**.

Part II Advanced Winamp

Always on Litestep Virtual Desktops

This box makes Winamp always appear on virtual desktops in Litestep. See **http://www.litestep.net** for more information on Litestep.

Default Extension for Unknown File Types

If you attempt to play a file with an extension that Winamp doesn't recognize, type an extension in this box and Winamp will attempt to play it. By default, the extension is set to mp3 and, for the most part, should remain as such.

Process Priority Class

Adjusts the priority class of Winamp when a track is playing. The priority class is set to Normal by default. If files are skipping because other processes on your machine are taking precedence, you can move this notch up for potentially better results.

Display Options

The second of the two options preference screens is the Display Options screen. This screen allows you to control the appearance of Winamp's interface (with the exception of skins, which are explained later).

Here are the options available to you on the Display Options screen and an explanation of each.

Always Show Clutterbar

The **Clutterbar** is the strip of letters that runs down the left side of the Vis menu. When this box is checked, *O, A, I, D,* and *V* display on the right side of the Vis window at all times. These helpful shortcuts can be removed, since some skins don't look right with it enabled.

Display ToolTips in Winamp's Main Window

When this box is checked, you can place the mouse pointer over an icon button for a few seconds and a small text box, called a ToolTip, will appear. The ToolTip gives you a brief description of the function of that button.

Scroll Song Title in the Windows Taskbar

This is a pretty simple function. Checking this allows the full title of the song to scroll on the button that Winamp places on the taskbar. This makes it easy to tell what is playing when the Winamp player is minimized. It does, however, consume a bit more CPU power. On slower machines, this is something that can be left off to help increase performance.

Use Winamp-Styled (Skinned) Cursors

When the mouse pointer is over the Winamp window, Winamp defaults to using the mouse pointers it has assigned or people have created with new skins. If you do not like the Winamp mouse pointers, you can disable them by unchecking this box and just having the normal Windows cursor used for all functions.

Dim Title Bars When Inactive

The title bar is dimmed when the Winamp window is not active and this box is checked. If you want Winamp to remain highlighted, uncheck this box.

Snap Windows at # Pixels

This function causes Winamp to snap to comfortable positions when moved. If this is not checked, you can get the same effect by holding down the Shift button when moving the Winamp window.

Use Bitmap Font for Main Title Display (No Int. Support)

This function causes Winamp to use the bitmap font that is part of the interface skins to display song titles. If you want to make Winamp use a normal Windows font, then uncheck this box. The main reason to do this is to have support for songs using international characters so that their title information displays properly. When checked, international characters will not display.

Show Numbers in Playlist

This feature allows the times of the songs to be displayed on the playlist. Turn this feature off if you don't want a numbered playlist.

Playlist Font Size

This sets the font size on the playlist, allowing users with large resolution desktops to make the songs more visible. The default size for this font is 10 pixels.

Winamp also allows users to decide where Winamp will be displayed when it is running. The bottom of the Options menu holds a box called Show Winamp In. In this box, there are four options: Taskbar Only, System Tray Only, Taskbar and System Tray, and None. Selecting Taskbar Only shows Winamp on the taskbar at the bottom of Windows when it is running. This is the default and is the way most programs run. The **system tray** is the area on the bottom right of the taskbar; Winamp can be just displayed there if you so choose.

Part II Advanced Winamp

You can have Winamp displayed in both areas, or in neither, although not displaying Winamp could be troublesome unless you know how to cycle through programs using Alt+Tab. (It can be easy to lose the program among all actively running programs.) If you decide to have Winamp show up in the system tray, you can select the icon that it uses to display itself, by using the slider in the System Tray Icon Box on the bottom right of the Options menu. If you run Winamp again, the running Winamp is brought back into view.

The Plug-Ins Preferences

One of the Winamp player's most entertaining features is the usage of plug-ins. The Plug-Ins Preferences section is the very guts of the Winamp player. Plug-ins interact with the file being played by Winamp in several different fashions. Most plug-ins add a visual component to the Winamp player, although some change the sound or even the interface of the player. The main categories of plug-ins are visualization, audio processing, audio input, audio output, and general plug-ins.

This series of options (each grouping is displayed under the main Plug-Ins menu choice) contains all of the settings for each plug-in type Winamp uses. This includes decoders and instructions that tell Winamp what files it can play, and how well it plays them, to how Visualization plug-ins are installed and their configuration.

On the main Plug-Ins Settings screen (**Figure 6.4**) you have several configuration choices that control how the entire plug-in subsystem of Winamp works.

Figure 6.4

Winamp's Preferences menu at the Plug-In Preferences tab.

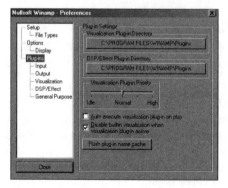

TIP

All plug-ins for Winamp are by default stored in the Plug-Ins directory in the main Winamp folder. Since Winamp defaults to the Program Files folder on Windows-based machines, you can usually find this folder at c:\Program Files\Winamp\Plugins. Plug-in files are stored as .DLL files in this folder. This contains both visual and audio plug-ins, and if you look in it you will see that this folder has at least 13 .DLLs in it, if not more. You will see the file name of the .DLL listed at the end of each plug-in preference settings area.

In version 2.10 and greater of Winamp, it is possible to set different directories for your Visualization and DSP/Effects plug-ins. All others will remain stored in the default plug-ins directory.

Visualization Plug-In Directory

Clicking this button brings up a directory selection dialog box in which you can change the specific directory Winamp looks for Visualization plug-ins. This is nice if you want to have separate directories for various plug-in types. Note if you want to have a new directory, you must create it first before clicking here to change it.

DSP/Effect Plug-In Directory

A new feature in version 2.10+ of Winamp is the capability to set a separate directory for your DSP/Effect plug-ins from that of your visualization and other plug-ins. Just as with Visualization plug-ins, click here to bring up a selection dialog box in which you can set a new directory to use.

Visualization Plug-In Priority

Use this slidebar to set the priority of any Visualization plug-in that is running. If a Visualization plug-in seems out of sync with the music playing, move it up a notch or two from the default Normal setting.

Auto Execute Visualization Plug-In on Play

Checking this box will automatically start whichever the current Visualization plug-in is when a song is started. It is by default not checked.

Disable Built-in Visualization When Visualization Plug-In Active

Checking this box will turn off the main player console's visualization when any Visualization plug-in is running.

Part II   Advanced Winamp

Flush Plug-In Name Cache

Used to flush the plug-in cache Winamp uses. This is a good button to press every now and then. By clicking on it, Winamp will remove any plug-in names appearing in the Preferences section that are no longer installed. It will also check to see if names and such have been updated due to new versions of plug-ins being downloaded and installed.

The Input plug-ins tell Winamp how to operate when processing sound. The Input Plug-In Preferences section will show you a list of each plug-in currently installed. Choose each one and click Configure to bring up the corresponding preference dialog box to configure how that specific Input plug-in should work.

Input Devices

Let's look at what each of these devices in the Input Plug-Ins box does, and then look at how to configure it to work optimally on your machine. Each plug-in allows Winamp to recognize and play different types of audio files. While Winamp is primarily used as an MP3 player, its audio plug-in architecture lets it support a number of other audio formats, past, present, and future. Each different format only requires that either Nullsoft or a third party construct the proper plug-in to decode or read the file format. This is how Winamp supports not only MP3 files but MIDI, .WAV, and MOD files, CD Audio, and more.

There should be at least five Input plug-ins in the Input Plug-Ins box. Make sure you have each of the ones listed here. You may have more, but these are the primary decoders:

▶ Nullsoft MIDI Player v0.53 (x86) [IN_MIDI.DLL]

▶ Nullsoft Nitrane MPEG Audio Decoder (x86) [IN_MP3.DLL]

▶ Nullsoft Waveform File Decoder v1.15 (x86) [IN_WAVE.DLL]

▶ Nullsoft CD/Line Input Player v0.100 (x86) [IN_CDDA.DLL]

▶ Nullsoft Module Decoder v1.21 (x86) [IN_MOD.DLL]

TIP

The wording in the brackets denotes the exact Dynamic Link Library (.DLL) file that contains the programming code which deciphers the various audio file formats. The (x86) wording denotes that the library is compiled for x86 Intel-based processors and not Compaq/Digital's Alpha processor.

Nullsoft MIDI Player v0.53 (x86) [IN_MIDI.DLL]

This plug-in allows the Winamp player to decode MIDI files. You will notice that the Configure and About buttons become accessible when you highlight this plug-in in the Audio I/O tab. Clicking on Configure pulls up a menu like that in **Figure 6.5**. This small menu allows you to do two things:

▶ Selecting the first box allows the Winamp player to query your sound card to display visualization. Your sound card must be able to record at 44KHz with 16-bit stereo quality while at the same time playing MIDI to do this.

▶ Selecting the second box prompts you when streaming MIDI files to save them on your hard drive.

> **TIP**
>
> It takes a good sound card to be able to change the MIDI file into a digital audio stream. If your sound card uses a software-based MIDI engine (a SoundBlaster PCI128, for example), it tends not to work. If you have problems playing MIDI files, disable this option.

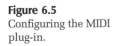

Figure 6.5
Configuring the MIDI plug-in.

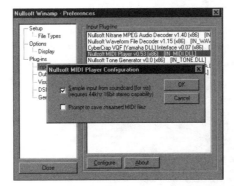

Nullsoft Nitrane MPEG Audio Decoder (x86) [IN_MP3.DLL]

This plug-in is the very heart of the Winamp player. This plug-in tells Winamp how to decode .MP3 files. This plug-in uses Nullsoft Nitrane, Winamp's powerful and efficient MPEG audio decoding engine. Select it and click Configure. You will see a menu with four tabs: General, Title, Decoder, and Streaming.

General tab—As seen in **Figure 6.6**, .mpeg1 allows users to select what types of files they want to be decoded using the Nitrane decoder. .MP3, .MP2, .MPG, and streaming files can all be decoded and used by this plug-in. It will also play any additional file types that are compatible if you place the extension of the file in the Additional Extensions box.

The Decode Thread Priority box controls how much CPU power is allocated to decoding the file. If it is set too low, it can cause skipping in file playback.

The Quality Controls box affects sound quality and equalization controls. You can select between setting your equalizer to act as +/-20db frequency control (Logarithmic EQ, like most home stereos), or as a Linear equalizer that can allow you to only boost frequencies up by +10db; it will remove frequencies entirely if the equalizer frequency is set to 0 (more for experimental use and neat effects).

Checking Blip Reduction will reduce noises that come from corrupted MP3 files. Sometimes when a file is a bit corrupted, it will contain small blips or pops. This will cause the Nitrane decoder to reduce that problem. It's recommended that you check this.

Aural Stimulation is an experimental setting that boosts the higher frequencies to generate a better sound image. It is under development, and not final, so opinions may vary on its effectiveness.

Figure 6.6
The General tab, which is found on Nullsoft Nitrane Preferences menu.

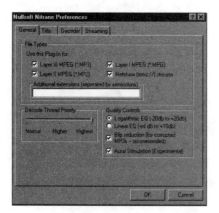

Title tab—This tab, seen in **Figure 6.7**, provides a simple but very neat way to customize Winamp. Winamp can read information from the song in a format called ID3 to determine the name and title of the song. It then displays this information on the Winamp faceplate and playlist. Through this tab, you can select how you want that information to be displayed by Winamp when it is playing the song. Of course, the information has to be in the song for Winamp to display it, so if the song was ripped from CD without specifying what album it came from, it won't appear until you enter that missing information. This menu lists how Winamp interprets the ID3 information.

Figure 6.7
The Title tab, which is found in Nullsoft Nitrane Preferences menu.

%1 = ID3 Artist
%2 = ID3 Title
%3 = ID3 Album
%4 = ID3 Year
%5 = ID3 Comment
%6 = ID3 Genre
%7 = File Name
%8 = File Path
%9 = File Extension
%% = If for some reason you want to display a % itself

All of these %x are just abbreviations for how Winamp will display the song either in the scrolling title bar or on the playlist. By changing the abbreviations in the writable area on this tab, you can customize the way songs display. Let's say you want to add the album and year to the display of a band's name and song title. Since Winamp defaults to displaying Artist—Title, you are going to need to add a couple abbreviations. For example, a song called SongX by the band, ArtistX, off the album AlbumX made in 1999 would be typed in like this:

%1–%2 off %3 in %4.

It would display like this:

ArtistX SongX off AlbumX in 1999

If you want no information, just use %7, which will just state the file name.

Decoder tab—The Decoder tab (**Figure 6.8**) controls how much of a load Winamp places on the CPU to decode and play .MP3s. The tradeoff in freeing vital system resources is diminished quality. Simply turning off Allow Stereo Output can cut processor usage in half on stereo-recorded .MP3s, since it only has to decode a one-

Part II Advanced Winamp

channel mono stream versus a two-channel stereo stream. The 16-bit Output box is included to make sure that Winamp will work on older sound cards, as some old sound cards can only accept 8-bit mode. (8-bit sound is noticeably worse sounding and uses more CPU time, though.) The Reverse Stereo box is provided for those who have their left and right speaker outputs reversed.

Figure 6.8
The Decoder tab, in the Nullsoft Nitrane Preferences menu.

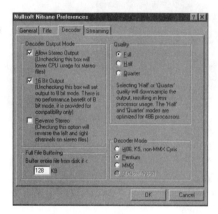

The Quality box on the Decoder tab allows you to set the processor usage, but it's set at the cost of sound quality. Full is the default setting. Half and Quarter were both designed to allow 486 processors to play Winamp. They **downsample** the original recording, losing accuracy from the original, but allow processor usage to be greatly reduced.

The Full File Buffering section simply loads a file into memory if it is equivalent or smaller to the size typed in the box on the bottom left. This is done to reduce skipping, ensuring smoother playback of smaller files. Users with more RAM can adjust this to whatever seems to work best for them. Generally (depending on how many other applications you typically load into memory at one time), if you have 64MB or more of RAM, you can raise this value to 4,000K or higher and get smoother playback.

The Decoder mode tells the Nitrane engine what special processor optimizations to use when reading .MP3 files. This automatically defaults to the Pentium setting. Simply selecting the proper processor to decode the music can make a large difference in the quality of playback for users with a Pentium or faster machines. On a test AMD K6-2 350MHz machine, using the 3Dnow! Instructions, CPU consumption drops from about 17% to 13% after changing from the i486, K5, non-MMX, Cyrix setting to the 3Dnow! setting. Pentium MMX, Pentium II, and MMX clone users should select the MMX mode. People with 486s and non-MMX clone chips should use the i486, K5, non-MMX, Cyrix setting.

Streaming tab—The Streaming tab (**Figure 6.9**) is designed to stream MP3 audio. There are many ways to do this, including plain HTTP (i.e., you can pass Winamp an URL to an MP3 on a Web site), Microsoft's NetShow streams, as well as through Nullsoft's own SHOUTcast radio. SHOUTcast allows music to be sent over the Internet in the MP3 format and received by Winamp. Much like a radio station, the Winamp user has no control over the songs being played, but he can select a broadcast that fits his connection and personal taste in music.

The Saving box allows users to save broadcasts and listen to them at a future date; however as noted, it is disabled for SHOUTcast streams due to copyright issues. When you join a streaming server, Winamp prompts you to save the data in an MPx output file on your hard drive. This saves the file as an .MP3 file. See Chapter 5, "Where to Get MP3 Files," for more on SHOUTcast.

Figure 6.9
The Nullsoft Nitrane
Preferences menu's
Streaming tab.

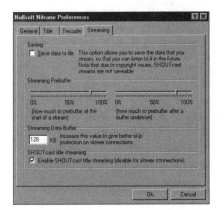

The Streaming Prebuffer box allows users to minimize gaps in the music due to Internet traffic when streaming an MP3 file like you do when listening to a SHOUTcast station. Streaming can be disrupted in many ways, and setting larger buffers can often slow the load time significantly. Users with unreliable connections and users in high-traffic areas, however, can often smooth playback by increasing how much they prebuffer at the start of a stream. This is done by increasing the Prebuffer amount by sliding the first Streaming Prebuffer slider more to the right. The second slider on the right, determines how much of a song to buffer after there has been a disruption in the connection. This also works to smooth out song play; increasing the buffer can eliminate further disruptions.

The Streaming Data Buffer is a numeric setting you can change to increase or decrease the amount of RAM used to buffer an incoming stream in memory. Increasing this value on machines with good amounts of memory can help provide better skip protection due to Internet congestion.

Finally the Enable SHOUTcast Title Streaming checkbox should be left blank on machines with slow Internet connections.

Nullsoft Waveform File Decoder v1.15 (x86) [IN_WAVE.DLL]

This plug-in is designed to decode .WAV files. When you select the Waveform File Decoder plug-in and click Configure, a small window is displayed (as seen in **Figure 6.10**). By adjusting the slider, the decoding priority can be adjusted to allow for slower machines. Slower Pentiums or i486 computer users can increase from the default Higher setting to the Highest setting. When the Prompt to Save Streamed Files box is checked, Winamp prompts the user about where to save streaming files when they are first downloaded over the Internet.

Figure 6.10
Configuring the WaveForm File Decoder.

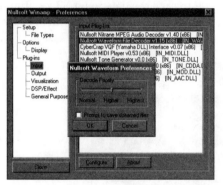

Nullsoft CD/Line Input Player v0.100 (x86) [IN_CDDA.DLL]

The CD/Line Input Player is an excellent plug-in that allows the Winamp player to read music directly from a CD, or even from a direct line in through the sound card. Click on the About button to get general information on how to utilize this plug-in. If you want to use the Winamp player to play music directly from a line-in on your computer, open Winamp and press Ctrl+L to get the Open Location box. Instead of typing in a normal URL, type in **linein://**. This pipes the music directly through the Winamp player.

If you want to use the Winamp player to play CDs, place a music CD in your CD-ROM drive. Open Winamp, press L to load a song, and go to your CD drive. You will note that the songs on the CD drive are all listed in a format like Track01.cda, Track02.cda, and so on. If you want to load all the songs, click on the first song once to highlight, hold down Shift, and click on the last track. This highlights all the songs. Click on Open and all the songs should be pulled into the playlist (if it is open); the first song on the CD to the last track will play. You can also make Winamp play audio CDs automatically. Just go to the File Types tab of the Winamp Preferences menu and check the Associate with Audio CDs option.

One of this plug-in's excellent functions is the capability to go out across the Internet and access sites such as CDDB (CD Database, located at **www.cddb.com**), which is a large database of all songs and titles on many compact discs. When Winamp contacts CDDB, it receives artist and song information for whatever CD is playing, provided the information is on CDDB.

To enable this function, open the Preferences menu, go to the Input Plug-In section, and highlight Nullsoft CD/Line Input Player v0.100 (x86) [IN_CDDA.DLL]. Click on Configure; a menu like that in **Figure 6.11** appears. In the Escient CDDB box, check the Use CDDB selection; when you load songs from a CD, Winamp will automatically go out, find the necessary information, and display it on the playlist and on the scrolling title bar. If you want to use another reference database to label tracks for you, click on the Change button and select from one of the databases listed; alternatively, enter your own in the space provided. If you want information from the selected database, enter your email information in the space provided.

Figure 6.11
Configuring the CD/Line
input player.

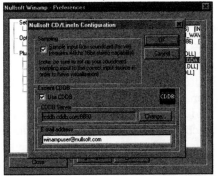

TIP

The Sampling box on the top of CD/Line Configuration menu enables users to add visualization components to music by allowing Winamp to sample your sound card's output. You must have a sound card that is capable of 16-bit sound and 44KHz quality. Make sure that your sound card sampling input is set to the proper input source in order to make visualization work. You can find these settings in the multimedia section of the Windows control panel. Check the CD device and the line input devices to make sure they are configured properly.

Part II   Advanced Winamp

Nullsoft Module Decoder v1.21 (x86) [IN_MOD.DLL]

The Module Decoder is an Input plug-in that allows the Winamp player to play module files. **MOD files** are best described as a cross between MIDI files and digitized music. Instead of using synthesized instruments like MIDI, MOD files play back specific samples in place of instruments. This format, which was started on the old Amiga computer system, has had a cult following ever since. For more on MOD files see Chapter 13, "Alternative Formats to MP3."

These files use extensions such as .XM, .S3M, and .MOD. On this plug-in's Configure menu (**Figure 6.12**), users can fine-tune the playing of modules for their computer. Here are the major options:

▶ In the Channels box, users can have modules play stereo or mono or reverse the stereo output.

▶ The Mixing Frequency box allows users to reduce CPU usage by downsampling the song to reduce the frequency from the default of 44100Hz.

▶ The voices box sets the maximum number of active voices used in a MOD file. Set this lower if MOD files seem to consume too much of your computer's processing power. The default setting is 64.

▶ The Bits per Sample box is included to provide compatibility with older 8-bit sound cards. The Streaming box, when checked, allows users to save streaming module files when they first play the song.

▶ Mixer options allow users to enable **interpolation** (which makes the music sound smoother); **surround sound** (which does some nifty stereo projection effects that make music sound better); **clickless mixing**, which can increase sound quality by improving volume issues; and **disable 8xx Panning Effects**, which gets rid of some annoying clicks and disables 8xx panning.

▶ Note that the first three mixer options tend to increase CPU usage, so try disabling them on slow machines if you have problems.

▶ Skipping problems can also be averted by increasing decode thread priority from the default of Higher to Highest.

▶ The final box offers the option to have Winamp prompt you to save MOD files that are streamed off the Internet rather than just played.

Figure 6.12
Configuring the Module
Decoder.

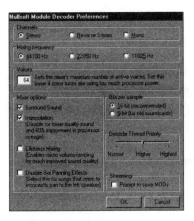

Output Plug-Ins

This section of preferences lets you pick and configure settings for any of
the installed output plug ins that are currently installed in Winamp.
While you may have more than three available, the main three to
configure are:

▶ Nullsoft WaveOut Plug-In v2.00 (x86) [OUT_WAVE.DLL]

▶ Nullsoft Disk Write Plug-In v1.0 (x86) [OUT_DISK.DLL]

▶ Nullsoft DirectSound Plug-In v.80b (x86) [OUT_DS.DLL]

Nullsoft WaveOut Plug-In v2.00 (x86) [OUT_WAVE.DLL]

This Output plug-in allows the Winamp player to play .MP3s by
converting them into .WAV files and playing them through your sound
card. Highlight this in the Audio I/O tab; you will notice that the
Configure and About buttons are now accessible. Clicking on Configure
pulls up a menu like that in **Figure 6.13**. If a song is playing, when you
bring up the configuration dialog box it will display information on what
amount of music is currently buffered, how much has been buffered total,
how many bytes have been transferred to the sound card, and the total
output recorded. Click the Reset button to set this data back to 0.

At the top of this menu there is a selection that allows you to control
what WaveOut device you wish to use to play the sound files. The
default selection is generally correct, but users with advanced hardware
may want to use other devices. This is especially true if you have two
sound boards on your machine (useful if you're mixing files using a DJ
plug-in like Pitchfork, or mixing other MP3 files). With this configuration
option, you can set different instances of Winamp to output to separate
cards.

Part II Advanced Winamp

Figure 6.13
Configuring the
WaveOut plug-in.

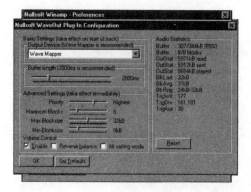

Under that is Buffer length. Setting the buffer length is very much dependent upon your machine. The default Buffer length is 2,000 milliseconds, or 2 seconds. This places two seconds of play time in memory in advance of playing and helps prevent skipping. Increasing this default allows slower machines to play without skipping when other programs take priority, but it uses more memory. The Separate Buffering Thread box is selected by default and allows the Winamp player to buffer more aggressively. This also makes for smoother playback on most systems. Disabling this option can be useful for some problematic sound cards.

Below the Buffer Length setting are Advanced Settings, which take effect immediately.

Priority determines how much precedence Winamp takes over other programs when playing files. Lower settings may cause Winamp to skip when processor usage is heavy.

The sliders for Maximum Blocks, Max Blocksize, and Min Blocksize control block size (in samples), which are the information blocks the Winamp player is using to output the music. Sometimes lowering this below the default of 9K samples can smooth out visualization and equalizer playback; increasing it can be helpful on some systems.

On the bottom of the WaveOut Configure menu, you can set Winamp to allow volume control directly from the faceplate. You can also reverse the balance controls if your speakers are reversed in playback by clicking on the Reverse Balance Control box. If volume control on the Winamp faceplate doesn't seem to work, you can try selecting the Alt Setting Method box.

TIP

If you've experimented with settings—especially the advanced ones, use the
Set Defaults button to recover.

Nullsoft Disk Write Plug-In v1.0 (x86) [OUT_DISK.DLL]

The Nullsoft Disk Write plug-in was designed so users can output .WAV
files from the Winamp player. Simply loading an .MP3 file, going to the
Preferences menu, selecting the Disk Writer plug-in from the Outputs
box, and clicking on the Configure button will allow you to pick the
directory you want the output of the song to go into. Playing the song will
then place a .WAV file converted from the .MP3 format. When the plug-in
is selected in the Output box, the Winamp player will not play .MP3,
only convert it to a .WAV file and save it to the location selected.

Nullsoft DirectSound Plug-In v.80b (x86) [OUT_DS.DLL]

The DirectSound plug-in allows the .MP3 player to utilize Microsoft's
DirectSound drivers to play files and communicate with your sound card.
This extends the Winamp player's capabilities a good deal, allowing for
more than one song to be playing concurrently. It also lets you play your
favorite MP3s, while games that may be using DirectSound are running.

TIP

You must have DirectSound installed on your computer to use this plug-in. If
you've ever installed the DirectX drivers from Microsoft (usually installed as
part of many of today's computer games), you will have it. If not, you can
download the DirectX drivers (which include DirectSound) from Microsoft at
http://www.microsoft.com/directx/ or from C I Net's Download.com.

You can also after that point install the latest sound card drivers from your
manufacturer. Check your card manufacturer's Web site for more information.

To configure the DirectSound output plug in, highlight it in the Output
box on the Audio I/O tab and hit Configure. A menu like that in **Figure
6.14** will be displayed. This menu allows users to set the default buffer
size, which controls how many blocks of information are stored in the
buffer. The default is 3; you may want to increase this if you experience
skipping during playback on slower computers. Block Size (In Samples)
allows the user to increase or decrease the block size stored in the buffer.
Sometimes setting the block size up from its default of 16K per block can
smooth out playback for some cards.

Figure 6.14
Configuring the
DirectSound output
plug in.

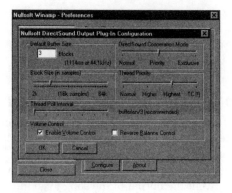

DirectSound Cooperation mode determines how your computer
prioritizes the music coming from Winamp, as well as from any other
source. Setting the slider bar to Normal tells your sound card that
Winamp's playback quality isn't critical. The overall quality of music
you'll hear will be pretty bad, since it will typically output it in 8 bits per
sample by default. Priority keeps Winamp playing in its intended quality,
and mixing with other DirectSound programs. Exclusive allows Winamp
to be the only program to use the DirectSound sound card. There is no
real benefit to doing so, however. Thread Priority tells your CPU how
much priority the DirectSound output portion of Winamp should get
when the computer is processing information, including other programs
running on your machine. Here are the settings you can choose:

▶   Normal is the lowest setting priority, which will allow Winamp's
    playback engine to sometimes be disrupted by other more important
    programs running on the computer.

▶   The Highest setting is the default.

▶   TC(!) is actually a step above highest. It should be used when
    Winamp is being used exclusively for recording or broadcasting.

After setting the Thread Priority, there is the Thread Poll Interval. This is
used to determine how often the Winamp player checks the threads being
sent to the CPU. The default setting is the first notch on the slider bar,
bufferlen/3. Setting this higher can sometimes allow slower computers to
do less processing at the cost of accuracy.

The Volume Control box allows control from the Winamp faceplate,
while the reversing stereo balance control option lets you switch the way
the balance works in case your speakers are not positioned in-sync with
the balance control on the Winamp main console.

TIP

A number of options in the DirectSound Output plug-in are there primarily for experimentation. The DirectSound Output plug-in is an in-progress plug-in, and the WaveOut plug-in is better in nearly every way on most systems.

Visualization Plug-In Settings

In this section of preferences (**Figure 6.15**), you can choose the Visualization plug-in that is run when you start the Visualization mode of Winamp. You can also start, stop, and configure various Visualization plug-ins here as well. Below the main window is a smaller drop-down list that lets you select specific types of variants a single Visualization plug-in might offer. Choose a plug-in (and the specific variant if ones are offered) listed in the top window and hit Configure to bring up the configuration dialog box for that specific plug-in. In Chapter 7, many of the most popular Visualization plug-ins are explained in detail.

Figure 6.15
Choose the Visualization plug-in you want and its variant and then press Start, Stop or Configure.

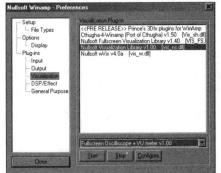

The Visualization plug-ins display some of the most incredible light shows available to computer users. With plug-ins that run in windowed form, at full screen, and plug-ins that utilize the newest 3-D graphics hardware, any Winamp user can find a plug-in to go with his musical choice and add a whole new dimension to how he listens to music. In addition to adding colors and sound, many plug-ins also add excellent features such as fading one song into the next and top-notch sound-wave imaging. There is a plug-in that allows you to add lyrics to songs. Plug-ins even allow you to run multiple plug-ins at once!

Part II Advanced Winamp

However, some of these spectacular visual displays and utilities come at a significant cost. Most plug-ins that run windowed have modes that consume fewer CPU cycles, which can allow most computers of Pentium speed to run without slowdown. These are very useful because they can run while you go about your normal computer pastimes. Surfing the Web, sending email, chatting, or even working on spreadsheets can all be performed while you have visual and auditory entertainment. Some of the fullscreen and 3-D–only plug-ins can consume all available processing power, making them only useful when you don't want to use your computer for anything else.

Finding and Installing Plug-Ins

Finding additional and third-party plug-ins is a snap. The Winamp community is very active, and new plug-ins are released quite frequently. Winamp's home page, **http://www.winamp.com**, gathers most of the plug-ins and makes them available for direct download. They organize the plug-ins into the basic categories of windowed, full-screen, 3-D only, general, effects, input, and output. They also offer a top 10 plug-in category that shows what plug-ins people seem to download and enjoy the best.

Winamp used to come with one plug-in already installed, but plug-ins have been removed from the newest version of Winamp removed to save on download times. The Nullsoft Visualization Library (by Justin Frankel) is the standard plug-in installed if you have an older version of Winamp.

Plug-ins stay even when you upgrade, so check to see which ones you may have.

Pull up the Winamp menu by right-clicking on the faceplate. At the bottom of the menu you will see a selection for Visualization. Click on this option; you will see a menu like that in **Figure 6.16**. Winamp's Preferences menu pulls up when you click on the last entry in the Select Plug-In menu. It comes up opened to Visualization tab. Chose The Nullsoft Visualization Library v1.0- [VIS_NS.DLL], if present. It should be present if you had an older copy of Winamp installed on your system before 2.10 was released as many earlier versions of Winamp contained it automatically in the download.

NOTE

If you have the latest version of Winamp and do not have this plug-in installed, connect to the Internet, and go to **http://www.winamp.com**, and download it. Go to the Winamp Downloads section and select the link for the plug-ins page; download the Nullsoft Visualization Library plug-in.

TIP

You should consider bookmarking Nullsoft's plug-ins page; it contains many useful plug-ins, and you will need to refer to it in order to get other plug-ins for trial (in addition to demonstrating the Nullsoft Visualization Library in this section).

Figure 6.16
The Preferences menu's Visualization tab with the Visualization Library v1.00 selected.

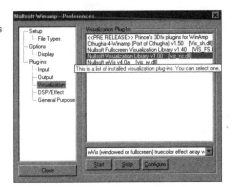

Part II   Advanced Winamp

NOTE

All plug-ins are stored in the Plug-Ins folder in the Winamp main directory (the default is C:\Program Files\Winamp\Plugins). This is unless you decided to change the directory as discussed earlier. Whenever you download any plug-in, simply placing the .DLL in the Visualization folder will allow Winamp to use it. The .DLL files are usually very small, so hard drive space is not a big issue; if, however, you need to trim down your plug-ins, you can simply delete the appropriate .DLL file out of the Plug-Ins folder. All plug-in file names are listed at the end of the name of the plug-in on its appropriate tab on the Preferences menu. This allows you to easily recognize what .DLL file is behind each plug-in effect you've added to Winamp.

Running a Windowed Plug-In

With the Nullsoft Visualization Library installed, go have some fun. Fire up Winamp and start some music. Pull up the Visualization menu, either by pulling up the main menu and selecting Visualization, or by clicking on the V in the Vis window on the Winamp player's faceplate. In addition to the Start, Stop, and Configure buttons at the bottom of this window, you can adjust the priority of the visualization display by increasing or decreasing the slider from the default of Normal. There are also two other boxes. The first one, Auto Execute Plug-In on Play, will automatically allow plug-ins to start as soon as you play a song. The other box, Disable Built-In Visualization, will stop the display on the Vis window on the main Winamp console itself. This can save extra CPU power while using plug-ins that either duplicate or obscure the Vis window's effect.

Click on Select Plug-In; you should see a plug-in called Nullsoft Visualization Library v1.0- [VIS_NS.DLL]. Click on it and then click Configure. This menu pulls up some information on the plug-in as well as instructions on how to configure it.

One of this plug-in's great features is its many types of modes. You can see what modes any plug-in has by simply clicking on the menu arrow on the Plug-In module. Nullsoft Visualization Library defaults to a Windowed mode that runs in the Vis window of the Winamp player replacing the Oscilloscope that shows the levels of each frequency in the current MP3 being played, and the time display. This mode, wVis (Windowed or Fullscreen) Truecolor Effect Array v4.11, has many functions. Start it and take a look at some of them.

Click on Start and then click on OK to close the Visualization menu. Check out the Vis window! If everything is working properly, you should see a light effect, consisting of two oscillating lines running horizontally and a yellow spinning star as seen in **Figure 6.17.** This display is the default display. To create this effect, the Normal Scope, Solid Scope, and Oscilloscope Stars functions are turned on from the Visualization Library menu. Once this plug-in is running, this menu is available simply by right-clicking on the visual display, allowing users to change any effects while the song is playing. **Figure 6.18** shows this menu.

Figure 6.17
The Nullsoft Visualization Library in action.

Figure 6.18
Right-clicking on the Vis
window brings up the
configuration menu.

The menu has many functions so let's look through them all. The first
selection on the menu is in fact not a selection at all— it's just the name
of the plug-in and its version. The second selection is Rendering Options
(**Figure 6.19**). This menu controls how the visuals fade, blend, transition
into each other and other functions. The Fading submenu allows you to
control how much visuals fade after being drawn on the screen. The
Fading menu allows users to set visuals to clear immediately, to fade
faster or slower, or to avoid fading at all. Setting fading to Clear can
sometimes use 10–20% less processing power than setting it to None.

Figure 6.19
The Rendering menu
with Fading options.

The Transitions submenu has three options: None, Blur, and Blitter
Feedback. The None option shows no fading between peaks and dips in
effects, while the Blur smoothes transitions. Blitter Feedback pushes
blurring to the outer edges of the window, causing the image to seem to
stream toward the user. It is a very cool effect when the fading is set to
Fast Fade and Blitter Feedback is turned on. Note that Blitter Feedback
has no effect when fading is set to Clear.

Foreground Blend

This Rendering menu submenu allows you to blend the visual displays
into each color displayed. The three settings on the Foreground menu are
Average Blend (wVis 3.0), Add Blend (wVis 4.0), and Peak Blend. Add
Blend is the default and allows the colors to fade into the background.
Play with these; some effects look better with different colors or displays.

Part II Advanced Winamp

Background

This submenu is pretty simple. It pulls up a spectrum menu, which allows you to set whatever color you want as the default background when the plug-in plays. This is a cool feature to play around with when you are using different-colored skins.

Spectrum Falloff

Here you can determine how quickly the visual displays take to return to the **zeroed**, or res, state after each musical peak and dip. The three settings on this menu are Slow, Medium, and Fast. A slower setting requires slightly more CPU power to calculate. Some effects look much funkier with falloff slower; some look better sped up.

Refresh Rate

This menu determines how often the plug-in samples the musical output to display visuals. This setting can allow most slower computers to display visuals by setting the rate from its default setting of Full, to Half (or even Third). On a test AMD K6-2 350MHz machine, setting the Refresh Rate from Full to Half can reduce the workload by 15%–25%.

Changing the Effects

The Rendering portion of the wVis menu holds the section that contains what visual effects are displayed. Each one of these effects can be either shown with other effects or individually. Some effects look better when they are run alone, some look better with other effects. Normal Scope, Solid Scope, and Oscilloscope Stars are all running when you first start this plug-in.

Normal Scope

This shows two horizontal lines that perform oscilloscope-like functions. Here you can either enable or disable this or change the colors of the lines.

Solid Scope

This shows the peaks and dips in two horizontal rows. On this submenu, you can enable this function or change the colors of the lines.

Line Analyzer

This option shows two vibrating lines that separate at higher volumes for each frequency, and collapse to center when the frequency is silenced. Here you can enable this function or change the colors of the lines.

Solid Analyzer

This option displays a single line, which represents playing frequencies, thickening, and returning to 0 as the song requires. You can enable or disable this function or change the colors of the line.

Flower Scope

This provides a neat effect by creating two circular shapes that pulse and contract with the music. You can enable this here or change the colors of either flower. You can also control the complexity of the flower shapes.

Spectrum Radar

This places two rotating lines in the left and right sides of the Vis display. They provide a radar-like look with the frequencies being played. On this submenu, you can enable this function or change the colors of the lines. A pretty cool effect. This effect looks better with fading set slower.

Bass Spin

This generates two spinning lines or triangles from points on the left and right of the Vis display. These lines expand and pulse with lower frequencies. On this submenu, you can enable or disable this function or change the colors of the lines. You can also set the bass from triangles, which can use a little more CPU usage, to lines. This effect often looks better with faster fading.

Oscilloscope Stars

This creates two stars made of five lines. When music is played, these two stars vibrate, rotate, and oscillate with the music, blending their colors to form a very cool effect. Here you can enable or disable this option or change the colors of the line. Changing the colors of the lines makes for some very entertaining eye candy.

Time Display

This option places the time remaining or elapsed (depending on what normally is displayed) back in the Vis window. You turn this option on or off here, as well as change the color of the display and control where the time is aligned on the Vis window.

Docking the Nullsoft Visualization Library

Docking is a term used to describe how the Vis window displays in relation to the Winamp faceplate. As you experiment with docking, don't forget that no matter how or where the visualization is displayed, you can get back to the menu simply by right-clicking on the area where the plug-in is displayed. The Docking selection of the menu has the following options:

► **Entire Window**—This turns the Winamp player into a visual display, leaving just a title bar and its controls.

► **Bottom**—This attaches a visual window to the bottom of the Winamp player, generally where the equalizer would appear.

Part II Advanced Winamp

▶ **Top**—This attaches a visual window to the top of the Winamp player.

▶ **Left**—This displays the window to the left.

▶ **Right**—This displays the window to the right.

▶ **Little Vis**—This displays the Visualization where the Spectrum Analyzer would normally be in the Vis window.

▶ **Little Vis w/o Time**—This is the default setting, replacing the Time and Spectrum Analyzer in the Vis window.

Fullscreen

This allows you to take any effect and have it run full-screen on your computer. You can choose from these resolutions:

320×200

320×240

512×384

640×400

640×480

800×600

To display some of these effects full-screen at 800×600 takes quite a powerhouse of a computer! That would be a machine with good CPU power (200MHz or better) and a graphics card with at least 8MB of memory and AGP 2X support.

Saving and Loading Visualization Presets is as easy as clicking on the Presets button in the Visualization Library. Nullsoft automatically defaults to saving these files in the Plug-Ins directory in the main Winamp folder. When you want to load them again, click on Load. Winamp will automatically look in the Plug-Ins folder for any preset files.

Running the Nullsoft Visualization Library in Full-Screen Modes

Are saying to yourself that these are some very cool effects? By no means is this the end of what this plug-in has to offer. The windowed effects of the Visualization Library have only been touched on. Now you need to explore what it has to offer in true full-screen effects.

Full-screen effects can consume a lot of the CPU's power. This can sometimes cause Winamp to skip or stutter through tracks. Turning the priorities up on the Input and Output plug-ins on the Audio I/O tab on the Preferences menu can resolve these problems some of the time. Slower computers may suffer from poor **framerates** (the effects will look jumpy or act slow), and there is not a lot that can be done about this except upgrading.

Go to the Preferences menu and pull up the Visualization tab. Click on the pull-down menu in the Plug-In Module box; you will see that in addition to the wVis Truecolor Effect Array, there are nine other modules! Take a look at what they do. To start any plug-in, select it in the Plug-In Module box and press Start. To escape from a plug-in, click the Esc button in the upper-left corner of your keyboard.

Fullscreen Spectrum Analyzer + VoicePrint v1.00

This module displays a full stereo Spectrum Analyzer and Voiceprint Analyzer. If you hit Configure before going into this module, you can adjust the colors and control the falloff rate of the bars.

Fullscreen Oscilloscope + VU meter v1.00

A stereo oscilloscope is displayed when this module is playing, as well as a VU meter at the bottom of the screen. A **VU meter** is simply a display that shows the volume of the left and right channels. If you click Configure, you can customize the VU meter's colors.

Fullscreen Oscilloscope + Spectrum Analyzer v1.00

This module combines the fullscreen oscilloscope from the previous module with the Spectrum Analyzer from the first module. If you click Configure before going into this module, you can adjust the colors and control the Analyzer's falloff rate.

Fullscreen Big Spectrum Analyzer v1.00

This module takes the Spectrum Analyzer, expands it physically, and runs the left channel on the top of the screen and the right channel on the bottom. If you click Configure before going into this module, you can adjust the colors and control the Analyzer's falloff rate.

Fullscreen Big Oscilloscope v1.00

The oscilloscope is displayed with the left channel on the top of the screen and the right channel at the bottom in this fullscreen module. The Configure menu does not change any function on this module.

Fullscreen Oscilloscope Flowers v1.00

This visualization effect creates a line, like a oscilloscope, but wraps it around itself until it makes a cool flower-like shape that spikes and dances with the music. Clicking Configure allows the user to increase or decrease the density or complexity of this display.

Part II   Advanced Winamp

Fullscreen 3-D Spectrum Analyzer Dot Plane v1.00

This cool full-screen effect creates a spinning plane of multicolored dots that rise and fall according to the frequencies being played (**Figure 6.20**). Configuring this module allows you to change the colors of the display and the falloff rate.

Figure 6.20
Dot Plane Analyzer in action!

Fullscreen 3-D Dot Oscilloscope Fountain v1.00

This is one of the best full-screen effects of any of the plug-ins tested. It creates a fountain of spinning dots that shoot up and change colors depending upon the music. Configuring this allows you to change the colors.

Fullscreen Trippy Blurred Rotozoomer v1.09

This entertaining effect pulses to the bass, spinning and blurring colors in conjunction with the music (**Figure 6.21**). This is the only module that has its own unique Configure menu. In addition to being able to change the image displayed, you can set the size of the full-screen image displayed, control the blurriness, and even control the rate of spin.

Figure 6.21
Funky effects from the
Trippy Blurred
Rotozoomer.

Part II   Advanced Winamp

General Visualization Overview

The Nullsoft Visualization Library is only one of many Visualization
plug-ins available on the Winamp home page. Some of these other plug-
ins are very simple; some of them can rival and even beat the
Visualization Library for complexity and general display capabilities. The
next chapter takes a look at some of the very best plug-ins available from
some very talented Winamp community programmers.

DSP/Effect and General Plug-Ins

Aside from Visualization, Input, and Output plug-ins, there are two other
types of plug-ins to generally discuss. DSP/Effect Plug-Ins let you change
the shape and characteristics of the outgoing waveform giving you the
ability to add echoes, vinyl rassy and other special effects to your music.
In Chapter 7, there is further discussion about these types of plug-ins and
in Chapter 12 there is a discussion of the SHOUTcast Source for Winamp
plug-in used to output your Winamp stream to a SHOUTcast server in
order to create your own Internet radio station.

General Purpose Plug-Ins

Two general purpose plug-ins are packaged with Winamp. The Nullsoft
Windowshade Docker Plug-In v0.7 (GEN_DOC.DLL) lets you force the
Winamp player, when it is in Windowshade mode to dock to the active
window. Just click Configure, check the box on the resulting dialog box,
and press OK to enable this setting.

The Tray Control Setup plug-in (**Figure 6.22**) provides a series of play/pause/track controls that you can have displayed in the system tray of your Windows taskbar and use to control the player. Simply place a check in the box of each control you want placed in the tray.

Figure 6.22
The Nullsoft Tray Control Setup dialog box lets you place common play controls in the system tray of your Windows taskbar.

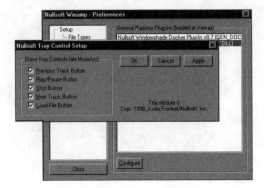

Power to the User

By understanding all the ins and outs of the program you should now be a Winamp superhero, able to tweak settings in a single bound. It's one thing to simply use Winamp; it's another to master it. The beauty of the product is that Winamp is so much more than a mere mild-mannered MP3 player. Winamp is really a platform upon which you can turn your PC into the ultimate audio system. By opening so many of the options in each Winamp system piece, and by offering the easy capability to expand it, Winamp puts the precise power of how you listen to your MP3s and other forms of digital music in your hands.

The tweaking and power capabilities don't stop with the built-in plug-ins and Nullsoft's Vis plug-in. Winamp users are provided with a wealth of plug-ins, both audio and video flavors, to ascend to the top tier of users and get the most out of your MP3 experience, You'll want to acquire, install, and then precisely configure the best of Winamp plug-ins. In the next chapter, you do precisely that.

7

All About Winamp Plug-Ins: How to Configure the Leading Plug-Ins

Plug-Ins and Winamp

In Chapter 6, you learn the basics of installing and operating the Nullsoft Visualization Library plug-in. In this chapter, you look at some of the other outstanding plug-ins available for Winamp. The Nullsoft Visualization plug-in was designed strictly to add a visual component to Winamp's performance, like the majority of plug-ins. While some plug-ins perform very similar tasks, there are also plug-ins that allow multiple visual plug-ins to run at the same time. There are even plug-ins that create graphical speakers that throb and respond to the music, VU Meters, Lyric Players—even plug-ins that allow you to output data to the serial port to flash external lights in time with music. A virtual DJ!

In addition to these outstanding visual capabilities, the Winamp player allows you to extend many of its functions through the use of **general** plug-ins. General plug-ins range a great deal in intent, allowing a huge amount of added functions and changes to the Winamp player. Some general plug-ins enable Winamp users to totally customize and rearrange the Winamp interface, hiding Winamp and adding new play controls, as well as many other functions. Some plug-ins allow Winamp to be controlled over a LAN, even one that allows users to control Winamp with a joystick! Want to use Winamp as an alarm clock? Want to put it on a sleep timer? There are plug-ins for those functions.

Many people have taken the time to design excellent audio plug-ins as well. From effects-plug-ins that allow you to run several DSP plug-ins simultaneously; to add reverb, filtering, or pitch adjustment; plug-ins to make beatmixing simple. There's an excellent plug-in that equalizes volume between MP3s. Winamp offers everything a budding DJ could desire.

Since there are so many plug-ins available from the Nullsoft guys and from third-party developers, we are going to take a look at only the most popular and useful. Since usefulness is very subjective matter, and you may find that the plug-ins covered may not be the ones you need to use, we'll give you a lot of helpful hints for use when downloading and using new plug-ins for the first time. Let's go look at the Visualization plug-ins.

Windowed, Fullscreen, and 3D-Only Visualization Plug-Ins

Chapter 6 contains a lot of details about downloading and installing a new plug-in, and it can provide a lot of information in case of any problems. The Nullsoft Visualization Library should already be installed in the Plugins folder in Winamp, but you need more than one plug-in to use Winamp to its fullest. Start Winamp and open the Main menu by right-clicking on the top title bar. Go to the Visualization menu and click Select Plug-In. You will then notice a blue link on the bottom of the menu that says Download Plug-Ins from **http://www.winamp.com/plugins/**. Click on the blue link to open your default browser to the Winamp Plug-Ins page. Click on the Windowed link under the Visualization section.

The Winamp page rates each plug-in on a one-to-five star rating. These plug-ins are then organized by their ratings. Any plug-in rated five stars is considered an essential Winamp power user visualization tool. Let's download FunkyFX by Paul Holden, Albedo by Imad Jureidini, and Prince's OpenGL plug-ins. Remember where you save the files you download, they'll need to be uncompressed and placed in the proper location.

Most plug-ins are compressed with a program such as WinZip or PKZIP, which you will need to use to extract these files to C:\Program Files\Winamp\Plugins (or wherever you installed your main Winamp program). The file that tells Winamp what to do is a .DLL file contained in the .ZIP file you downloaded. All plug-ins are stored in the Plugins folder in the Winamp main directory; whenever you download any plug-ins, simply placing the .DLL in the Winamp\Plugins folder allows Winamp to run the plug-in. You will notice that all of these .ZIP files have at least two files in them: a .TXT file that tells about the plug-in and where to place it as well as the .DLL file that tells the Winamp player what to do.

When unzipping the FunkyFX plug-in, make sure that the .ZIP file's directory structure is maintained by checking Use Folder Names when extracting through WinZip; alternatively, you can use the –S switch when using PKZIP. The FunkyFX plug-in creates three subdirectories in your Plugins folder when unzipped properly:

▶ FFXSkins

▶ FrequencywurX

▶ FyreWurx

If you want to uninstall this plug-in, remove these three directories as well as the vis_funkyfx.dll from the Plugins folder.

Once you have unzipped all of these plug-ins into the Winamp folder's Plugins directory, close your Preferences menu and reopen it to the Visualization tab. You will notice that the following plug-ins are listed alphabetically:

Albedo v1.07	[vis_albedo.dll]
FunkyFX plug-in	[VIS_FUNKYFX.DLL]
Nullsoft Visualization Library v1.01	[VIS_NS.DLL]
Prince's 3D OpenGL plug-ins	[Wa3DGL.dll]

FunkyFX Plug-In

The first plug-in you are going to learn how to use to the fullest is the FunkyFX plug-in by Paul Holden. This impressive plug-in creates visualization to go with the music playing on the Winamp player. The Web page address for FunkyFX is **http://www.javigate.com/FunkyFX/**, and the current version of this plug-in is v2.00b.

FunkyFX should work with most hardware and software, but it will run best on Pentium 133 or higher machines. i486 machines will run this, but with reduced effects and frame rates. Video cards that can display in 32- or 24-bit color show off the spectacular visuals of this plug-in the best. Note that Microsoft's DirectX is required to run this plug-in.

The FunkyFX plug-in consists of three modules that generate different effects: FyrewurX, FrequencywurX, and FlamewurX. Start the plug-in and take a look at these modules by starting the Winamp player and loading your favorite music. Pull up the Visualization menu either by pulling up the Main menu and selecting Visualization, or clicking on the V on the Vis window in the Winamp player's faceplate. Click on Select Plug-In; you should see a plug-in called FunkyFX Plug-in [VIS_FUNKYFX.DLL]. Click on it to highlight and then select Start.

The FunkyFX plug-in should now be running somewhere near your Winamp player. The plug-in defaults to using the FrequencywurX module when it starts. This plug-in has two display modes: a Windowed mode designed to link to the normal sized Winamp player and a Fullscreen mode.

TIP

If you have Winamp displayed in Doublesize mode, this plug-in will not automatically adjust size to match the larger Winamp display, but it can be easily resized by putting your cursor on the edge of the display and dragging the window to a larger size.

Increasing or decreasing the size of the display window can greatly affect processor usage. It also will not display in the Vis window; it will, however, snap and lock to the Winamp player in whatever position you place it, like the equalizer or playlist functions.

The FrequencywurX module displays a colored spectrum analyzer that starts with a line across the center of the screen that expands up and down on the display, fading and blending with the peaks in the music frequencies. **Figure 7.1** shows this effect in action.

Figure 7.1
FunkyFX's default visualization, FrequencywurX.

Each of the three modules in the FunkyFX plug-in has its own menu for configuring each plug-in's properties. Like the Nullsoft Visualization Library, each module's Configuration menu can be accessed while the plug-in is in operation; do so by right-clicking on the visual display window. You can pull up a menu like that in **Figure 7.2** by right-clicking on FrequencywurX. While this menu is pretty self-explanatory, some of its functions aren't immediately obvious.

Figure 7.2
The FunkyFX menu.

Clicking on the Properties tab can pull up the Properties menus for each module. You can choose between the FyrewurX, FrequencywurX, and FlamewurX modules by clicking on Module and then selecting the appropriate effect from the drop-down menu. You can restore any of the modules to its default setting, or even create and save your own by selecting Load Preset or Save Preset. Some of the saved presets that come with the plug-in can give you an excellent idea of how each visual display can be changed to create visuals that are very unlike those shown when you first start each module.

Clear Screen clears the display window, while Recover resets the plug-in to its original start position and settings. These are handy if the display gets corrupted while adjusting settings in the Properties menu.

Mode allows you to select between Windowed and Fullscreen modes, as well as setting the visual window's display status. If the Always on Top setting is checked, the display window will always remain visible on your desktop, above any other windows.

FunkyFX allows skins to be used in conjunction with its modules. If you put a FunkyFX skin file (.FFS) and all its bitmaps in the same directory as a Winamp skin, the plug-in automatically changes to the matching skin when you select it in Winamp. However, you need to turn on Check for Winamp Skin Changes in Properties->Display (which is enabled by default) for it to work. Load Skin allows the plug-in to load a skin onto the Winamp player, and Use Skin makes the module use the skin in its display.

Exploring the Properties Menus

While each module has its own Properties menu, there are three tabs on each Properties menu that are the same on all the modules. FyrewurX, FrequencywurX, and FlamewurX all have Amp, Rendering, and Display tabs. Each of these tabs works the same way in all the modules, so let's take a look at them now.

The Amp tab on the Properties menu controls how much visual information is displayed from base volume of the song, and you should definitely try adjusting this to suit your computer's capabilities and your personal taste. Some songs are recorded quieter, some louder. If your display bar seems to be displaying too much sound—it seems to be constantly peaking to the outer edges of the visual display, for example— try setting the Linear Frequency Amplification slider bar down (to the left). If music visualization is minimal, try sliding it to the right. The Drop Off slider controls how long music information like the peaks and bars remains displayed on the screen. Setting this to Clear Sounds Quicker (sliding to the right) can speed performance slightly.

> **TIP**
>
> The Rendering tab can also increase performance when Blur is turned off and the Fade slider is set to Maximum. When checked, the Enable Blur box smoothes out peaks and valleys in frequency visualization, while the Fade slider controls how long the column colors and effects remain on the screen.

Part II   Advanced Winamp

The Display tab allows the user to control the way the window is displayed on your desktop. The Always on Top box can be used to set the window to always be on top of your desktop. On this tab, you can control the fullscreen resolution of the FunkyFX display. Only very fast computers using displays of 640×480 or 800×600 will get decent framerates. If you have downloaded skins, the Display tab will allow load skins for the FunkyFX plug-in.

FrequencywurX Module

The FrequencywurX module has a large Properties menu with seven tabs! Each tab controls a different aspect of the display, and with a little bit of tweaking, each display can be changed into a variety of colors and very cool special effects. Let's look through each of the tabs not already covered on the FrequencywurX Properties menu as seen in **Figure 7.3**.

Figure 7.3
The FunkyFX Properties menu with the FrequencywurX module.

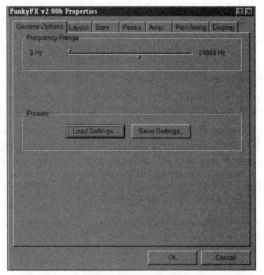

The General Options tab allows you to control the range of frequencies sampled for visual display. This defaults to a sampling range of 0Hz to 24,869Hz. The generally accepted range of human hearing is a low of 20Hz to a high of around 20,000Hz. The slider bar on this tab allows you to sample frequencies up to 44,000Hz! You may not be able to hear it, but you can see if those frequencies are there in the music. From this tab, you can also load or save presets.

On the Layout tab, users can define how the frequencies are displayed in the window. If you select Mono, the display will change to a long single bar equalizer. If Flip Horizontal is on, the display will have higher frequencies to the left and lower frequencies to the right. If Flip Vertical is checked, the frequencies are displayed starting at the top and shoot toward the bottom of the display with each peak. If Diamond is selected (this is the default setting), frequencies start at the center of the window and flow toward the top and bottom during peaks. If Stereo is selected, it displays a stereo spectrum analyzer that you can set up however you like with the Flip Horizontal and Flip Vertical boxes.

The Bars tab controls the geometry settings, as well as drawing mode and color selection. The Geometry box contains sliders that control bar width, horizontal spacing, and bar height. These sliders control how many frequency bars are displayed in the visual display window, as well as the base width and horizontal spacing. By default, these are set to the highest detail, with all the sliders set to the left. When checked, the Columns box tells the display window to draw columns under each bar; this is on by default, but it can change the appearance a great deal when turned off. The display's colors can be adjusted by clicking any of the four corners of the multicolored box in the bottom of this menu. Doing so pulls up a menu of colors to select from, and up to four colors can be used for special effects.

The Peaks tab allows you to control how peaks in the frequencies are displayed on the visual window. The Enable Peaks box displays frequency peaks with a white dot when playing music. Peak DropOff controls the rate at which those Peaks fall back into the center. Peak Aging controls how long each dot takes before it changes to another color. Hang Time controls how long each peak remains at its maximum before it starts to fall back to the center. The colors of the dots can be adjusted by clicking on the corners of the Color box. The top two colors control how each dot is first displayed; the colors on the bottom of the box determine the color as each peak ages.

Part II Advanced Winamp

FyrewurX Module

The next module FunkyFX offers is called FyrewurX; it is shown in **Figure 7.4**. This displays visuals that are very similar to its name. Jumping sparks and explosions are delivered in outstanding colors and variety. The FyrewurX module adds two other tabs to its Properties menu in addition to the three tabs for Amp, Rendering, and Display: General Options and Particle Sources.

Figure 7.4
FunkyFX's spectacular FyrewurX module.

General Options is the first tab on FyrewurX's Properties menu. This tab allows you to control the physics of the explosions and particles. The first slider, Particle Cull Rate, controls the rate at which particles disappear from the display window. The Animation box allows you to enable Air Resistance, which slows the particles as they stream off an explosion. Jitter allows the particles more movement. Stationary Source keeps explosions from imparting any inertia to particles, causing explosions to be rounder and to respond to gravity settings equally. The Type allows you to select from normal explosions, ring-shaped explosions, or a colored frequency display that works much like a spectrum analyzer with bouncing particles. Adjusting the Gravity slider allows you to control how the particles react once they stream off the explosion. Antigrav pushes the particles up to the top of the display, while Sun pulls them strongly toward the bottom.

The Particle Sources tab allows you to control the colors of the explosions, the types and the frequencies they respond to, and the number of particles displayed with each type of explosion. There are three types of explosions or particle sources displayed by default: Bass, MidRange, and Treble. You can create new particle sources by clicking on New Source. Rather than simply adjusting those explosions displayed by default, let's create a new type of explosion for the MidBass frequencies.

First select Bass under the Particle Settings pull-down menu. You are going to allow this to reproduce frequencies from 0Hz to 765Hz. Adjust the frequencies by using the sliders on the Frequency Response box.

Once this is done, click on New Source to create a new explosion; click on Set Name to name the new particle source **MidBass**. Adjust the low end of the frequency response to 688Hz and the upper end to 1,453Hz. Click on the Color button to set the color of the particles. Now you need to adjust the MidRange frequency settings. Pull down the menu on the Particle Settings box and select Midrange; use the Frequency Response box to set the lower frequencies to 1,453Hz. If you look back at your display window, you should have a new explosion throwing off particles any time any MidBass is played.

Creating new particle sources is pretty simple as is controlling those sources. Adjusting the Sensitivity slider for each particle source can allow more or fewer effects to be played. The settings in the Explosion Characteristics box allow you to adjust particle size and particles per explosion and you can even control how fast those particles shoot off the explosions by adjusting the Speed slider.

FlamewurX Module

The last part of the FunkyFX plug-in that you need to explore is the FlamewurX module. This module generates a window of flames that leap to beats in the music; you can see them in **Figure 7.5**. This plug-in is very simple, but with a little tweaking it can produce a cool special effect that goes with any song. The Properties menu on the FlamewurX module is simple; it only adds one tab, General Options, to the Amp, Rendering, and Display tabs.

Figure 7.5
Streaming flames dance to the music in the FlamewurX module.

The General Options tab is very simple. The Frequency Range slider allows you to adjust what frequencies are shown on the display window. Since most .MP3 file formats filter out sounds that humans cannot hear, frequencies above 25,000Hz rarely exist in songs that are not recorded at 256kbps. Setting the top end of the frequencies displayed on the Frequency Range slider to around 20,000–25,000 can allow the entire display area to show the visual effects. The Flame Color box allows you to set the color of the effects. A bright green flame goes very well with the base skin color, but this can be adjusted to whatever skin you are using.

Play with the settings on the Amp tab; try setting linear amplification to the third or fourth notch from the left; use the Rendering tab to set the fade to the second notch from the left and turn off Enable Blur. Check out those excellent effects!

Part II Advanced Winamp

The "Electromagnetic" Albedo Plug-In

The Albedo plug-in (**Figure 7.6**) by Imad Jureidini is another outstanding example of how far we have come with the personal computer. Ten years ago, it would have taken huge mainframe computers designed to specifically produce graphics to generate these dazzling effects you can now have at home. This plug-in is definitely designed to give most modern computers a good workout, and a Pentium II or Celeron computer is recommended to get the best performance, but any MMX-enabled processor should be able to run Albedo. Albedo uses Microsoft's DirectX to generate its effects, so make sure that you have downloaded and installed the most current version from **http://www.microsoft.com/directx/**. The Web page address for Albedo is **http://www.tripod.com/albedoplugin/**, and the current version of this plug-in is v1.07.

Figure 7.6
One of the cool effects generated by the Albedo plug-in.

The Web page contains useful information on the plug-in including the Readme.txt file included in the .ZIP file with the plug-in and a handy FAQ. Once you have installed the Albedo files by unzipping all the required files into the C:/Program Files/Winamp/Plugins folder above, you must select it within Winamp. The simplest way to do this is to press CTRL+K with the Winamp window activated, and to select Albedo in the Visualization Plug-In menu. Press Start to run the plug-in and get ready to be dazzled.

TIP

Albedo means "the fraction of incident light or electromagnetic radiation that is reflected by a surface or body." When you see this plug-in in action, the reason behind its name becomes clear.

Albedo is a plug-in that has many different types of visual effects and as it cycles through them all, it will very rarely repeat any patterns. Its geometric creations (**Figure 7.7**) combined with outstanding smoothing effects and hypnotic movement make this a great plug-in for your home system, or for DJs who are looking to add color to their music.

Figure 7.7
Cool geometric effects
are part of the Albedo
plug-in.

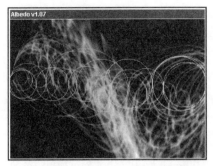

When Albedo starts up, it defaults to a Fullscreen mode that runs at
640×480. Changing to a Windowed mode by pressing F2 will allow you
to adjust the resolution to suit your computer's speed. Once you have
Albedo in a Windowed mode, you will notice that a small icon, which
looks like a red circle with a yellow X overlaying it, has been added to
the taskbar in the lower-left corner of your desktop. Left-click this icon
and it will pull up the Albedo Configuration Panel, or click the Tab
button while the plug-in is in operation.

On the Albedo Configuration Panel (**Figure 7.8**), you can easily adjust the
Display Mode default, from Full Screen to Windowed, and the resolution
to whatever works well on your computer. The Scene options box
displays the name for every different music renderer and scene
transformation while they are being displayed. You can select Next to
skip to the next one, or turn it off by unchecking the On box.

Figure 7.8
The Albedo
Configuration Panel.

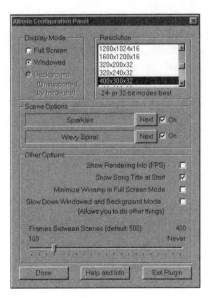

To show frames per second and some other information on the display window while the plug-in is in operation, you can select Show Rendering Info (or click F4 if the Albedo Configuration Panel isn't open). The check box next to Show Song Title at Start can be turned on or off in the Configuration Panel, or by pressing F9 during operation.

Minimizing Winamp in Full Screen Mode should be checked if you have problems with Winamp flickering behind the display window in Fullscreen mode. Checking the box next to Slow Down Windowed and Background Mode should be checked if you don't have a fast computer, and you will be doing a lot of other functions on your computer while the plug-in is displaying visuals. The slider bar labeled Frames Between Scenes allows you to select how long Albedo goes between switching from one scene to the next.

Albedo has hot keys that allow you to issue commands in Fullscreen mode without accessing the Albedo Configuration Panel. We covered some of the most used hot keys, but the following table is a complete listing of all of the hot keys available for Albedo.

SPACE - Randomly picks a new scene.
TAB - Brings up the Configuration Panel.
ALT_ENTER - Switch between Windowed and Fullscreen modes.
F1 - Switch to Fullscreen mode.
F2 - Switch to Windowed mode.
F4 - Shows some info, including frames per second.
F5 - Change to next music renderer.
F6 - Change to next scene transformation.
F7 - Lock the music renderer.
F8 - Lock the scene transformation.
F9 - Show song title when it starts.
F12 - Insanity mode (all renderers on...) Not very pretty.

Amazing 3D-Only Plug-Ins

With the advent of all the new 3D accelerated games and all of the 3D hardware required to go with those games, programmers have found other ways to utilize these excellent developments in technology. 3D-only plug-ins are designed to work on computers equipped with 3D hardware video accelerators. Are you unsure whether your video card is 3D accelerated? Those listed here are. If your card is not in the list below, check with your card's manufacturer to determine if it can play OpenGL or 3D programs.

3DFX Voodoo3/Voodoo2/Voodoo1/Rush/Bashee
ATI Rage Pro/128
Intel I740
Matrox G200/G400
nVidia Riva128/Zx/TNT/TNT2
Permedia 2/3
Rendition 2x00 (V2100,V2200)

The whole reason for having a 3D accelerated card is for the visual improvements it offers over unaccelerated cards. Faster, cleaner, and smoother graphics are the cornerstones of 3D acceleration and no plug-in demonstrates this as well as Prince's 3D OpenGL Plugins by CJ Cliffe. If you do not have a 3D accelerated card, this plug-in will not work for you. (You can make it work, but it will do so very slowly.) 3D cards are becoming very inexpensive, widely available, and almost mandatory for any new game, however, so most users will find them easy to obtain and install.

The minimum specification for running 3D-only plug-ins will depend greatly upon what type of 3D card you have. Generally, a Pentium 90 or higher is required to run 3D-only cards; the original 3DFX chipset-based Voodoo card is an example.

Installing Prince's 3D OpenGL Plug-Ins

Prince's 3D OpenGL plug-ins are available both on the Winamp home page under the 3D-Only section and directly from **http://3d.technonet.com**. This plug-in creates a display window using OpenGL.

> **NOTE**
> Certain cards are incapable of displaying windowed 3D acceleration. For example, 3DFX's Voodoo- and Voodoo2-based chipsets can only display fullscreen video effects.

Part II   Advanced Winamp

Once you have downloaded this plug-in, unpack all the contents of the
.ZIP file into your Winamp/Plugins directory. Load some music and take
a look at what Prince's OpenGL plug-ins can do to make your computer
show off its capabilities.

TIP

Once the plug-in has been installed, you may need to check with your
graphics vendor to see what steps are necessary for OpenGL support. Most,
but not all, graphics cards' installation programs will automatically install
sufficient OpenGL support.

The Prince of Plug-Ins

Open Winamp, load some of your favorite music, and open the
Visualization tab on the Preferences menu. You should see a listing of
plug-ins. Select Prince's 3D OpenGL Plugins [Wa3DGL.DLL]. This plug-in
has four modules:

▶   3D Sound Wave

▶   3D Sound Block

▶   3D Sound Tunnel

▶   3D Cube Plug-in

Each of these modules uses Winamp sound to affect visual displays.
Unlike the other plug-ins you've explored—the Nullsoft Visualization
Library and the FunkyFX plug-in—Prince's OpenGL plug-in can be
adjusted from the Configure button on the Visualization tab in the
Properties menu; alternatively, you can select Visualization, Configure
Plug-in from the main Winamp menu. When Prince's OpenGL plug-in is
set as the default plug-in, the quick key combination of Alt+K will pull
up the Configuration menu for whatever module is set as the default.

The Configuration menu of each module contains a button at the bottom
for graphics options. This button pulls up a menu that controls the
default display resolution and the setting for automatic fullscreen display.
Texture mode is designed to allow different 3D cards to be compatible if
they do not support features or perform too slow to use higher settings.
Off, Low (no perspective), Med (perspective), and High (Bilinear) settings
allow you to adjust the performance speed. Shading settings are Flat or
Smooth, and setting Shading to Flat can help performance.

Figure 7.9
Prince's OpenGL 3D
Sound Wave module.

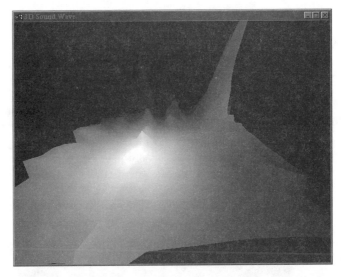

Start the 3D Sound Wave module, shown in **Figure 7.9**, and click the
Configure button to look at the menu. This menu allows you to change
between styles of visualization using Oscilloscope or Spectrum. You can
hold the image stationary, add rotation, and even control that rotation
with the Mode and Rotation pull-down menus and the Rotation Amount
slider bar. Sensitivity controls the size of peaks on the display. You can
adjust the colors assigned to frequencies by clicking on Light Color 1,
Light Color 2, or Light Color 3. Turning off Dynamic Lighting can help
lower CPU usage. If you don't like what changes you make while
experimenting, you can simply click the Reset button or click on the
Presets button to load the default settings.

Figure 7.10
The Sound Block
pounding out the bass.

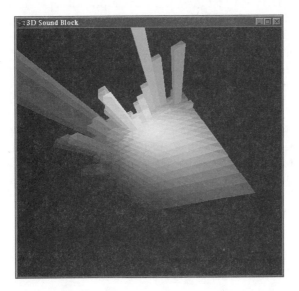

Part II   Advanced Winamp

The next module of Prince's OpenGL plug-in is the 3D Sound Block plug-in (**Figure 7.10**). This module creates a square grid that extends columns to the music pulsation. When you configure this module, lighting, color rotation, and sensitivity are controlled the same as in the prior module. This menu adds another slider bar, Grid Resolution, which sets the number of block columns per side. For example, a setting of 4 results in a square four blocks by four blocks. Setting this lower than the default can decrease CPU consumption. This module has two presets: Default and High Performance. Selecting High Performance is a pretty good way to see how powerful your machine is. Only a very top-end computer can deliver smooth frame rates while this gorgeous display is fullscreen!

Figure 7.11
Spinning and shimmering, the 3D sound tunnel adds outstanding effects.

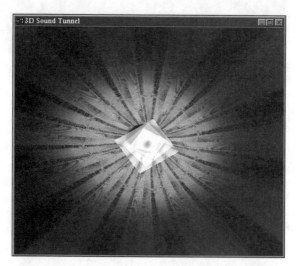

The 3D sound tunnel is a very graphically spectacular spinning vortex of colors that dance, rotate, and shimmer to the music; you can see it in **Figure 7.11**. While most will agree that Prince's OpenGL plug-in is the favorite 3D plug-in for visualization, we think that this module produces the most impressive display this plug-in has to offer. To configure this module while running, pull up the Configure menu with Alt+K quick key. The menu for the 3D sound tunnel is very thorough. You can control rotation amount, default tunnel brightness, and **flare speed** (the rate at which flares shoot down the tunnel towards you) with convenient sliders. Light flares can be turned on, turned off, or randomized. Bass, Middle, and Treble boxes allow you to control the sensitivity to which the tunnel or flares responds to music peaks, as well as the color for each frequency. The 3D sound tunnel has some pretty cool presets, including a default setting in case you do not like the results of tinkering with this module.

The 3D Cube plug-in is very simple. No Configuration menus, no controls—just start it and enjoy. It creates a textured cube that glows in various colored lights, pulsing and spinning to the music. Take a look at **Figure 7.12**.

Figure 7.12
The 3D Cube module at work.

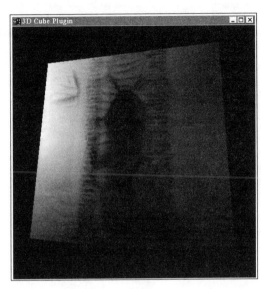

NOTE

Another 3D-only plug-in very worthy of downloading is Tripex by Ben Marsh. This very cool plug-in is available at **http://tripex.technonet.com/** and from Winamp's Plug-Ins Download page. The plug-in is designed to take advantage of Glide, the API used exclusively by 3DFX-based chipset video cards such as the Voodoo1, Voodoo2 and the Banshee. The 3DFX chipset is specifically designed to handle 3D graphics by doing many of the complete and intensive tasks that would normally just be handled by your computer's processor. Tripex is designed to run fullscreen only, and it has some very spectacular effects. The Configuration menu on this is very well designed and easy to use. After using the Nullsoft Visualization Library, the FunkyFX plug-in, and Prince's OpenGL plug-ins, you should be ready to tackle any windowed, fullscreen, or 3D-only plug-ins out there!

Sound and DSP Plug-Ins

We've only covered visualization programs that create cool visual effects, which utilize the music to provide some awesome eye candy. Now it's time to learn about plug-ins that extend the Winamp player's audio capability. The plug-ins covered do a variety of things.

Part II Advanced Winamp

The first plug-in you take a look at is AudioStocker Pro by Leif Claesson. This is a very useful program designed to equalize sound volumes. Then you take a look at DeFX plug-in by Franco Catrin L., a great sound-modifying plug-in. Next in line is MuchFX^2 by Marc S. Ressl. This is a plug-in that allows multiple DSP (Digital Signal Processing) plug-ins to be run simultaneously. There are programs that allow you to run multiple visualization plug-ins, most notably Visualization Mux by Jason Crawford, which is designed to allow you to stack programs that affect the sound output.

Volume Equalizing Plug-Ins

How many times have you been playing music, only to have to adjust the music volumes when new songs load because of different recording levels when the .MP3s were made? There is now a very handy utility called AudioStocker Pro, which allows Winamp to automatically equalize volumes when loading the next .MP3.

AudioStocker Pro can be found at **http://www.users.one.se/liket/ mp3stock/audiostocker.htm** and at the Winamp Plug-Ins page. Once you have downloaded and uncompressed this plug-in to the Winamp/Plugins directory, start Winamp, load a playlist (or a bunch of songs), and try it out. Follow the steps described here to do so:

Open the Preferences menu and select the Misc. Plug-Ins tab. This tab just basically lists DSP plug-ins like the Visualization tab. One of the limitations of Winamp, is that it was designed to only support one DSP plug-in at a time. Fortunately, the designers had the foresight to provide the capability for people to develop plug-ins that allow the usage of multiple audio plug-ins. When you install the AudioStocker Pro, it loads a program that allows it to work with any other DSP plug-ins currently on your system—a very handy feature. You will see that it has added several items to the Library pull-down menu on this tab, and these items will vary depending upon what DSP plug-ins are already in your Winamp/Plugins directory.

Use the pull-down menu on the Library box to load the AudioStocker PRO [DSP_AUDIOSTOCKER.DLL] selection. There is only one module to this plug-in and clicking on the Configure button pulls up a menu like that shown in **Figure 7.13**. This plug-in is very simple to use. The Range box limits the amount of amplification the plug-in can add to any song.

TIP

Quieter songs will require a higher range value to maintain equal volume level with the other songs playing in the playlist.

Max EQ allows the plug-in to actually change the levels of frequencies within the song itself, not just change the overall volume. This plug-in can, to a degree, equalize the sound for songs that were recorded with over-bassy tones or muted highs. Compression controls the overall amount of change or sound processing the AudioStocker can add to all songs when playing. Your personal preference for this can vary depending upon your listening material and sound system. Try them all and see how they sound on your machine. For a very big sound, try setting Max EQ to +6dB and Compression to Medium. Now that's what makes plug-ins so much fun!

Figure 7.13
The AudioStocker PRO Configuration menu.

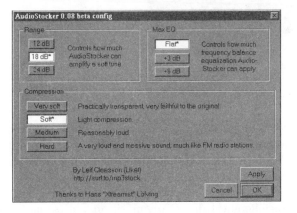

Modifying Sound with Plug-Ins

Playing recordings of live, or any other type of music can be given a new dimension of sound with plug-ins like DeFX plug-in by Franco Catrin L (**Figure 7.14**). You can get it from Winamp's plug-in page (**http://www.winamp.com/plugins**). Download the .ZIP file, uncompress it into the Plugins folder, start Winamp, load some music, and go to the Misc. Plug-Ins tab on the Preferences menu. Select DeFX Plug-in v0.8 for Winamp 2 [dsp_DeFX.DLL] from the Library pull-down menu and press the Configure button.

Figure 7.14
The DeFX Configuration menu.

DeFX allows Winamp to change the effects of the sound being played in several ways. The Pitch Modulation box allows you to choose between Chorus or Flange and to control rate, depth, and amount. Playing around with these is the best way to find out what works well for different songs. Did you ever want to be a karaoke star? Give it a shot with help from the Voice Removal slider. Any musician knows that reverberation is the key to making a room sound great with live music. You can adjust the length and amount of reverb in songs with DeFX. This plug-in can help a lot when recording or when performing as a DJ.

Not all plug-ins have to be useful. Some are just plain fun or cool. For example, VinylRassel by Per-Olov Jernberg is great. Have you ever found yourself missing the nostalgic sound that vinyl records used to produce? Maybe you are tired of all the crisp, clean music today that doesn't seem to have any character? Here's a neat little program that adds that crackle and pop you are looking for. VinylRassel is available at **http://winAmp.lh.net/htdocs/Effects-2.html**. Download the .ZIP file, uncompress it into the Plugins folder, start Winamp, load some music, and go to the Misc. Plug-Ins tab on the Preferences menu. Select Illuminator's VinylRassel v1.0 [DSP_VNYL.DLL] from the Library pull-down menu. Click OK, sit back, and enjoy!

Stacking or Running Multiple Plug-Ins

MuchFX^2, whose logo is shown in **Figure 7.15**, allows you to stack DSP plug-ins. It even allows you to use versions of DSP plug-ins designed to run on the older versions of Winamp 1.X. Since Winamp is now version 2.X, you can no longer use some older plug-ins unless you use a utility like this. This is an essential tool for any Winamp power user.

Figure 7.15
The MuchFX^2 logo.

This very useful plug-in can be found on Winamp's Plug-Ins page and at **http://www.geocities.com/SiliconValley/Lakes/2382/**, along with some other very cool plug-ins for Winamp. You can also get Q-Filter, DiabloDJ, and RealReverb—all excellent plug-ins for Winamp from this Web site.

Once you have downloaded this plug-in, uncompress it to your Winamp Plugins folder, start Winamp, load some music, and go to the Misc. Plug-Ins tab on the Preferences menu. Select MuchFX^2 0.9901.1 [DSP_MFX2.DLL] under the Library pull-down menu and click OK.

MuchFX^2 is a very simple DSP plug-in. It essentially provides a framework for all other plug-ins in which to operate and be accessed. A window that looks a lot like the Playlist window (**Figure 7.16**) has opened near the Winamp player and provides an excellent tool for seeing what DSP plug-ins are currently running.

When this window is on top, you can press F1 or the question mark key (?) to get a Help menu that tells about the plug-in and its hotkeys.

Figure 7.16
The MuchFX^2 plug-in operating on the Winamp window with playlist.

Press the + (plus) button to load DSP plug-ins, or the – (period) key to unload plug-ins. The CFG button quickly pulls up the Configuration menu for whatever plug-in is highlighted in the MuchFX^2 window. The up and down arrows scroll the list of plug-ins up and down. The About button pulls up the same menu F1 brings up. You can load or save DSP plug-in setups by clicking on either button.

Part II   Advanced Winamp

Plug-Ins That Are Just Useful

Piloting Winamp

It is a very common occurrence to have Winamp playing music while you work or surf the Net. One thing that all users will recognize is that Winamp would be much better with some form of external control. Well, Nullsoft has provided just that in the form of a plug-in that allows users to control Winamp with a joystick without having to stop working, open windows, or click on little buttons and icons.

Let's go to Winamp's home page and get the Nullsoft Joystick Control 1.0b plug-in by Justin Frankel from the General Plug-Ins page. Once it is downloaded, and unzipped into the Winamp/Plugins folder, open Winamp, load a song, press CTRL+P to get the Preferences menu, and select the plug-in's General Purpose menu. You should see a listing for Nullsoft Joystick Control Plug-In v1.0b (GEN_JOY), select it, and click Configure to bring up the Configuration dialog box (**Figure 7.17**).

Figure 7.17
The Nullsoft Joystick Control Plug-in Configuration dialog box.

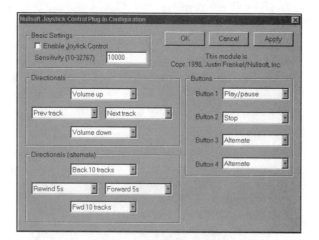

This plug-in works with all major joysticks, but you need to have a joystick attached to your gameport on your sound card, and configured to work correctly with your computer. On the Nullsoft Joystick Control Plug-In Configuration dialog box, check the box labeled Enable Joystick Control and click Apply. If your joystick is set up correctly, you should be able to skip from one song to the next by moving the stick left or right.

CAUTION
In the Nullsoft Joystick Control v1.0b plug-in zip file, there is no Readme.txt file included to help you with any questions you have about the plug-in.

Most of the buttons on the joystick can be assigned to control Winamp comfortably for you. The Directionals box controls how Winamp responds to movements of the joystick. By clicking on the pull-down menus next to each of the directions, you can set how your joystick will affect Winamp. The Directionals (alternate) box is designed to send instructions to Winamp when the alternate button is held down, and the joystick is moved. Buttons can be assigned to do functions in the Buttons box. Button 1 usually is the trigger button, Button 2 is usually assigned to the left button on the top of the joystick. Locations of Buttons 4 and 5 can vary.

Hints for Using Different Plug-Ins

There are many plug-ins that do different things. Most of them are listed on the Winamp home page, where you can easily download any that suit your needs. As you can see, some plug-ins are very, very simple—just install and turn them on. Some are a bit more complex. Most first-time users will probably run into significant problems or questions. There are several resources that you can turn to if you are having problems.

In addition to the help that is provided at the Winamp home page, most plug-ins have a home page that can provide very useful operation information. FAQs and help guides are available on most plug-ins, especially the more popular ones. One thing that you should never overlook if you are having problems is the Readme.txt (or .TXT) help file that comes with most .ZIP files when you download the plug-ins. These Readme files usually have a good deal of information on how to operate the plug-in, as well as some information on what kind of machine the plug-in works best on.

Visualization plug-ins such as Aquamarine 3 by Pablo Rewak (**Figure 7.18**) have many features and appear to be very complicated; they are often very similar in layout and operation to the Visualization plug-ins examined in depth in this guide. This can make using them much simpler, but the best way to use them is to get into the Configuration menus and see the effects as you change settings.

Part II Advanced Winamp

Figure 7.18
Pablo Rewak's Aquamarine plug-in creates very cool spectrum equalizer effects.

There are also plug-ins that appear simple but require a great deal of knowledge to work properly. PitchFork by Leif Claesson (**Figure 7.19**) is an outstanding plug-in for the experimenting DJ who wants to use Winamp to beatmix. The Readme.txt file included in the .ZIP file is an essential guide for using the plug-in. It explains how to beatmix and how to use all of the plug-in's features. Without this guide, it would be very difficult for any but the most experienced DJ with a solid computer background to use this plug-in. Appendix B has more information on PitchFork's and Virtual Turntables' two MP3 tools for DJs.

Figure 7.19
The tool for virtual DJs:
Leif Claesson's
PitchFork.

If all else fails, most of the people who have spent the time to develop and design these plug-ins can be reached by email. Winamp's Plug-In page lists emails for the people who programmed these plug-ins. If you are going to contact a plug-in programmer, be sure to include the following information. It will help him or her diagnose your problems:

    Operating system (Win 3.1, Win 95, Win98, NT)
    CPU speed
    RAM
    Video card
    Sound card
    Winamp version
    Plug-in version

If you have to email the programmer to get help, you should include other details that could help diagnose your problem: when a plug-in causes crashes, what other programs are running at the same time, what it seems to do, and details that could be relevant to the misoperation of the plug-in. Some of these plug-ins are made by people just like you, and many programmers don't have access to all types of operating systems and hardware configurations. If you have exhausted all other alternatives, many of the programmers will be happy to help determine if it is your computer hardware or their plug-in that is causing problems.

The last thing you can do to learn about plug-ins is to use them. Go one-by-one through all the configuration options and play with them. Learn every option and how it affects the plug-in. Experimentation is the key. Use different songs to see which ones react well with plug-ins (we find anything by Rob Zombie seems to work real well) and just have fun.

Plug-Ins and Tune Up

Plug-ins, especially the visualization ones really exemplify the difference your computer, .MP3 files, and Winamp can have over your traditional stereo. .MP3 files don't necessarily carry the fidelity of a good CD or record, but your stereo isn't infinitely expandable like Winamp with its plug-in architecture. Whether it be a particular DSP plug-in that you use or a Visualization plug-in you sit back and watch, this expandability adds more to the audio. There is no question that songs are at first meant to be heard as the artists intended, but music isn't just for the artists themselves, it's also for you. With Winamp, the music in-effect becomes something you can adjust and create new things with. That's a power heretofore unseen.

So use plug-ins and turn the tunes up and watch what happens!

Part II   Advanced Winamp

Part III
Digitizing Audio

8

Digital Audio

When it comes to digital audio, there is a lot more than just the sound that comes out of your speakers or headphones. Chapter 2, "Inside the MP3 Format and Players," covers the details of the MP3 file format and the technology that created it. However, MP3 is usually the result of an encoded raw digital audio file or CD track. In the cases where you are encoding from the raw CD track, you don't need to understand much about the actual digital structure of that file in order to maintain CD-like quality. MP3 creation isn't always done from a pure digital source like an audio CD. In many cases you may be encoding from a .WAV file that was created from a computer-based program, recorded from an analog cassette tape, or some other non-digital source.

As the saying goes, garbage in, garbage out. This chapter explains many of the ins and outs of digital audio that allow you to create the highest quality MP3 files from imperfect sources.

Digital Sound Basics: How Computers Capture Sound

At the most basic level, computers capture sound by taking a stream of analog music and converting it to a digital form using special chips known as **ADCs** (**analog-to-digital converters**).

NOTE

To be more exact, you will see ADCs typically referred to as either **A/D converters** or even just **AD converters** (without the forward slash). Conversely, there are also digital-to-analog converters—known as either **DACs**, **D/A**, or **DA converters**—as well as converters that handle both (AD/DA converters).

ADCs take a signal from a microphone, audio tape, or some other analog source and convert it to a digital signal that computers can understand and save. Nearly every soundcard available today includes one or more ADC.

As the soundcard reads the audio signal, the ADC passes the digital information to your computer as raw data. This information passes through the sound card driver software, to the operating system and to whatever recording program you are using. This process is called **sampling**, because the computer is actually taking tiny samples of the audio stream and turning it into a numerical equivalent it can later use to re-create the audio it has captured.

Sampling

While sound is a continuous stream of information, a computer needs to take small samplings of sound at constant intervals in order to record. If you sample the input more often, you'll be able to reproduce a more accurate, better sounding output when the time comes to play it back. The rate at which you sample (or the **sampling rate**) is usually measured in Hertz (Hz) or kHz, which is 1000 Hz. One Hz means once per second. Sixty Hz means 60 times per second (which happens to be the rate at which fluorescent lights buzz). A 44.1 kHz sampling rate means that the audio was sampled 44,100 times per second.

The more often the sound is sampled, the more accurate the sample gets (meaning it sounds more like the original), but you also accrue more data, and thus a larger file results. Most high-quality, CD-style samples are collected at a 44.1kHz sample rate. When sampling at a lower rate for smaller files, most programs offer 22.05kHz (one half) or 11.025kHz (one quarter) rates.

Channels

A **Channels** count refers to how many different unique audio signals there are in a file. For example, most tapes and all CDs include a stereo signal, which means there are two channels—left and right. AM radio, for instance, is usually a mono signal. Stereo signals tend to require twice as much data as mono signals, since there are two separate signals.

Resolution

While sampling determines how often you capture a segment of sound, it doesn't determine the precision of the sample. Precision is usually determined by the resolution of the sample, which is measured in bits per sample. Having increased resolution makes sounds have less background noise. For example, 16-bit samples allow sounds with nearly no noticeable noise to be reproduced, while 8-bit sound tends to have a pretty noticeable amount of noise. The only downside to 16-bit samples over 8-bit samples is they take up twice as much information.

One thing to be sure about is that your system is set up properly to provide good quality sampling. Some pieces of audio sampling software don't automatically default to using the highest quality settings of your sound card. To ensure that your sound card is providing you the best quality audio it can, be sure to read the section on sound cards later in this chapter.

Later in this chapter we discuss checking out the multimedia section of your Windows Control Panel where you can potentially set your card to a higher sampling rate.

> **NOTE**
>
> Many popular consumer level, and some professional level, audio sampling software will typically by default sample at 8 bits during simultaneous recording/playback. Be sure to change to 16-bit samples for adequate sound quality.

File Size

How do sample rate, sample resolution, and channels affect file size? Table 8.1 shows the approximate number of megabytes (before encoding to MP3) that each style of recording requires. MP3 size varies based on the quality of the input recording as well as the quality selected during the encoding process. For high-quality 16-bit stereo recordings sampled at 44.1kHz, you can figure on a 10:1–12:1 compression ratio when converting to the MP3 format.

Table 8.1–File Sizes for One Minute of Sound Recorded at Various Frequencies, Bit Rates, and Channels

Bit Rate	44.1kHz		22.05kHz		11.025kHz	
	(stereo)	(mono)	(stereo)	(mono)	(stereo)	(mono)
8-bit	5.0MB	2.5MB	2.5MB	1.3MB	1.3MB	.6MB
16-bit	10.1MB	5.0MB	5.0MB	2.5MB	2.5MB	1.3MB

Acquiring Sound Files

There are two ways to acquire the original source audio for your MP3 files. The most direct way is to **rip** the audio right from the CD audio track file. Ripping involves no digital-to-analog and analog-to-digital process; the computer simply reads the CD information and either writes a .WAV file or encodes directly. Programs that do this are known as **rippers** and are discussed in more detail in Chapters 9, "Creating Your Own MP3 Files," and 10, "Creating Your Own Custom CDs."

The other common way to acquire audio for creating MP3s? Convert any analog audio source that's coming into your sound card into a raw digital form (such as .WAV). To do that, you need to understand the intricacies of sound cards, line noise, and digitization software.

Part III Digitizing Audio

The .WAV format in and of itself is not a CODEC. Rather .WAV is a file format that can encapsulate sounds that are compressed using different CODECs including PCM (Pulse Code Modulation), ADPCM (Adaptive Pulse Code Modulation), TrueSpeech, and more. Usually .WAV files use PCM data. This sound is stored in a nearly or completely uncompressed format, which is why .WAV files tend to be big in comparison to some other formats. If you're interested in reading more on various other CODECs used by .WAV files, check the documentation or Help file that accompanies your sound-recording software of choice.

What You Should Know About Computer Sound Cards

Not all sound cards are created equal. Because not all computer users are audiophiles, a good Sound Blaster-style card should be fine. For those who are audiophiles, there are higher-end cards to consider. The analog-to-digital conversion quality will be higher with higher-end cards. If you plan to do a lot of transferring to MP3 from DAT, cassette, or LP, then a higher-end sound card offers better dynamic range; the signal-to-noise ratio will produce discernably better files.

Here are some cards to consider. How do they stack up against each other?

Antex Electronics

www.antex.com

If you are looking for the top of the high-end sound cards, Antex Electronics is a great place to go. They have staked out a niche selling sound cards to demanding musicians and computer audio engineers. The Antex StudioCard 2000 and StudioCard A/V Pro sell for $800–$1,100 and feature the kind of quality you'd expect from a card that costs 4–10 times more than mass-market cards.

These cards feature 20-bit DAT-quality capabilities. The cards also have multiple input capabilities. For example, the StudioCard 2000 can record or play back eight stereo tracks (using four physical ins and outs). The 20-bit A/D and D/A converters allow you record and play back nearly perfect sound; with a high signal-to-noise ratio, there is no background noise or hum whatsoever. The card claims less than .003% total harmonic distortion and features a sampling range of 6.25kHz–50kHz— more than anything you'd find on lower-end cards.

Turtle Beach

http://www.voyetra-turtle-beach.com

Turtle Beach Multisound card is an excellent product for users who want a great sound card that features much less noise and better sampling capability than the Sound Blaster standard but who don't need to go to the upper echelon. The product costs less than $400 and features 20-bit A/D and D/A converters and a 97dB signal-to-noise ratio (total harmonic distortion is claimed at .005%). The sampling rate for the card ranges from 5.5125kHz–48kHz.

Gadget Labs

http://www.gadgetlabs.com

Gadget Labs makes two cards that are among the top favorites of PC musicians everywhere. Its Wave/4 card features four separate inputs and outputs, excellent signal/noise ratio, and extremely fast data transfer. The card also features 64 times oversampling and the architecture of the card is constructed to provide as little noise as possible to your incoming audio. This card sells for under $260 and is available.

Gadget recently introduced a newer card the Wave/8•24, which supports true 8 channel, 24-bit sampling with 128 times oversampling. This card sells for $499.95 and is getting rave reviews.

Sound Blaster

www.creativelabs.com

There are many varieties of Sound Blaster cards. Millions have been sold or bundled with computers since the late 1980s, when they became the de facto standard for PC sound cards. Standard doesn't necessarily mean best in terms of quality. Sound Blasters aren't bad cards; they've been engineered to sell for a low price, a fact that helped the company pioneer the market and achieve the success it has. However, as prices have come down and more demanding users have pushed for better features, Sound Blaster and compatible cards have gained better capabilities.

Most people probably use a Sound Blaster 16 or 64 style card. These cards typically have some level of noise associated with them and feature 16-bit A/D and D/A converters with a sampling range of 5kHz–48kHz. They're fine cards for most purposes. They are noisy and not ideal for creation or capturing audio to convert into MP3 files (unless you are doing some serious conversion for your band or personal listening). If you do want to upgrade or are considering getting a new card, the current high-end Sound Blaster Live is an excellent choice that demonstrates how capable even the low end of the PC sound card market has gotten. For under $200, Sound Blaster Live is a great choice.

Part III Digitizing Audio

More Notes About Sound Cards

True PC audiophiles will debate sound cards like traditional audiophiles debate their amplifiers, speakers, and turntables. The truth is as a regular user you're probably fine with any 16-bit audio card because the sound will be good enough for you. However, as you've seen, there are superior cards out there in comparison to the commonly found 16-bit "Sound Blaster Compatible" card. However, for the common user who is thinking of upgrading to a higher-end card because of MP3, it is important to understand some of the issues involved with high-end vs. traditional multimedia soundcards.

1. Mass market cards tend to try and condense the chips on the card to save money. They include the digital-to-analog converters in with other electronics, raising noise ratios. Higher-end cards try to isolate the D/A converters.

2. Higher-end cards are positioned for the music market, and thus aren't necessarily "Sound Blaster" compatible. This can make them difficult to work with games, especially older DOS-based products. It is possible to use them with games, but if you're a heavy gamer consider this first.

3. It is possible to have more than one sound card in your machine. However, check to see if you can support it. Each sound card will need at least four DMA channels to provide full-duplex recording. That means two cards need a total of four DMA channels for full duplex sound. To check for available DMAs, go to your Windows Control Panel, click on System, highlight Computer, click on Properties, and then click on the Direct Memory Access (DMA) choice at the top of the Computer Properties dialog box.

4. Another issue with installing two sound cards is that drivers may not be written to support two cards very well. Some people get around this by installing cards from two different manufacturers, which brings its own set of problems. The best way around this is to install cards that have drivers, which support more than one card, or to purchase a card with multiple-channel support.

5. Mass market cards tend to mix all the streams they can produce, CD, input, internal audio, all into one stream. This, in addition to extra amplification that some add, can increase noise to recordings.

6. Be careful about how card capabilities compare to driver capabilities. Cards with 24-bit, and 20-bit sampling better have state-of-the-art drivers capable of supporting these higher resolutions. It's not uncommon to find 20-bit cards that end up, due to of software limitations, really only producing 16-bit sound that has been "dithered" down from 20-bit sound. This, of course, isn't true 20-bit sound. Many newer cards are using Microsoft's DirectX/DirectSound system to increase performance, which requires up-to-date DirectX-compatible drivers.

7. If you do have a higher-resolution card and drivers, make sure your sound-editing software supports it too.

8. Know the difference between PCI and ISA cards. PCI is a newer card slot architecture that is faster, and easier to install than older ISA technology. If your computer has an available PCI slot, make sure to get a PCI-compatible card.

The Issues That Control Good Sound Acquisition

Buying the best sound card you can afford does not guarantee good sound acquisition. The sound card quality is just one step among many that will help ensure that you're generating clear source sound files for encoding into the MP3 format. The following sections introduce the other steps.

Kill Background Noise

One of the most important things is to find ways to kill the background noise that can be associated with your recording setup. Background noise can be a slight hum or another form of noise that distorts the sound coming through your sound card. You can see whether there is background noise in your setup by doing a 20–30 second recording of sound with no music (**Figure 8.1**). You can then decide whether you have too much noise. Noise shouldn't be a problem for the most part.

Figure 8.1
Record moments of silence with your digitization software to see how bad background noise is.

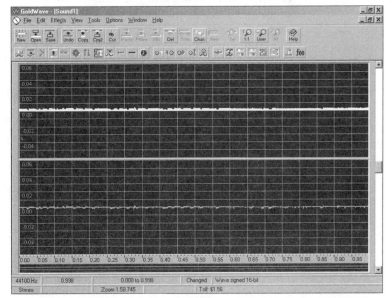

Part III Digitizing Audio

Clean Tape Heads and Records

One of the most critical things you can do when coming off a regular tape or record is to clean everything as much as possible. Tape decks can use a quality tape-head cleaner, which can be found in many record stores for $10–$15. Wiping records clean of dirt and dust and buying a new needle will help as well.

Get Good Cables

Trying to talk about cabling with stereo fanatics, engineers, and audiophiles is bound to drive you crazy. There are many opinions and ideas, as well as hype, about who and what types of cabling you should use to connect various audio devices. In most cases, you will use a simple RCA-style cable to connect out-jacks to in-jacks on your sound card.

By far, the most commonly used quality audio cabling is Monster Cable (**www.monstercable.com**). The problem with this cable is that it is so prevalent; it has its share of supporters and detractors. Overall, this cable's quality is very good—probably better than anything you'll find that comes from a mass market no-name or low-end cabling company. The construction is sturdy and the price is reasonable. If you want to go an extra mile to provide your card a quality signal, using Monster Cable to patch your audio into your sound card isn't a bad step.

If you're interested in alternatives and higher-end options to Monster Cable, try two other well-known audio cable manufacturers. Nordost (**www.nordost.com**) and AudioQuest (**www.audioquest.com**) are two recommended cabling manufacturers used by audiophiles worldwide.

Optimize Your Hard Drives

Once sounds are captured in digital form, they are stored either in memory or directly on the hard disk. This is somewhat important because quality sound files take up a lot of space. A normal CD track length can be 40MB–50MB. The computer memory fills up as your sound card and the program you use to capture audio digitizes sound. If the memory is insufficient, the sound spills onto your hard drive. The hard drive will capture the sound as fast as it can, but poorly optimized hard drives might not offer optimal quality. Optimizing your hard drive provides for the best performance.

Some hardcore recording types recommend getting a separate hard drive that is as fast as possible. It should have a transfer rate of 2.5MB/sec and a rotational speed of 4800 rpm (revolutions per minute) or higher. Keep it separate from other programs and operating system needs and it will provide very good capture for incoming recordings. It doesn't matter whether you get an IDE or SCSI interface for your card, although SCSI drives tend to be faster. The downside is you'll have to buy a special SCSI interface card for a drive of this type as almost every PC using an IDE-based interface system for hard drives. (Note: Buy Adaptec only.)

Recording Your Files

When you aren't ripping a track directly from a CD, you have to record from your sound card and store it in a format that is a perfect representation of the sound captured. For PCs, that means a .WAV file; for Macintosh platforms, that might be an .AIFF file. Both these formats can store raw captured sound with no encoding or loss of data in return for compression. In the next two chapters you'll learn how to create MP3 versions from these files.

You need sound-recording software to record your audio into a raw file. Many cards come bundled with various products, but in many cases this software might not be as robust. In some higher-end cases, digitization programs can offer a range of effects and an audio-tweaking capability.

Part III Digitizing Audio

Table 8.2 outlines some of the better sound-capturing and editing packages. In this book, we use Sonic Foundry's Sound Forge XP, a great, inexpensive program for capturing raw audio (**Figure 8.2**).

Figure 8.2
Sonic Foundry's Sound Forge XP is one of a number of good programs that captures audio prior to encoding it to the MP3 format.

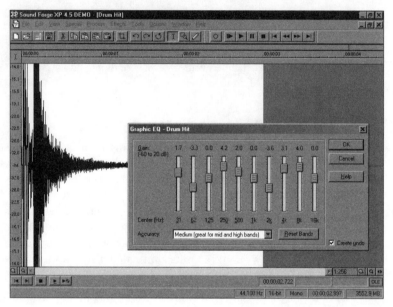

Table 8.2–Sound Capturing and Editing Packages

Product Name	Manufacturer	Platforms Supported	Retail Price	Comments
Sound Forge	Sonic Foundry	Windows	$499.95	The best higher-end editor for Windows 9X/NT systems.
Sound Forge XP	Sonic Foundry	Windows	$59.95	A light version of its top-line editor that is good for everyone but the more demanding developer.
Sound Edit 16	Macromedia	Macintosh	$349.95	Solid Macintosh editor with many higher-end features.
Goldwave	Chris Craig	Windows	$40.00	A good shareware product. The interface is a little clunky but the system has lots of power and supports MP3 encoding.
Cool Edit	Syntrillium	Windows	$50.00 (Basic) $399.00 (Pro)	Well-liked shareware editor with many features.
Peak LE	Bias, Inc.	Macintosh	$99.00	The best of the lower-priced Macintosh sound-editing tools.

Once you have your desired package, it certainly will pay to become familiar with it. Some of the higher-end packages have an incredible range of features and effects. Some even let you record and mix several streams of files, which can be great for creating your own digital recordings directly on your computer. For the purposes of this book, we're going to touch on some basics that should be common to every program (**Table 8.2**).

Capturing and Enhancing Audio

Capturing audio in almost every program is about as simple as pressing the Record button. Once you've conditioned your setup and queued the music on your tape, record, MiniDisc, or DAT, you should hit Record on the capture software and then initiate play. Later you trim the file to capture the sound only.

> **TIP**
>
> Approximately 10MB of space is needed on your hard drive to store the file for every minute of high-quality audio. Be sure to calculate the length of your song and prepare the necessary space accordingly.

In some cases, the software you use saves the file as it digitizes the incoming the sound source. However you will want to be sure that once you have your captured file that you do indeed ensure it is saved. Much can go wrong and your PC can crash when working with large sound files during the editing and enhancing period.

With all the major packages listed in Table 8.2, you have a wealth of effects. In many cases you'll probably want to leave the file as is. Have you managed a good, clean capture? Why fix something that isn't broken? There are, however, processes common to all the major sound-editing packages worth being familiar with. As you gain expertise with them, you will find yourself better able to improve various recording styles.

DC Offset

One of the top items that you can look for to help improve the quality of your digitized audio is known as DC offset. **DC offset**, one of the noise types talked about earlier in this chapter, happens when the equipment and lines feeding into your sound card aren't properly grounded. DC offsets are usually caused by electrical mismatches between your sound card and microphone. This is common with lower-end sound cards. You can see how bad DC offset is on your setup by digitizing a few seconds of silence.

Bad DC offset forces the baseline of your audio to be slightly off the 0 axis or centerline of your digitized audio. You may have to zoom in on your audio to see how bad it is. If there is a significant offset, you can easily correct this with your editor. Every decent sound editor (like those mentioned in Table 8.2) has a DC adjustment function.

Once you've zoomed in on the file, look to see what the offset is. Your editor should have numbers along the side or a graph overlay that helps. After you've digitized a file, you can improve the sound and apply the opposite amount of offset. (If the offset is 85, for example, apply a –85 DC offset filter.) Some programs can automatically calculate it and adjust accordingly.

Equalizing

Just like a graphic equalizer on your stereo or the one included in Winamp, most sound-editing packages let you adjust the various frequency bands and apply that to the file. Equalizing really depends on what you think sounds best.

TIP

Since the MP3 format uses a perceptual encoding technique, it will drop out very high-end and low-end frequencies in the file. An increasing of the middle frequencies just a hair by using your equalizer (2kHz—3kHz) can sometimes be a nice adjustment that specifically takes into account how the MP3 format changes the audio upon encoding. You may have to experiment and encode a few files to be certain.

Normalization

Normalization helps you maximize a file's volume without distorting it. The function scans the audio data and then applies a gain to the levels in the file to a specified amount of increase. Every good package has a normalization (sometimes called **maximize**) function.

You can set a normalize factor between 0–100% of the maximum value when running this process. It is possible for a normalization process to maximize the frequencies out of range. For the most part, you can avoid this by setting the process to hit the 90–95 percentile. Play the resulting file and listen for any clicking sounds; they indicate that the process caused some frequencies to shoot out of range.

You'll want to perform this step at the end of your enhancement process. Once maximized, you can create distortion if you run filters.

What About Output?
Drivers and Speaker Issues

Just because you captured it correctly, touched it up, and encoded it perfectly doesn't mean you have achieved sonic nirvana. Here you should take some time to understand the role of speakers and sound drivers on your setup.

Most computers today come standard with multimedia speakers. However, the majority of speakers that come with computers aren't as good as those you'd get with even a modest stereo system. In addition, positioning them to close to your monitor or other computer equipment might add interference. Some computer audiophiles solve this by running their computer's sound output through their stereo system, while others purchase computer speakers with above average quality, such as those produced by Boston Acoustics or Bose.

> **TIP**
>
> Many people feel headphones are good tools to use when tweaking a sound. However, higher-end audiophiles feel that when enhancing and mixing a recording, you need what are known as "studio monitor speakers." According to the mixing information at **homerecording.com:** "Headphones tend to have better bass and treble response than speakers, your final mix will thus sound dull and lifeless when you hear it 'normally'."

Boston Acoustics

Boston Acoustics offers a complete line of add-on multimedia speakers. The speakers range from its lower-end BA-635 system, which runs $99, to its higher-end MediaTheater line, which runs $299 and includes a subwoofer and optionally (for another $99.00) a surround-sound speaker (**www.bostonacoustics.com**).

> **BOSE**
>
> Bose produces two specific products, both of which are two-speaker setups (**www.bose.com**). Its high-end Acoustimass multimedia speakers cost $499 and are highly rated by a number of computer magazines. Bose also has a lower-end offering. The MediaMate line runs $199 for a pair.
>
> In terms of sound card drivers, you should familiarize yourself with the options your drivers allow. Some can affect the way sound is played back. Check the manufacturer's Web site for your card and make sure you've updated your drivers to the latest versions.

TIP

For some reason, sound card companies like to post beta drivers a lot. While these drivers are more advanced, they're not final release drivers. Be careful about updating to what appears to be the latest driver. They may in fact be beta releases. Always look for the last fully released update. When checking for new driver updates, it's best to check your computer manufacturer's Web site before checking the sound card manufacturer's site.

With some sound cards and their drivers you may have special features that add effects to how your audio playback sounds (**Figure 8.3**). These can include wide spectrum effects, surround sounds, and extra vibrato. You should turn these features off when capturing and tuning your audio; this will prevent you from being confused by the adjustment to the sound produced by the special effects of your particular sound card.

Figure 8.3
Some sound cards have special playback settings that you want to reset to normal when tweaking your recorded sounds.

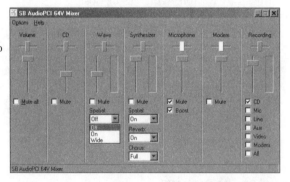

Check your card's recording properties using the volume control found in your Windows system tray (**Figure 8.4**). This controls the amplitude and balance of incoming audio streams during recording.

Figure 8.4
The volume properties control found in your Windows taskbar lets you tweak amplitude and balance of incoming audio. Double-click to activate the taskbar.

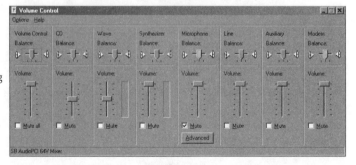

Bring up the volume properties control by double-clicking on the speaker icon in your Windows system tray; this will take you to record properties. Choose Properties, which is under the Options menu. This brings up the Volume Control Properties dialog box (**Figure 8.5**).

Figure 8.5
The Options menu lets you switch volume control mode between Playback and Recording.

Choose the recording option from the Adjust Volume menu in the Volume Options dialog box, and make sure in the checkboxes below that you have selected at least CD, Microphone, and Line Balance. Press the OK button; your volume control panel changes to the recording volume controls as seen in **Figure 8.6**.

Figure 8.6
The three recording volume levels that are most important: CD, Microphone Balance, and Line Balance.

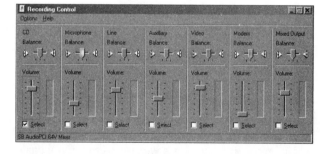

TIP

Most of the time you'll record through the line input. If you have a microphone attached to your sound card at the time, mute the mic input to reduce possible noise interference during recording.

Part III   Digitizing Audio

You'll also want to check the multimedia control on the Control Panel and see if you've set your sound card settings optimally. For example, the Sound Blaster PCI card driver shown in **Figure 8.7** has a setting that lets you increase the quality of the card's sampling rate—a sure way to improve sound-capture quality.

Figure 8.7
Check your sound card's driver settings in the multimedia control panel of your system. Adjusting these settings can improve the quality of the card's sampling ability.

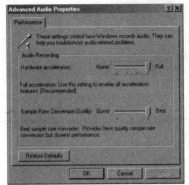

Depending on your sound card's features, you may have additional playback and recording options. By thoroughly checking out both your control panel settings and the volume and balance adjustments to your sound card, you ensure that you're creating the optimal conditions for recording and tweaking your digital audio prior to creating the final MP3 files.

Conclusion

There is so much you can learn about audio, digital audio, and how computer audio recording works that it could fill a book in-and-of-itself. However, in a few pages we've covered many basics, and many advanced tips that should certainly make you a better digital audio expert. When ripping a track from a CD (as will be demonstrated in the next chapter), there is little to be gained from knowing how to record audio. One of the great uses of MP3 as a format though is to create files of music recorded from other sources like DAT, MiniDisc or old records or tapes. In these cases a good knowledge of digital/computer audio and how it is captured will be incredibly useful.

If you want to learn a lot more about recording at home or with your computer, a highly recommended site is **homerecording.com**. There you can find a wealth of useful articles, reviews of critical tools, software, and pointers to other useful articles and FAQs on digital audio and home recording. Much of it is applicable to creating great audio that ends up creating great MP3s.

9

Creating Your Own MP3 Files

As explained previously, MP3s are mostly created by converting digital audio that is stored in some other file format to the more compressed MP3 file format. This process is known as **encoding** and requires a specific program that can convert a viable audio file into the MP3 format. Many different encoders exist; all are based off the original Fraunhofer specification for the MPEG Layer III format, if not the specific sample programming code Fraunhofer developed. Fraunhofer itself offers an encoder that is actually used by a number of other products, including AudioActive's Production Studio, which is discussed in the "Using AudioActive" section later in this chapter.

Creating your own MP3s is about more than just an encoder, however. Other things discussed in this chapter include compact disc **rippers** (such as AudioGrabber), which are used to read a CD audio track and directly transfer it to either .WAV or MP3 format and several utilities you can use during the encoding process to improve your MP3's quality.

The Basic Process

Creating an MP3 file basically involves identifying an audio file you want to convert into MP3 format and then determining the steps needed to get that file into the MP3 format. If it's a CD track, you can use a ripper and encoder program to convert the CDDA data to an MP3 format. If it's not a CD track, you need to record it as a .WAV file and then run an encoding program to convert the product into an MP3 file. Prior to encoding to an MP3 file, you can change the file's characteristics (as discussed in Chapter 8, "Digital Audio"); there are a couple of programs that can help you do this.

Part III   Digitizing Audio

The Programs to Use

There are a number of programs that aid you in creating MP3 files. We have chosen what we feel are the best programs and utilities that are widely available. The MP3 scene is vast and constantly evolving; thus, new products or alternatives may have been overlooked. Rest assured, however, that these products get the job done well. While we have focused on Windows-based utilities—especially in the step-by-step section later in the chapter—we have gone out of our way to point out similar products on other platforms you may be using, including Macintosh, Linux, and BeOS.

Xing MP3 Encoder (for Windows)

▶   Xing Technology Corporation (**www.xingtech.com**)

The Xing MP3 Encoder is a standalone encoder program for the Windows platform. The program supports a wide range of MP3 formats and is quite a bit faster than the standard Fraunhofer MP3 encoder program.

AudioCatalyst (Mac and Windows)

▶   Xing Technology Corporation (**www.xingtech.com**)

AudioCatalyst is the leading ripper/encoder product for Macintosh and Windows. The program is the result of a marriage between a popular CD ripper known as AudioGrabber and Xing's own MP3 encoder software. AudioCatalyst is available in a demo form (you'll find it on the CD included with this book). The full version, at the time of this writing, costs $29.95. (You can order the full version directly from Xing's site.)

> **TIP**
> An alternative ripper to AudioCatalyst, but one that doesn't come with a built-in encoder, is ASTARTE's CD-COPY 2.0 (**www.astarte.com**). The ripper is available at **ftp://ftp.astarte.de/pub/astarte/CD-Copy_2.0.2/English/CD-Copy2.0.2_w_manual.hqx**. CD-COPY 2.0 is specifically for the Mac.

AudioActive (Windows)

▶   AudioActive (**www.audioactive.com**)

AudioActive is an alternative encoder program that uses the Fraunhofer CODEC for the MP3 encoding process. The program operates very similar to that of the Xing encoder program but also supports AudioActive's MPEG encoding and broadcasting hardware systems from parent company Telos Systems.

AudioGrabber (Windows)

▶ Jackie Franck (**http://www.audiograbber.com-us.net/**)

The original CD ripper program that Xing adapted and merged with its MP3 encoding technology works almost exactly as AudioCatalyst. AudioGrabber, however, lets you specify the specific third-party encoding technology you care to use. It can also support other alternative encoding formats, such as AAC.

AudioGrabber ($25.00) is a little cheaper than AudioCatalyst ($29.95).

> **TIP**
>
> Your CD can be defective or scratched. Because of that, small pops or hisses might be captured in the .WAV file. If this happens to your file, a utility known as Antipop 1.0 by Vladimir V. Bashkirtsev can help. Available on AudioGrabber's download page (**www.audiograbber.com-us.net/ download.html**), the program takes a pass through a .WAV file grabbed from the CD, analyzes it for the distinct data pattern that makes up a pop, and removes it from the file.

Using AudioCatalyst

AudioCatalyst combines the best of the AudioGrabber application with Xing's own MP3 encoder product. You can download a trial version of AudioCatalyst from Xing's site, or you can buy the full version for $29.95 from C|Net's BuyDirect.com. The trial version limits you to six tracks, which you convert off the CD with the tracks randomly determined at runtime. The trial version doesn't support .WAV file encoding of MP3 files.

Using AudioCatalyst is a fairly easy process—although there are a number of options and other configurations beyond selecting tracks from your CDs and then converting them to MP3.

The main AudioCatalyst window (**Figure 9.1**) consists of a track-listing window and a menu bar composed of seven key function icons. The menu bar also shows fields in which to type the artist and album name. Whenever you pop in a CD, you can request that the program connect the CD database (**www.cddb.com**) and search for the CD's album information, including track listings, artist information, and album name. The CDDB has a very updated and broad listing of tracks, which makes it easy to avoid having to manually enter this information. If the program hasn't automatically offered this search, press the CDDB icon on the menu bar or choose Get From CDDB from the CD menu.

Figure 9.1
The main AudioCatalyst
program screen.

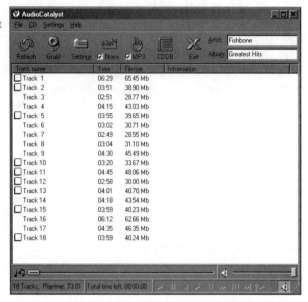

You can begin creating an MP3 file once you have your track listing
information. There is a checkbox next to each track listing. Check the
tracks you want to convert (**Figure 9.2**).

Figure 9.2
Check the tracks on the
CD you want to encode.

You must first access two critical configuration dialog boxes—the Normalization and MP3 dialog boxes. The options found in these dialog boxes control most of the key output issues you need to deal with when constructing an MP3 file using AudioCatalyst.

The MP3 Dialog Box

The MP3 Settings dialog box (**Figure 9.3**) can be displayed by clicking on the MP3 icon on the menu bar or by choosing MP3 Options from the Settings menu.

Figure 9.3
The MP3 Settings dialog box.

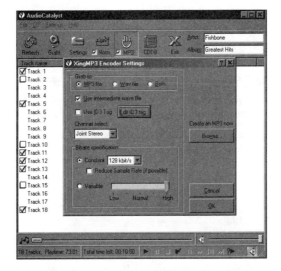

You can choose from the Grab To section to convert the CD tracks straight to the MP3 format, to a .WAV file, or to both. Just beneath that option is the Use Intermediate Wave File checkbox. Choosing this option enables the program to run a normalization routine on the .WAV file during the construction of an MP3 file, which helps better enhance the volume settings within the song to bring out the fullest sound prior to encoding. By not checking this, you can have AudioCatalyst skip this step; this speeds the creation of your MP3 files.

The next option in this dialog box is Use ID3 Tag. If you select this option, at the end of the encoding process, AudioCatalyst will append an ID3 tag to the MP3 file.

Part III Digitizing Audio

The next option is an important one. The Channel Select drop-down list offers you the ability to configure how stereo tracks are encoded. You have four choices:

▶ **Stereo** separates the left and right channels in the normal Stereo mode. Overall, the file conforms to the total bit rate selected, but the program splits the bits between the channels to improve the overall quality of the MP3 file. It does so by allocating more bits to the channel, which requires more range based on the sound wave flowing through that specific channel. The Stereo setting gives you the best quality stereo audio at higher bit rates.

▶ **Joint Stereo** forces the encoder to share certain bits between high-frequency left and right channels. The result is higher compression, but it may decrease the quality of the stereo playback of the sound. Xing recommends this setting for better quality at mid- to lower bit rates.

▶ **Dual Stereo** forces the encoder to split the bit rate constantly in half as opposed to the dynamic appropriation of the Stereo Mode. Xing recommends this for multilingual audio programs.

▶ **Mono** fuses the stereo channels into a single channel of audio. It's best used for either achieving high compression or when encoding a mono sound source.

After the Channel Select option is set, you need to deal with the bit rate specifications. Xing's encoder supports two types of encoding: Constant and Variable.

Constant Bit Rate Encoding

Constant Bit Rate encoding (CBR) means that the bit rate setting you choose is maintained throughout the length of the file. This is done regardless of the specific needs of any portion of the song, whether it's a very noisy and dynamic section or a period of complete silence. The result is twofold: Parts of the song that could use extra bits won't get them and areas of the song may include bits that are essentially unused.

The benefit of CBR is that you can consistently guess the resulting file size because it is an exact outcome of this formula:

```
bit rate/per second ✕ duration of file
```

Select the actual bit rate you want to use from the Constant drop-down list. You may check the Reduce Sample Rate (If Possible) checkbox; the reduced sample rate is for use when you are encoding files that do not have to be of CD quality. When doing this, the sample rate of the file is reduced by half at lower data rates (32kbps–80kbps), which results in a higher-quality file (with a sacrifice of dynamic range). The sample rates are kept within a better range for the bit rate setting.

Variable Bit Rate Encoding

Variable Bit Rate encoding (VBR) differs from CBR because it
intelligently applies the bits in the file based on the needs of the audio at
any moment in the file. This is useful, especially when encoding music
that has wide variances between stereo channels. For example, if one
portion of the stereo channel will benefit from extra bits allocated to it
(beyond the 64kbps), Constant Bit Rate-encoding will allocate more bits
to render it better. Meanwhile, the other channel, which may need less
bits to render properly, will be given less. Overall, the 128-bits per second
never changes, just the amount allocated to each stereo channel changes
relative to the needs of the audio source.

VBR files can be smaller and provide a higher-quality file that sounds
better as a result of its encoding process. However, because the bit rate
varies throughout the file, predicting the overall size of the file is nearly
impossible. In addition, not all MP3 players can accurately determine the
timing of a file within the total file, and thus, seeking may also be
difficult. (It is worth noting, however, that Winamp supports these files
perfectly.)

When choosing to use the VBR option, you need to set the sliding scale
from Low to High. When set at Low, you get a file that usually averages
96kbps; Normal represents 128kbps, and High represents 192kbps. The
scale sets the highest range that the file will go to when encoding any
section of the song—sections that can get by with lower bit rates are
subsequently encoded at the lower bit rates.

Finally, the Create an MP3 Now browse button will open a dialog box
from which you can select .WAV files for encoding into MP3 files (not
available in demo version).

TIP

I've encoded music with VBR. Why won't it run on my player?

Being the first person on your block to encode VBR has a few short-term
drawbacks. It's so new in the MP3 world that only a few really hip players
support it properly. The latest versions of Winamp, Freeamp, and Sonique
will work. (Go get them!) As for the others? We're distributing the files
needed by the player developers to support our VBR files. If the player you
use doesn't support VBR just yet, it should soon.

Part III   Digitizing Audio

The Normalizing Dialog Box

When you choose to have a file Normalize, you ask AudioCatalyst to convert the track to a .WAV file first (a setting offered in the previously discussed MP3 settings dialog box), after which it normalizes the file prior to encoding it to an MP3 file. Clicking the Normalize icon brings up the Normalizing settings dialog box (**Figure 9.4**).

Figure 9.4
The Normalizing
settings dialog box.

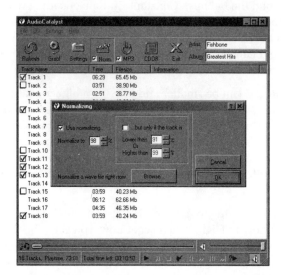

For the most part, the track to track volume settings on a CD or any good record will be the same. This is because they've been engineered and mastered as such. All CDs, LPs, and tapes are not recorded at the same levels, however; thus, if you are encoding from a mixed group of CDs, normalization in AudioCatalyst can help you create a more even flow of volume between tracks.

Most CDs levels are set from 95%–99% of the recording level. Tracks from most CDs will have the same level of loudness when you set the normalization routine in AudioCatalyst just below the 95%–99% level (91%–92%, for instance). A normalization setting just below 95% is recommended; you may otherwise lose some of the inherent loudness that a track should have.

TIP

Remember in order to normalize tracks in AudioCatalyst, you must first set the program to rip the CD track to a .WAV file.

Other Settings

Clicking the Settings icon on the menu bar brings up the basic Settings dialog box (**Figure 9.5**). You can ignore most of the settings that pertain to the CD-ROM access method used to rip tracks. The two most common CD-ROM control technologies are **ASPI**, a newer and more advanced system, and **MSCDEX** (Microsoft CD Extensions), an older technology that debuted alongside CD-ROMs in the earlier days of DOS. AudioCatalyst will most often attempt to auto-configure your CD. If you experience problems accessing your CD tracks, you may need to switch from the ASPI to MSCDEX system, tweak either settings, or update your drivers. The Help file included with AudioCatalyst goes into good detail about this process.

Figure 9.5
The other settings dialog box for AudioCatalyst.

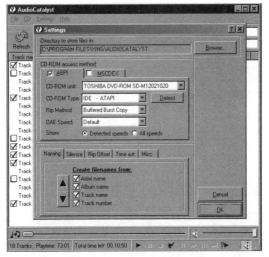

TIP

When running on Windows NT, AudioCatalyst reads data using ASPI calls for both IDE and SCSI CD-ROMs. The problem is that no ASPI manager is distributed with Windows NT. In some cases this might mean manually installing an ASPI manager driver. Check the Help file included with AudioCatalyst for specific information about setting up ASPI drivers for Windows NT.

Part III   Digitizing Audio

The second group included in the Settings dialog box is a series of tabs that manages several things: how tracks are named; song silence trimming; some ripping and track time-estimating functions (which, for the most part, should be left alone); and the Miscellaneous tab, which lets you turn on or off some features concerning track playback and the encoding process.

The Naming tab is the one you might want to give some attention to. Turn on or off the various information you want included in the MP3's file name and use the arrows to the left to set the field order.

Performing the Encoding

With your settings taken care of, you can now begin grabbing and converting the tracks. Again, make sure the tracks you convert are checked. Click the Grab icon; AudioCatalyst instantly displays a status dialog box (**Figure 9.6**) as it goes about ripping and converting the tracks.

Figure 9.6
AudioCatalyst displays a detailed status dialog box while ripping a CD file.

Rip and Go

AudioCatalyst couldn't be much easier to use. Its rip and go process and decent encoding speed make it a great MP3 tool to own. If you have a few (or more) CDs you want converted to MP3, AudioCatalyst is the way to go.

Using AudioGrabber

AudioGrabber—a shareware utility that is the basis of Xing's own AudioCatalyst program—works nearly the same way as does AudioCatalyst with a few notable exceptions.

The most significant differences between AudioGrabber and AudioCatalyst are the MP3 settings. AudioGrabber doesn't include the Xing MP3 encoder and instead uses—if it's installed—the Fraunhofer encoder or BladeEnc encoder. The configuration of the MP3 encoding system to use is found on AudioGrabber's MP3 Settings dialog box (**Figure 9.7**), which is different from the dialog box of the same name found in AudioCatalyst.

Figure 9.7
AudioGrabber's MP3 Settings dialog box has a different set of options than Xing's AudioCatalyst.

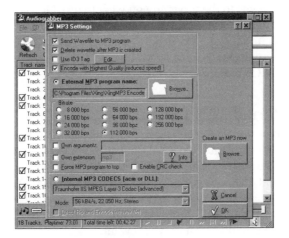

The first settings contain four checkboxes.

▶ The first checkbox, Send Wavefile to MP3 program, is unavailable unless you are using the Internal MP3 CODECS (acm or DLL) option (which is also contained in the dialog box). If you are using that option, click the Send Wavefile to MP3 program checkbox. AudioGrabber automatically sends the completed .WAV file to the CODEC for compression into the MP3 format after the .WAV file has been grabbed.

▶ The next checkbox, Delete Wavefile After MP3 Is Created, deletes the .WAV file after the resulting MP3 file is created.

▶ Use ID3 Tag and the accompanying Edit button to display the ID3 Tag Editor for the files.

▶ Finally, the Encode with Highest Quality (Reduced Speed) checkbox tells the program to take more time to analyze the .WAV file and produce a higher-quality sounding MP3.

Part III Digitizing Audio

Next, you choose what third-party system you're going to use to encode your MP3 files. Two choices are offered: using an external MP3 program (including a DOS command-line encoder) and using an internally installed Windows MP3 CODEC.

External MP3 Program Name

When using this method of interfacing with the encoding system, you must provide a path to an external program that encodes your MP3 files. The Browse button lets you wade through your computer to find an installed system. After that, you have a series of buttons and checkboxes with which you can set the bit rate or offer various command-line arguments to the program you wish to use. Of course, you must be familiar with the program in order to know what to do here. Either consult the Help file, Readme documents, and the manual that accompanies the encoder you want to use, or use the Internal MP3 CODECS option.

Internal MP3 CODECS

Rather than switch between programs, setting an automatic internal MP3 encoder is a much more elegant solution when encoding your MP3 files with AudioGrabber; the program interfaces with an installed .DLL or ACM CODEC to create your MP3 files. Installed CODECs appear in the drop-down list; below that list are the various MP3 encoding modes each particular CODEC supports. Make the choices from either list for the CODEC and MP3 quality you want.

If you've installed the Windows Media Player version 6.0 or the Net Show development from Microsoft, you should have the advanced Fraunhofer IIS MPEG Layer-3 CODEC available on your system. This CODEC, which can decode 128-bit or better MP3 files, supports encoding only up to 56K at 22,050Hz, stereo. In order to get the Advanced Plus CODEC that supports 128-bit, you need to purchase it from Opticom Solutions (**www.opticom.de**) for $49. A separate Professional MP3 Encoder CODEC, which supports a wider variety of methods plus better than 128-bit encoding, runs $199.

You can also download the freely available BladeEnc (**http://www.bladeenc.cjb.net**), which works through the internal method (though our experiences with BladeEnc give mixed results in terms of quality).

Other encoder choices include the previously mentioned AudioCatalyst, which combines AudioGrabber with Xing's MP3 encoder (which is very good) for $29.95. You can also get the separate standalone Xing MP3 encoder for $19.95.

AudioGrabber or AudioCatalyst?

Other than some icon differences and the way the MP3 encoding options are set, AudioGrabber and AudioCatalyst are identical. The big reason to use AudioGrabber instead of Xing's AudioCatalyst is if you want to use an encoder other than Xing's MP3 encoder.

Using Xing's MP3 Encoder

The basic Xing MP3 encoder (**Figure 9.8**) is a $19.95 utility that you can order and download directly from Xing. If you have the full version AudioCatalyst, you don't likely need this separate utility. If not, and you want a good MP3 encoder, then this standalone encoder is a worthwhile purchase.

Figure 9.8
Xing's basic MP3
encoder program.

The program is very straightforward. You can either choose Add (or Ctrl++) from the File menu or press the Add button at the bottom of the dialog box to bring up a modified Add Jobs dialog box (**Figure 9.9**) that lets you choose .WAV files to add to the encoding job list. You can also click the Set Profile button in order to choose the encoding options you want; choosing the Set Directory button lets you select the desired output directory for your MP3 files.

Figure 9.9
The Add Jobs
dialog box.

Setting Profiles

Each file in your Jobs to Encode queue can have its own profile. This lets you set different files to different encoder settings as needed. To set a profile for any file, select it from the list, right-click on the item, and choose Properties from the menu. This brings up the Encode Properties dialog box (**Figure 9.10**).

Figure 9.10
The Encode Properties
dialog box.

This dialog box provides two tabs: Target and Source. The Source tab provides nothing more than details on the source .WAV file you're attempting to encode. The Target tab offers you two buttons: Set Directory, which lets you individually set a specific target directory for each file, and Set Profile, which brings up the MP3 encoding options that Xing offers.

The Select a Profile dialog box (**Figure 9.11**) provides a drop-down menu system that houses your encoding options. The two major branches of this menu are the XingMP3 Profiles and the StreamWorks Profiles.

The StreamWorks Profiles give you the ability to encode your .WAV files to Xing's proprietary StreamWorks streaming audio format—an older system, based on MPEG, that the company launched in the earlier days of audio on the Web.

The XingMP3 Profiles offer you eight specific encoding options, from 16-bit mono to 128-bit CD-quality stereo, to full-blast 320-bit stereo. Choose the profile you want (128 bit is normal MP3 setting) and then press OK. You return to the Encode Properties dialog box, where you can view the statistics for the to-be encoded file showing expected file size and other profile settings. Hit the OK button to return to the encoder and repeat this process as necessary for each file.

Figure 9.11
The Select a Profile dialog box is where you set the MP3 encoding style.

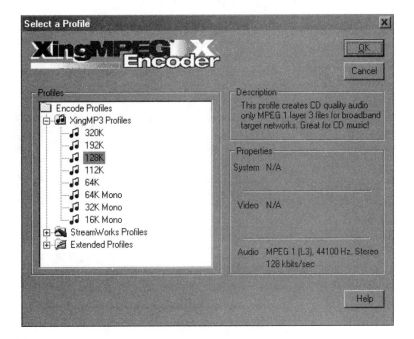

Part III Digitizing Audio

Once you have added all the files you want to the Jobs to Encode list, press the Encode button to begin the process. As each file is completed, its status changes from Waiting to Done. Once complete, you can choose Play to test the resulting MP3 file. To delete a file from the list, select Remove from the buttons at the bottom of the dialog box.

TIP

You must reset the Done status to Waiting in order to re-encode a file at a different profile. Highlight the file in the list and then choose Reset Status Waiting from the File menu (or by pressing Ctrl+W).

Using AudioActive

An alternative program to Xing's MP3 encoder is AudioActive's Production Studio (**Figure 9.12**). This program works in a fashion similar to Xing's MP3 encoder. You can add files to a job's list from the menu. Select each file and press the Encoding Properties button to bring up the Encoding Properties dialog box.

Figure 9.12
AudioActive's Production Studio encoder program.

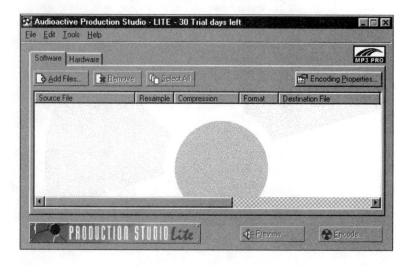

From this dialog box (**Figure 9.13**), you can delete the source file after encoding, as well as set the compression scheme and the output format. The output format, which in addition to supporting MP3 also supports Microsoft's Active Streaming Format (.ASF for use with NetShow Server) and Macromedia's Shockwave streaming audio (.SWA). Choose the Faster Encode option for speed or the Higher-Quality Encode (not available in the demonstration version) for better-sounding files.

Figure 9.13
AudioActive's Encoding Properties dialog box.

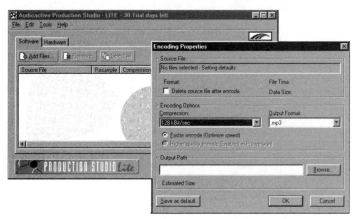

Select the output file name and directory and press OK to return to the main screen. Press Encode to begin the process.

AudioActive Production Studio also supports hardware-based encoding using parent company Telos's MPEG encoding hardware.

Alternative Platform Programs

Most of the programs talked about thus far run on either Windows or the Macintosh platform—but what of other platforms, like Linux? Here is a rundown of various rippers and encoders that work for other non-Windows or non-Macintosh platforms.

Linux

You have a choice of several encoders for the Linux platform:

▶ The MP3Enc from Fraunhofer (**www.iis.fhg.de/amm/download/mp3enc/**) is available directly from the site. You can order the professional version of this encoder from Opticom (**www.opticom.de**) for $199.00.

▶ The BladeEnc is also available (**home8.swipnet.se/~w-82625/encoder/DL.html**).

▶ For a ripper, try cdparanoia (**www.mit.edu/afs/sipb/user/xiphmont/cdparanoia/**).

Part III Digitizing Audio

BeOS

The BeOS platform has one encoder: Encode .2. It is available from Halfast Software (**www.halfast.com/products.html**), which also created the BeAmp product.

At this time, however, no CD ripper exists for the BeOS platform.

Unix (Various)

▶ The BladeEnc encoder from Tord Jansson is available for FreeBSD.

▶ The Fraunhofer MP3Enc is available for Solaris, Sun OS, IRX, and Alpha/OSF1 (**www.iis.fhg.de/amm/download/mp3enc/**).

▶ Opticom is selling a $199 professional version of the Fraunhofer encoder as mentioned earlier.

For rippers:

▶ Tosha .6 (FreeBSD) by Olli Fromme (**dorifer.heim3.tu-clausthal.de/~olli/tosha/**).

▶ CDDARead (Irix) from Tim Kokkonen (**http://www.jyu.fi/~tjko/projects.html**).

▶ Gallete (Solaris) by G. Boccon-Gibod (**www.cybersoft.org/galette/**).

Open the Music

As millions of users discover the MP3 format, people from all over are quietly digitizing their music collections from tapes, from CDs, and from vinyl. Perfect copies can be made in a digital software form, and unlike the false promise of CDs, the music never wears out, gets scratched, or skips. Once archived on your hard drive, you can instantly call up songs. You can download it to one of the portable MP3 players (such as Diamond's Rio), transfer it to a car-based MP3 system, serve it out over your personal LAN, or load it into Winamp or into another MP3 software player.

Unlike formats such as RealAudio or Active Streaming Format, MP3 is an open format supported by a number of far-reaching products from Winamp, to SHOUTcast Radio, to Freeamp, to Virtual Turntables (a DJ program that supports MP3 files). This can make old music new again, new musical styles available like never before, and more.

Therein lies the true power of the open MP3 format: By encoding your music to the MP3 format, you've essentially opened it up to a whole world of possibilities.

10

Creating Your Own Custom CDs

While most people try to convert their CD collection to the MP3 format for listening on their computer, portable MP3 device, or MP3 car stereo, others will want to create custom CDs of their MP3 files. If you're collecting original MP3 files, putting your files onto CD is a great way to share new work with people who don't have computers or portable MP3 devices. In addition, archiving your collection to CD-ROM (keeping it in the MP3 format as opposed to making it into a common audio CD, for instance) is a good way to build your MP3 collection without necessarily having your hard drive overcrowded with MP3 files.

This chapter covers the basics of creating your own custom audio and data CDs. From purchasing a quality CD-R (Recordable CD) device to using the most common CD-R software packages, we cover how to use CD-R technology to expand your MP3 experience.

Purchasing a CD-R Device

CD-R drives were once the province of a privileged few who could afford them and needed to create their own CDs. These people, however lucky to be an early adopter of recordable CD technology, also had to deal with unreliable drives—and the creation of more than a few $8–$10 coasters. What's more, it was easy to create a CD that worked on one type of drive but didn't work on others.

Today, after several drive generations, not only have prices come down, but reliability has gone up. In fact, many new machines shipping from the likes of Gateway and Dell are making CD-R drives standard.

Despite lower prices and manufacturers inclusion in systems, there's a good chance you might not have purchased a CD-R drive. The first place to start is to learn the basics about recordable CD-ROM technology and how to get a drive.

Part III Digitizing Audio

Drive Types

There are four types of drives you can consider when purchasing a drive. The first two types are CD-R and CD-RW. **CD-R** stands for CD-Recordable. These were the first type of drives created. They are essentially write-once drives. Once data is written using these drives, you can't erase and write over the data.

Most drives today are the second type—**CD-RW**, or Read-Write drives. These drives allow you to rewrite to the CD as many as 1,000 times before the disc itself is worn out. The problem with CD-RW drives is that their discs can only be read by multiread CD-ROM drives, which aren't as prominent as regular CD-ROM drives. Another major concern is that audio CD players can't handle CD-RW but can usually handle CD-R discs. CD-RW drives are better but can be a bit more expensive. Make sure when you use a CD-RW drive that it's creating a CD with other CD systems. The software you use handles this.

The other major issue to consider is external versus internal drive. If you're not the type who finds it easy to open your machine and install new equipment, then go for an external drive. While many external drives require you to install a card in your system, installing a card is easier than installing the entire drive which requires you to hook up the power, and screw it into place (it's actually not that hard but you be the judge). However, there are some external drives that connect via the parallel port on your machine. These drives are the easiest to install and use, although they tend to be much slower than internal, card-based drives.

If you are planning on purchasing an internal drive, you can choose between an IDE/EIDE drive and a SCSI drive. The difference is the interface that connects the drive to your computer. IDE/EIDE is a mainstay for PCs that is cheaper but slower than a SCSI drive. SCSI is important for Macintosh machines, which unlike the PC, use the SCSI interface exclusively. SCSI drives will require a separate SCSI adapter card be installed in your machine. Be careful to make sure you buy a SCSI card if your drive doesn't include it to begin with (many don't).

Finally, consider speed. Each new generation of recordable drives will get faster and faster, just like the read-only CD-ROM drives have for years. Right now it's common to find 2-6x drives. Be careful not to confuse a drive's read speed with its write speed as read will almost surely be higher. Also, look at a drive's overall throughput when writing. Just because it spins the disc really fast doesn't necessarily guarantee it's as fast as similar drives.

Some people avoid buying the fastest drives because newer, faster drives can be a bit unreliable in creating CDs that other drives will read with ease.

Looking for Drives to Buy

The best place currently on the Web to find any computer hardware for purchase is at one of the two major hardware purchasing Web sites: **Computers.com** or **Computershopper.com**. With these sites it's easy to enter some criteria for the type of drive you want and narrow it to a model and a location within driving distance. For example, on Computershopper.com (**Figure 10.1**) you can enter basic speed, interface, and pricing criteria. On Computers.com (**Figure 10.2**), which is run by C I Net, you can enter that criteria as well as sort it by price and release dates.

Figure 10.1
Computershopper.com lets you spec out the type of CD-R drive you want and then search for available makes and prices.

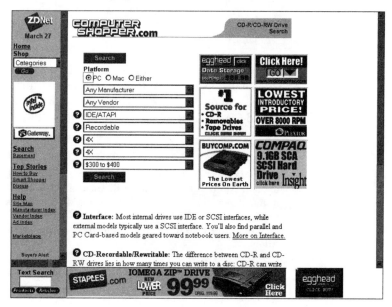

Part III Digitizing Audio

Figure 10.2
C | Net's Computers.com
offers a similar service.
It makes buying the CD-
R drive of your choice a
snap.

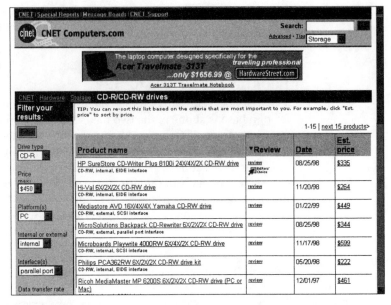

On average, drives run (at the time of this book's writing) between
$220–$500, depending on features such as writing speed, external versus
internal, and reading speed. By Christmas of 1999, many are predicting
low-end CD-R drives will be down to $100–$150 a piece!

TIP

When it comes to CD-creation software, the choice is fairly easy. Almost 90%
of the drives out there include a slimmed-down version of Easy CD-Creator
from Adaptec (for Windows) or Toast (for Macintosh) also by Adaptec. Both
pieces of software are very good and if you're not satisfied with the version
included with your drive, you can upgrade to the full version available from
Adaptec.

Preparing an MP3 File for CD Audio

MP3s cannot be laid down as audio tracks on a CD as is. Instead, you have to decode the files into .WAV files so that Easy CD-Creator can write the files to your CD. Doing this is fairly simple using the Winamp Disk Writer plug-in:

1. All files loaded in the playlist will be made into .WAV files when the Disk Writer plug-in is selected as the output system to use. Go to the Preferences menu in Winamp, select the Output options, and choose the Nullsoft Disk Writer Plug-In v1.0 (x86) option (**Figure 10.3**).

Figure 10.3
Using the Preferences dialog box to select the Nullsoft Disk Writer plug-in.

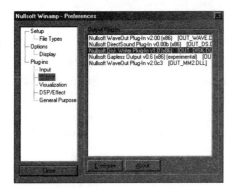

2. You can configure the Disk Writer plug-in to output the .WAV files to any directory on your machine. Pressing the Configure button brings up a dialog box in which you can select the precise directory to store MP3 files converted to .WAV files.

3. Make sure you have enough disk space (one minute of an MP3 file will take one megabyte of space on your hard drive). Do this before pressing Play Winamp (when you have selected the Disk Writer as the output system to capture the output). Also make sure that you aren't set in Repeat mode; otherwise, the Disk Writer repeats and overwrites files unnecessarily.

4. Create the playlist you want to put on CD. (Remember that a CD holds about 72 minutes worth of music.) Hit Play. The Disk Writer plug-in runs through the playlist, and each song will be written out as a .WAV file.

5. Once written to disk, your files are ready to go onto a recordable CD. You can load them into a sound editor and change them around, but that isn't recommended because, unless you know what you're doing, you're likely not to help them sound any better.

Using Easy CD-Creator

Easy CD-Creator can be used in two basic ways: via its step-by-step wizard interface or its more advanced mode. For the most part, the Creation Wizard system is very easy to use and takes you through all the choices you need in order to burn a new CD.

> **TIP**
>
> Burn, baby burn. Because a laser is used to heat up the blank CD and write the information to it, recording a CD is also referred to as **burning** a CD. *Burning* is thus used interchangeably with *recording* by CD recording junkies.

Follow these steps to create an audio CD:

1. Load Easy CD. If the Adaptec Easy CD-Creator Wizards doesn't display, select it from the menu (File, Wizard or Ctrl+W). The Wizard will display.

2. The Wizard prompts you to choose to create either a data or an audio CD. Choose Audio CD and click Next.

3. The Wizard lets you select songs to lay down onto the CD. The dialog box (**Figure 10.4**) lets you move throughout your directories and select files. Pressing Add Now puts them in the layout. You can move around your hard drive, adding files until there is no space left on the CD. The dialog box also includes a Play button in the upper-right corner, where you can preview files to make sure you have the song you want selected. Click Next when you are done selecting songs.

Figure 10.4
It's easy to add files and check remaining room with the CD Creation Wizard. Choose the .WAV files you want and hit Add Now.

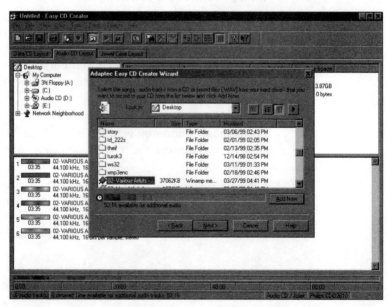

> **TIP**
> You don't have to fill the entire CD at this point. As long as you don't close the CD, you can add to it over time until it is filled.

4. The next screen on the Wizard (**Figure 10.5**) lets you create a title and artist listing for the CD. Simply type in the name of the CD and the artist(s).

Figure 10.5
Name your CD and type in the artist(s) names.

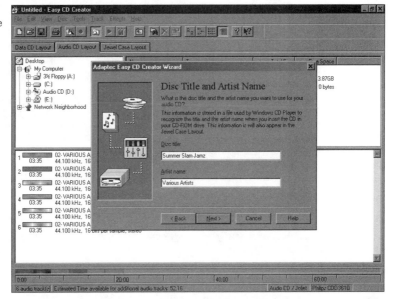

5. After naming the CD, you must choose to either Leave the Session Open or Close the Session. You can record more data to the disc if you leave the session open. Closing the session prevents you from adding more data to the disc. If you keep the session open, the CD won't play on a standard audio CD player. Choose Close the Session if you're sure you're not going to add any more tracks to the CD; otherwise, keep it open until you're done. Click Next when you've made your choice.

6. The Wizard asks if you want to test before writing to the disc. When creating a CD, it helps to first have the entire system do a test before writing. This ensures the best quality and chances of perfect success. While testing nearly doubles the time it takes to create a CD, it gives you a better chance of a successful burn. Adaptec recommends testing at least the first few times you use the program. Click Next after making your choice.

Part III Digitizing Audio

7. Now you are ready to create your CD. You can choose to go ahead with your layout and choices or to create the CD later, which gives you a chance to edit the layout (**Figure 10.6**). If you choose to create the CD now, the CD Creation Status dialog box comes up as the drive begins burning the CD.

Figure 10.6
Decide whether to start recording right away or leave to edit.

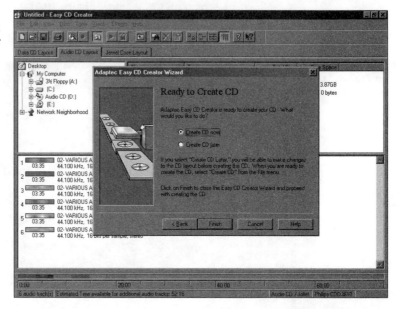

TIP
At any point when using the Web, you can backtrack to previous choices by selecting Back.

Using Toast

Follow these steps to create a personalized audio CD:

1. **Getting Started**—Once you have installed the proper software, as well as attached your CD-Recorder to your Mac, launch Adaptec Toast. Go ahead and place a blank CD in your recorder at this time.

2. **Choosing Your Format**—From the Format option in the menu bar, pull down to "Audio CD" (**Figure 10.7**). The main Toast window will scroll to reveal the options related to your chosen format.

Figure 10.7
Choosing the format

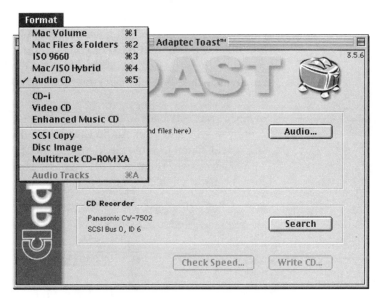

3. **The Selection Process**—You now have the option of either dragging and dropping your selected titles directly from the original audio CD to the Toast window, or you can import them into Toast via the Audio button. If you desire to import as opposed to "dragging and dropping," click on the Audio button (**Figure 10.8**).

Figure 10.8
Click on the Audio button to make selections.

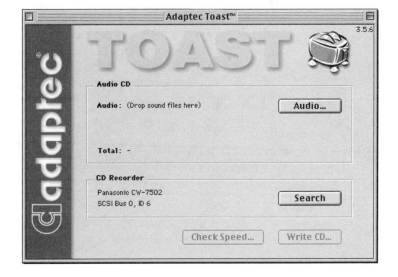

Part III   Digitizing Audio

By clicking on the Audio button you will be given the Audio Tracks window. Once here you still have the option of either dragging and dropping from your audio CD or you can continue to import "traditionally." The bottom left hand button on the Audio Tracks window is labeled "Add." Click on this once to begin importing tracks.

Navigate your way back to the desktop, through the import window, where you will find your Audio CD (that is, if you have placed it in your drive). Open (double click) the Audio CD, select the first track you wish to record (**Figure 10.9**) by clicking once, and then click on Open, or just double click on your selection.

Figure 10.9
Select the track you
want to record

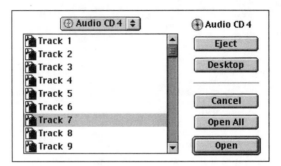

The importing window will close and bring you back to the Audio Tracks window. Your new selection will now be listed above while the total number of tracks chosen, as well as the total elapsed time will be displayed in the lower left hand corner. To choose another track, repeat the above procedure by clicking on "Add" etc. If you wish to select a track from another CD click on "Add" once and, when your importing window appears, click on Eject and replace the new CD with the old when your CD drawer opens.

NOTE

If you do select tracks from various CD's, Toast will ask you to name the "Source CD" for it's own reference purposes during the recording procedure.

From within the Audio Tracks window, if you select a track by clicking once you will then have a few options available. These include playing the track to make sure you have the right song by clicking on the "Play" button; saving the entire file (in AIFF format) to the drive of your choice by clicking on the Extract To button; or you can remove it from your list by clicking Remove.

If you double click on a track in the Audio Tracks window, a second window (**Figure 10.10**) will open where you can then name the track.

Figure 10.10
Name the track

At the end of the selection process, if you have chosen songs from more than one CD, Toast will show you a message displaying the names of the Source CDs (**Figure 10.11**) and will advise you to have them available once the recording session has begun. Click OK.

Figure 10.11
You will need
to have the
Source CDs
on hand.

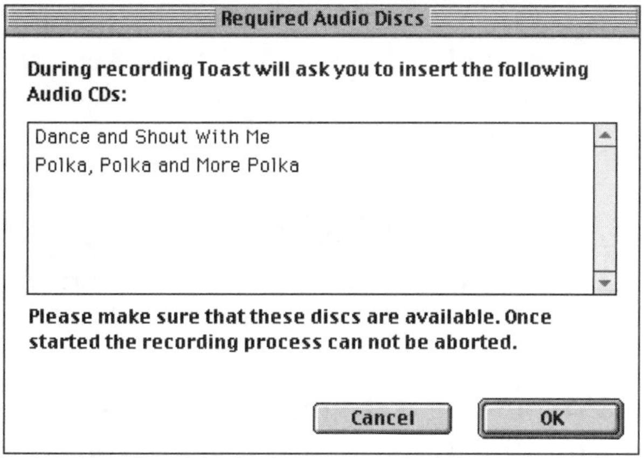

Part III Digitizing Audio

4. **Recording**—You are now ready to burn your custom CD. Click once on the Write CD button on the lower right corner of the main Toast Window. A new window will appear (**Figure 10.12**) asking you to indicate recording speed as well as the option to either Write Session or to Write Disc. For the speed, select the fastest speed possible for your writer. You can choose either Write Session or Write Disc, but remember that choosing Write Session will allow you to add more songs on your custom CD at a later date. While selecting Write Disc, Toast assumes that you will not be adding to this disk and therefore considers the CD complete once the recording session is over.

Figure 10.12
Writing Options

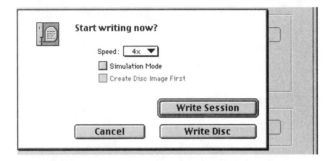

Once you have chosen either Write Session or Write Disc, Toast will begin the burning process. When a different source CD is required during the recording process, your CD drawer will open and a message will appear indicating which CD should be inserted.

5. **Your Disk Is Ready**—Once finished, a message will display stating that the new CD is ready with a button to eject. Eject and enjoy your customized audio CD.

Advanced CD Creator Options

The CD Creation Wizard makes using Easy CD-Creator a snap, but there are some advanced program features worth understanding.

Previewing, Editing a Track Name, and Rearranging the Track Order

When you've created a layout you like, you can do several things before recording the CD. Click on a track to highlight it and then right-click on the highlighted track to bring up a menu. Choosing Rename from this menu lets you rename any track listing. Choosing Properties from this menu lets you see that file's properties.

To preview any track on your computer, just double-click to play the .WAV file.

When you've created a layout and are in the Audio Layout mode, drag any track up or down the list to rearrange the order of the songs.

Saving and Loading a Layout

Sometimes you'll want to save a good layout to your hard drive for repeated use. If you've made a particularly good mix of songs and want to burn it for friends from time to time, it is a good idea to save the final layout. That way you don't have to re-create it every time someone wants a copy.

To save a layout to disc, choose Save from the File menu (Ctrl+S). You can load previously save layouts by choosing Open CD Layout from the File menu (Ctrl+O).

Recording Your CD

You can set up the Wizard to begin recording your CD. However, sometimes it pays to use the Wizard to set things up only, allowing you to take some extra steps to perfect things.

1. If you haven't told the Wizard to immediately burn the CD and instead decided to tweak the layout before recording, you can hit the Record button on the toolbar or choose Create CD from the File menu. This brings up the CD Creation Setup dialog box (**Figure 10.13**).

Figure 10.13
The CD Creation Setup dialog box lets you make final choices before hitting Record.

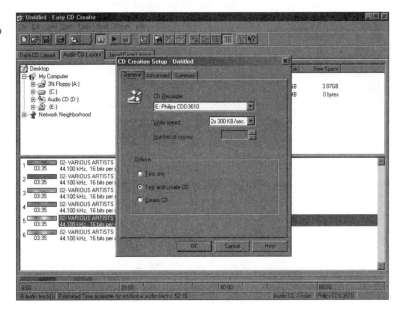

Part III Digitizing Audio

2. The CD Creation dialog box is composed of three tabs : General, Advanced, and Summary. The General tab shows you the various recordable CD drives you have attached to your system (most only have one). A drop-down list below that shows the available write speeds that the selected CD drive has. You can leave these unchanged.

    Directly below the drop-down lists is an Options area with three choices: Test Only, Test and Create CD, and Create CD. These options let you decide whether the burn process will be a test run, a creation only, or a combination test burn and recording. Testing and creating is the best choice. If speed is a necessity, choose Create. Remember, however, that the likelihood of a perfect recording is increased with a test.

3. The Advanced dialog box lets you choose the status of the recording session when the recording is complete. You have four distinct choices. (Note: there are more provided here than were provided in the simplified Wizard process described earlier). The options are divided between Track-at-Once and Disc-at-Once. In the Track-at-Once options, you can choose Leave Session Open, which lets you add more songs to the CD within the same session. Remember that you have to close the session at some point in order to listen to it on a typical audio CD player.

    If you want to listen to the CD on a home or car CD player, you must close the session once you have added all the songs you want to the CD.

    Close Session and Leave Disc Open lets you create multi-session CDs. This option closes the current session, but not the overall CD. This lets you record more data to later sessions. Only audio discs in the first session, however, can be heard.

TIP

Use this method to create a first session that are the audio versions of the songs; close the session with room left over. Open a new session and record the MP3 files in a data format to the second session. These are for people to load and listen to on their computers without having to rip the audio tracks all over again.

The Close Disc option completely closes the disc at the end of the write. There can be no more data recorded to the CD after a disc is closed.

The Disc-at-Once option writes and closes a CD in one move, without turning the writing laser on and off between tracks. By not turning the laser on and off between tracks, there is no two-second gap between tracks; it also write-protects the CD. This creates one long mix of a track, which may be useful for CDs of DJ mixes and the like.

4. Press OK to begin the burn after you've chosen Record and set the options. The CD Creation Process dialog box (**Figure 10.14**) shows progress. If you've chosen to test and then write tracks, the entire testing process is looped through first; an identical loop, which actually writes the data, is then run. Press the Details button to see more information as the CD progresses.

Figure 10.14
The burning process in action and recording details are shown.

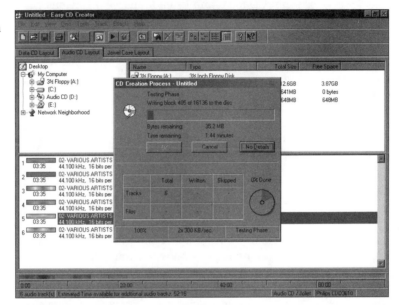

TIP
To avoid hiccups in the burning process—especially for audio CDs—it is recommended you don't use your machine intensively while burning a CD. Burning a CD should be the last thing that remains going when you retire from your machine for the day or for a lunch hour.

Writing MP3s to a Disc

If all you want to do is create a CD-ROM version of your MP3 files, Easy CD-Creator can do that. This is useful if your hard drive is filling up to the brim with MP3 files and you want to archive them to CD. While you can't play an MP3 file stored on a CD-ROM on a separate CD player (at least not yet), you can insert the CD into any computer with a CD-ROM drive and retrieve files from it to listen via Winamp.

With the files stored in the MP3 format, a single CD can hold approximately 650 minutes of music. Imagine storing an artist's complete discography on one CD in the MP3 format.

Part III Digitizing Audio

What's more, you can mix audio tracks with a data component if you created what is known as a **multi-session CD**. In the first session of a CD, you store the tracks as traditional CD audio. You then close that session and store the same songs in the MP3 format on the remaining portion of the disc in a data format. Now you never have to be without either version. Pop the CD into your car stereo on your way to work, and into your CD-ROM and listen to the MP3 versions via Winamp when you're at your PC.

Follow these steps to create a data CD:

1. Load Easy CD. If the Adaptec Easy CD-Creator Wizard doesn't display, choose it from the menu (File, Wizard or Ctrl+W).

2. The Wizard prompts you to create either a data or an audio CD. Choose Data CD and click Next.

3. The Wizard lets you select files to lay down on the CD. The dialog box is just like the one used for choosing audio files. It lets you move throughout your directories and select files. Pressing Add Now adds them to the layout. You can move around your hard drive selecting and adding files until there is no room left on the CD.

4. Sometimes a file name on your machine may be incompatible with the CD's file-naming convention. If this is the case, the program will catch the problem when you click the Add Now button; an Alert dialog box comes up (**Figure 10.15**) and suggests a new name for the file. If you agree with it, either press the Change button or type in a file name. Click Next when you are done selecting files.

Figure 10.15
The Alert dialog box tells you to rename files whose file names aren't recognized by the computer.

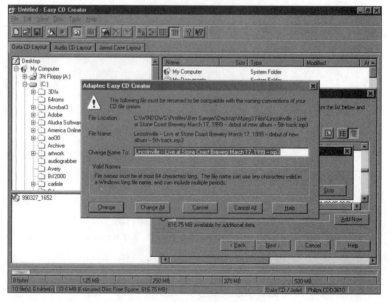

5. The Wizard asks if you want to test before writing to the disc.

6. Now you are ready to create your CD. You can go ahead with your layout and choices or create and edit it later. If you choose to create the CD now, the CD Creation Status dialog box displays as the drive begins to burn the CD.

Closing a Session or Disc Separately

Sometimes you will need to separately close a session and the CD as a whole depending on the status you asked to have after the recording was done. In this case, you need to specifically perform these operations by calling the Disc Information dialog box.

1. Choose Disc Information from the Disc menu. The Disc Information dialog box (**Figure 10.16**) displays, and you are greeted with a list of the last current session opened or closed on the disc in your drive.

Figure 10.16
The Disc Information dialog box gives you a status on any CD and its sessions. It also lets you close a session or the disc as a whole, so it can be played on other CD players.

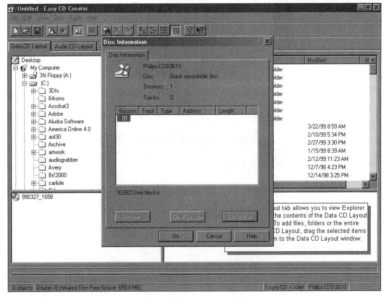

2. To close a session, highlight it and choose Close Session.

3. To close a disc, choose Close Disc.

Part III Digitizing Audio

Creating a Jewel Case Printout

After you've burned the perfect CD, you'll want to create a printout to insert in the CD jewel case (for track listings and the like). To activate the automatic Jewel Case Layout mode, click on the Jewel Case Layout tab at the top of the screen. Using the current active track layout, the program creates a simple jewel case layout that you can print and cut out for your CD (**Figure 10.17**).

Figure 10.17
Easy CD-Creator automatically creates CDs covers for you.

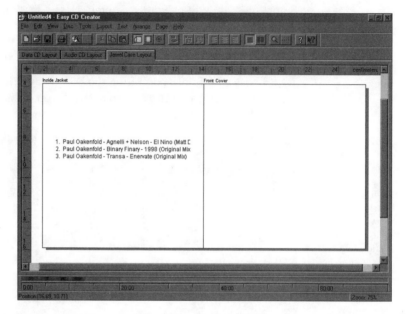

Click on any section of text to activate it. You can move the text around when it's highlighted. Double-clicking on any object of text lets you edit it and its font characteristics (**Figure 10.18**). If you have a color printer, you can select colors for the text here as well.

Figure 10.18
You can select any piece of text and change color, size, or font type via the Font Characteristics dialog box.

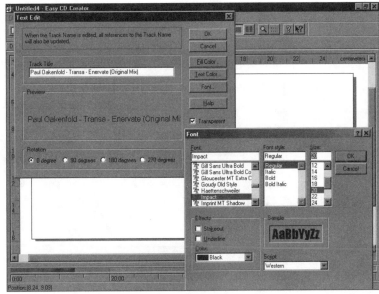

To change the background color and other options, choose Options from the Layout menu. This brings up the Jewel Case Preferences dialog box. You can change the cover colors and overall default fonts for the layout.

> **TIP**
> There is no easy way to insert graphics into the jewel case layout with the version of Easy CD-Creator that ships with most CD drives. You need to activate a graphics program in order to do this. Select a graphic you want to use, return to the Easy CD-Creator program, and then Paste (Ctrl+V) the graphic into any area of the layout (**Figure 10.19**).

Part III Digitizing Audio

Figure 10.19
To easily place graphics on your jewel case layout, open a graphic in a program such as Paint Shop Pro, copy it to the clipboard, and paste it in the Layout mode.

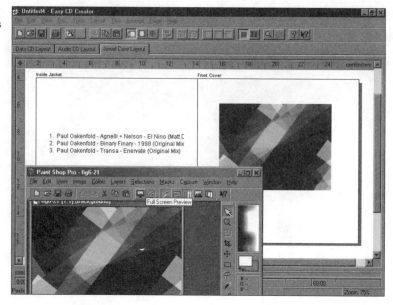

To MP3 and Back Again

So much music today is created for CD. Then along comes a compelling digital file format named MP3 and millions of people begin moving their CD collection to an electronic file format. As digital formats like MP3 progress, you have to wonder if the CD's days are numbered. Hardly—just as CDs didn't end the reign of tapes, MP3 files won't necessarily end the need for CDs. Audiophiles, as well as the simple engineering principles discussed in Chapter 2, "Inside the MP3 Format and Players," describes to you that an original CD audio track has quality superior to an MP3 file. As this chapter has shown you, recordable CDs also help you extend your MP3 power. By creating CDs of your favorite MP3 files, you can share new songs and artists you've discovered on the Internet with people who don't yet have a computer or understand how to use MP3 files. You can also create huge MP3 file archives on CD for friends with slower Internet connections; for the real MP3 freak, you can create a dual disc containing both audio and MP3 versions.

CDs may have originally been seen as the prey of the MP3 movement, but that couldn't be further from the truth. The traditional CD you purchase in a record store will perhaps take a dent as digital music catches on, but recordable CDs offer an inexpensive way to transfer and expand the realm of online music.

11

Artists and MP3: Make It Work for You

Much of the media's coverage of MP3 has focused on how musicians can be robbed of royalties by unscrupulous MP3 Web site owners who give away commercially released tracks in MP3 format. However, MP3 can also work as an outstanding promotional tool for musicians—especially lesser known bands who, in search of a record deal, would otherwise be forced to go through the arduous and more expensive process of cutting, making, and shipping demo CDs to Artist and Repertoire (A&R) people across the country.

Public Enemy's Chuck D, one of the most outspoken proponents of MP3, says that the day of the demo as we know it is nearing the end. Musicians can record a song, convert to an MP3 file, and have it up on the Web in a matter of hours or days, not the several months it would take to move a demo tape or CD.

This chapter covers how to use MP3 to your advantage; how to get your songs posted on MP3.com; where to set up a free or a commercial Web site to post your own MP3s; how to link your promotional Web site to MP3.com; and all about the upcoming MP3 watermark technology, which informs listeners that a given MP3 file is one produced by you, not by someone else.

MP3.com

Even artists as successful as the Beastie Boys are turning to MP3 to promote their music. While the Beasties have the power of a major label, most musicians don't. It is this group of artists—those seeking all possibilities for getting their music heard—who can benefit most from the promotional power of MP3 and (specifically) MP3.com.

Part III Digitizing Audio

MP3.com says it averages more than 200,000 visits to its download area each day. The download area has music divided into more than 30 genres, including alternative, blues, industrial, rock, and hip hop. Songs in each genre are ranked by popularity and may be featured as the "Song of the Day" on the front page, which sometimes increases downloads by more than 500%. There is also the weekly Top 40 and Bottom 40, as well as a spotlight on new songs and new artists. Artists may also be featured on MP3.com Radio and on MP3.com compilation CDs.

Each artist gets a Web page at no cost. The site can include songs, band logos, album graphics, lyrics, and any other information about your band (or yourself) that you want to include. MP3.com offers an interface that allows artists to create a Web page without having to know HTML.

Signing Up as a New Artist

Before you sign up as a new artist, you must have at least one song ready to upload to MP3.com's server. Do not fill out the application form until you have an MP3 file ready to go. Duplicate band entries are deleted.

A band name, email address, and genre are also required in order to sign up as a new artist. Other information that will help you have a more descriptive listing? A list of your musical influences; a list of popular artists that you sound similar to; a band history; list of band members and which instruments they play; albums; concert dates; press releases; and any other relevant information. You should also include your Web site address (if you already have one), a band logo, a picture (270×180 pixels), and contact information.

For your song, you can include the title, a one-line song description. If applicable, you can include the CD that the song is taken from, your record label, credits, lyrics, and a picture of the album cover (70×70 pixels).

Signing up as a new artist is a simple process:

1. Go to the New Artist Sign Up area by clicking on the New Artist Signup link under Artists/Labels on the MP3.com front page; you can alternatively go straight to **www.mp3.com/newartist/**.

2. Click on Get Started Signing Up.

3. Read the MP3.com Music Submission Agreement.

4. Electronically sign the agreement and click the Continue to Step 2 button.

5. Enter your artist information and click Continue to Step 3.

6. Confirm the artist information and click Continue to Step 4.

7. Upload your band picture.

At this point, you are finished with the artist information sign up process. However, you still need to upload your MP3 file:

1. Click on the Song Admin link.
2. Click on Add New Song.
3. Enter song information (title, description, and credits).
4. Find the MP3 file stored on your hard drive and upload it.
5. Upload the album cover image that will accompany your song. Indicate whether your song needs a parental advisory warning and where you want to make the song available.

That's it. Your MP3 will be in Unverified status for a short time until MP3.com verifies that it is encoded correctly.

Digital Automatic Music CD Program

MP3.com also offers the Digital Automatic Music (DAM) System that intends to put all of the control and more of the money from record sales into musician's hands. Artists can sell and market their music without any start-up costs and receive 50% of the CD sale price. MP3.com takes care of the CD manufacturing and mailing for no charge. The contract is a nonexclusive agreement, so you can cancel your DAM agreement with no obligation if you sign a record deal. You can sign up for the DAM system after entering your band information into the artist database.

1. Log into the Artist Area with your username and password.
2. Upload the songs in MP3 format that you wish to sell on your CD.
3. Set a price for your CD (from $4.99 to $9.99).
4. Select at least one song to give away for promotion.
5. Order the first copy of your CD for publication.

The artist must buy one copy to verify the validity of the CD, to verify that the files can be decoded, and to test the quality. MP3.com says there is nothing to lose: Sell no CDs and you owe no money. You receive 50% of the sale price for every CD sold. There are no fees; artists receive a weekly report listing sales and promotional downloads. Payouts occur quarterly once the minimum amount of $50.00 is reached. Artists can opt to leave the program at any time. If you need your CD encoded into MP3 format, MP3.com will do it for a $5.00 fee. DAM CDs are in both Redbook Audio and MP3 files so that people can listen to your music in their homes or cars, as well as via their computers or Rio players. As of this writing, MP3.com did not offer cover art with the DAM CDs, but said it was working on making this possible.

Setting Up a Free Web Site

As mentioned earlier, MP3.com allows participating artists to create free Web sites using MP3.com's tools. MP3.com obviously isn't the only place to set up a free Web site, however. There are a number of Web communities that cater to the novice, intermediate, and even expert Web builder. You have a number of choices if you want to build a Web site to promote your music and offer songs in MP3 format.

The leaders, GeoCities and Tripod, offer free, easy-to-use Web-building tools, free space, free email, and a community of millions—all potential listeners.

GeoCities

GeoCities (**www.geocities.com**) is certainly one of the most popular Web communities and suppliers of free personal Web publishing tools. GeoCities, which was founded in 1994 and was recently purchased by Yahoo!, has more than 3.5 million members.

GeoCities is one of the most visited sites on the Web and offers a tools package that allows even technical novices to publish a Web site. GeoCities is divided into 41 themed communities. You can be sure people visiting your community and your site will be music fans.

The free personal home page program offers, at the time of this writing, 11MB (megabytes) of space, a full set of Web-building tools, and technical support. With 11MB, you can offer approximately 10 minutes of music for download at any given time and still have room to put up a Web site with plenty of pages.

NOTE

If you do want to have your site hosted on a service such as GeoCities or Tripod—but also want to make all of your songs available for download—you can simply store your MP3 files at MP3.com and provide links from your outside Web site via MP3.com.

TIP

While you need a megabyte of space to store one minute of MP3 music at the 128bps rate for demonstration purposes, you might encode at a lower bit rate. Try 64bps, which sounds very good and doubles the amount of music you can store on your site.

GeoPlus

If that isn't enough space for you, the GeoPlus program offers at the time of this book's writing, 25MB and enhanced features for $4.95 a month. Among the advanced features that GeoPlus members receive: an extensive library of interactive features such as surveys; a Java applet library; dedicated technical support; and a help center.

While the available space won't allow you to constantly offer several CDs worth of music, you can use this to your advantage by offering songs on a rotating basis. Having your fans regularly check back for new music helps build loyalty.

GeoShops

If you are interested in investing the money, you can become a GeoShops member for $24.95 per month. This allows you to sell your CDs over the Web while accepting credit card payment. (Credit-card payment processing is an extra charge, and you'll have to qualify to accept it, read up on the site, and check with your bank to see what is necessary.) Again, no experience is necessary and, like GeoPlus, you receive 25MB of space.

GeoShops has store templates and other helpful materials that can make it easy to set up your online record store.

TIP

For more information on GeoCities, check out *Creating GeoCities Websites* by Ben Sawyer and Dave Greely.

Tripod

Tripod (**www.tripod.com**) was founded in 1992. It has 14 zone topics and approximately two million members. Among Tripod's free membership services are 11MB of space and access to Tripod's Homepage Studio Web-building tools.

Homepage Studio includes QuickPage, which allows beginning Web page designers to use Build by Topic and Build by Design templates. The Build by Design template is the most useful for your purposes. It allows you to choose a layout template and fill in the blanks with text, photos, graphics from your album covers, and links through which to download your MP3 files.

If you have HTML skills, you can also use the Freeform Editor, which allows a bit more flexibility and creativity for the more technologically advanced.

Tripod's community is divided into **pods**. You can become a member of as many pods as you want; they focus on a specific topic, such as alternative music, electronica, and folk music, as well as plenty of non-music issues. Pod members can take part in chats, post to message boards, and interact with other members with similar interests. This gives musicians the opportunity to bring fans to their site and to sample MP3 music.

Chat Central is the place to go not only for pod chat, but for personal and public chat as well. You can create a member profile, which allows members to find out more about each other. Here is where you can let people know about the type of music you create, your interest in MP3, and any other tidbits that might send people to your Web site for more information—and to hear those MP3s.

Premium Membership

For $3.00 a month, Tripod's premium membership services offer 22MB of disk space (enough for a little less than 20 minutes of MP3 music and several Web pages), as well as a number of other features. You can get rid of advertisements for an extra $3.00 a month!

Tripod premium members also can promote their pages in the Tripod *Insider* zine, a status page that shows you how much space you have remaining, which is important for someone who will be posting MP3 files. It also gives you the ability to upload your pages quickly with your own FTP address.

Setting Up a Standard Web Site

While free Web site services, such as GeoCities and Tripod, let you get your work onto the Web for no cost, they're limited in terms of space and the advertising that will accompany your page. You may therefore decide to seek a better site setup. Try purchasing a hosted site. There are hundreds of Web-hosting providers that let you rent server space upwards of 20MB–40MB for as little as $19.95–$29.95 a month. The site is yours and there is no advertising.

Setting up your own standard Web site is not difficult:

1. Locate a Web-hosting provider who offers a price and the space you want. There are several sites on the Internet that list and even rank various hosting providers. Several large providers commonly used include **Hiwaay.com**, **Webcom.com**, and **Interland.com**.

2. Sign up with the host provider. Most providers have a simple Web-based form that you fill out to start your site. These forms let you submit billing information, choose from among the various plans, and select a domain name for your site.

3. Select a domain name. Most host providers' basic package includes allowing the site a unique domain name. The **domain name** is the address people type to reach your Web site; **www.winamp.com**, for instance. These providers then submit that name to Internic, the company that approves and sets up your domain name on the Internet. Your domain name must be original in order to be approved. Most providers check the domain name when you register and will reject your application until you submit an acceptable domain name. If you want to determine whether your domain name is already taken, you can search the database at **www.internic.net**. Domain name registration will cost you $70 (for two years) and usually is billed directly by Network Solutions, the company behind the Internic site. Some, but not all, host providers may charge an extra $20–$30 one-time fee for your domain registration. Don't use host providers that charge you more than that.

4. Once the name is approved, your site account is open and you can begin building your pages. Every host provider works differently in terms of how you set up your site. The process is, for the most part, similar. You develop your pages using various Web-page building programs and then using an FTP program with which you will transfer your data (pages, MP3s, graphics, and the like) onto your site. You can hire a local Web designer; most charge between $25–$75 an hour. A basic site includes 5–10 pages; with some MP3s you encoded, it should cost between $200–$500 to have someone else develop the pages.

Building an Effective Web Site

This chapter isn't the place to go into HTML and the specifics of Web design; there are entire books written on those subjects. If you decide to go with GeoCities or Tripod, all of the tools and templates are there and they make it easy for you.

However, there are a number of things to consider when building a Web site to promote your band or yourself.

Design

You needn't be a Web design wizard to build an effective site. You simply need to make your site clean, easy to read, and well organized. Here are some quick tips that will help your site look good:

▶ **Keep it simple**—The best Web sites are not loaded with large graphics (which can make a site frustratingly slow to load), flashy colors, or crazy design. Instead they use imagery that works for the site and is optimized for quick loading. Lay your page out with links to other pages within your site. Put the links in one area, such as down the left side of the page.

One site that is fairly well done is that of Lucas, a technomusic-oriented artist from Argentina (see interview at the end of this chapter). His site (**Figure 11.1**) is located at: **http://www.ireal.com/lucas/LTCode.cgi?WEB**

Figure 11.1
Lucas' site is a good example of what you might do to promote your work.

▶ **Choose colors wisely**—Background and text colors should work well together. It doesn't have to be black and white, but stay away from colors that have little contrast. For example, a site with a white background and yellow text will be difficult to read. Primary colors such as white, black, red, and blue work well. Use colors that reflect the mood of your music. If your music is dark and foreboding, black and red are better choices than pink and white!

▶ **Anchor your page with a primary photo or graphic**—This can be a picture of yourself, your band, the cover of your most recent CD, or your logo. Place it in the top third of your page for maximum impact. Use smaller photos or graphics to balance the page and add professionalism.

Content

The content of your site is of the utmost importance. No matter how nice your layout looks, your fans will quickly become bored and stop visiting your site if you don't have interesting, fresh content. Your site is a reflection on you and your music.

► **Text**—You may have some written promotional material. Use it. Fans are interested in your background, your musical influences, the names of band members and the instruments they play, discographies, concert/appearance dates and locations, and what your music means to you. Keep your content fresh by updating your schedule and offering any current news. For example, let your fans know if you have a big performance coming up or are heading into the studio to work on new music. They'll appreciate the information and will keep checking for more.

► **Photos and graphics**—Band photos, whether promotional shots or performance pictures, are a must. You should also use your logo, pictures of album covers, or other photos or graphics that capture the feel of your music.

Promoting Your Music with Your Web Site

A Web site is a great way to promote your music, especially by allowing fans to download either entire songs or shorter clips in MP3 format—but there is more to a Web site than simply slapping up a handful of MP3 files. You have to promote your site and attract visitors in order for your site to be an effective promotional tool.

TIP

The easiest way to get fans to your site is to include your Web address on all of your real-world promotional materials. Direct your fans to your Web site by including the address in your CDs' liner notes, placing it on promotional posters, flyers, bios and media kits, and mentioning it to reporters in interviews.

Part III Digitizing Audio

Promoting Your Site Online

Promoting your site online can be difficult given the millions of Web sites out there. There are a lot of things you can do to help Web surfers find your site. With the phrase *MP3* currently the second most frequently entered phrase on search engines (trailing only *sex*), it is obvious that there are hundreds of thousands of people surfing the Internet for music.

Links

Links allow people visiting other Web sites to click and immediately be transported to your site. As a musician, you should seek to swap links with musicians of similar stature and genre. For example, if you are an independent rock band, it is unlikely that a major band will have any interest in linking to your site. If you are a techno artist, you might not be interested in trading links with a blues musician. There are, however, thousands of other bands and musicians who will likely have fans that are interested in your music. Explore relationships with bands in your region who play a similar style of music and who are interested in drawing some of your fans to their site.

If you have a record deal, you can also pursue links with other bands from your record label. You can contact artists via email, phone, or even when you bump into them on the road.

Web Rings

A **Web ring** is just what it sounds like: a group of related sites that are linked together so visitors can hop from one to the next, eventually returning to the first site in the ring. The best thing about Web rings is that they generate visitors who are interested in your site's topic. A ring is managed from one site.

If you have relationships with a number of artists, consider building a Web ring. WebRing (**www.webring.com**) is a service that allows you to build a Web ring that includes their site. One site will act as the host of the Web ring.

Search Engines

Search engines are those sites like Yahoo! (**www.yahoo.com**) and HotBot (**www.hotbot.com**) that allow visitors to search for information by entering phrases or words such as *MP3*, *music*, *electronica*, *punk*, and so on. You can submit your site to search engines by visiting them and following their simple instructions.

Here are some other major search engines that you should submit your site to:

▶ AltaVista (**www.altavista.com**)

▶ Excite (**www.excite.com**)

▶ InfoSeek (**www.infoseek.com**)

▶ Lycos (**www.lycos.com**)

▶ WebCrawler (**www.webcrawler.com**)

Announcement Sites

Announcement sites do just that—announce new sites to the Web world. The major announcement sites include these:

▶ Netscape's What's New
(**http://netscape.yahoo.com/guide/whats_new.html**)

▶ What's New Too (**http://newtoo.manifest.com**)

▶ Nerd World What's New (**www.nerdworld.com/whatsnew.html**)

MP3 Watermark Technology

As a musician who is using MP3, you should make sure that the MP3s you put out are good and remain the only ones with your songs out there. Not everyone will encode your songs as well as you, and you also want to make sure that you have some control over who distributes your MP3 files. While pirates can't be stopped completely, one potential distribution problem are people who think it's acceptable to distribute your MP3s on their site without your consent—or against your specific wishes.

As the number of legal MP3 sites proliferates on the Web, you might choose to have only your music posted on sites that you authorize. However, how do you tell, and how do your fans tell, if the MP3 file on any given site is one you've personally authorized and created? It's currently impossible, but a new technology called the **Genuine Music Mark** will make it possible for you to digitally watermark your MP3 files.

The mark technology is coming together as of this writing, but it should be up and running later this year and included as an option in many of the major encoding programs and players. The mark was developed by Liquid Audio, a developer of online music and audio delivery systems. The company got together with 48 record labels, software, hardware, and MP3 vendors, rights societies, retailers, and MP3 music Webmasters to develop this system under the auspices of the Genuine Music coalition. The coalition is making the Genuine Music Mark an open standard enhancement to digital music formats, including MP3, to provide digital authentication of the origin and ownership of music.

Part III Digitizing Audio

Once you have watermarked your MP3 file, listeners using an option on their favorite player will be able to check for it, As part of that view, a certificate that lists who created the file, the musician(s) behind it, and other vital information are visible. With this system, it will be very tough for someone to pose as someone they're not.

With the Genuine Music Mark added by the artist or record label, consumers will finally be able to confirm the legitimacy of music downloaded over the Internet. Again, while this won't stop piracy, it will help inform loyal fans which content to obtain .

E-Labels Galore

Every band—garage or Grammy winner—can create its own personal music distribution system with the combination of MP3 technology and Web site publishing. In addition, a whole other group of companies (MP3.com and E-music.com, for instance) are creating complete electronic MP3 labels, which some day might become the Internet equivalent of Columbia Records. The movement to MP3 and digital distribution of music may mean there will be thousands—even millions—of music labels. Some will be run by full-time professionals, some will be run by part-time musicians or lovers of music, and many will be run by bands themselves, big and small.

While not every e-label will be a major success, who would have thought ten years ago that every musician in the world with access to a computer could publish his or her music—and that anyone on the planet could hear and purchase it?

Interview:

Lucas

Publishing your own music on the Web is a very new thing. As far as it's come in the last few years, however, there remains much more to learn and discover about how music, MP3, and the Internet will change how musicians promote themselves and their music. Lucas is one of the early MP3 movement success stories. A 24-year-old techno/electronica musician based in Buenos Aires, Argentina, Lucas has had several of his songs on MP3.com's Top 40—for nearly six months combined. At the time of this interview, he had the number 1 and 2 top songs on the Top 40 list. **Figures 11.2–11.4** display various shots of Lucas and his albums.

Figure 11.2
Lucas.

Figure 11.3
Plug-n-Play, an album
by Lucas.

Figure 11.4
Neo-Gen, Lucas' follow-
up self-developed
album.

Q *When did you first hear of MP3 and what were your first trials of it like?*

A: It started as talk about this sound compression technique on Internet. That technique was MP3 technology and I heard about it for [the] first time in 1995. My first trial with MP3 encoding of my songs was in 1997.

Q *How does the MP3 format work for you as a musician? Do you like the fidelity? Do you do anything specific with your music before encoding it to make it sound better?*

A: The fidelity is great for digital distribution, but the compression noise is still there. I work with Parametrics EQ presets and a Dynamics presets to improve the response in the standard PC speakers.

First, I make a dynamic normalization of the entire track. Then I set the graphic dynamics at 2 to 1 starting at –12db to put more power to the sound, and finally I put a shine and contrast in the mix with a parametric equalization by adding level to the following 80Hz, 2500Hz, and 10000Hz frequencies.

Part III Digitizing Audio

Q *How has the MP3.com site worked for you? What other things are you doing to promote and sell your music online?*

A: I permit Webmasters to put my music in their sites if they respect the original copyright and links. At the moment, I haven't seen much money off of my DAM CDs. I think that for now it is a good idea, but I need a better marketing strategy. I have received lots of emails asking me where people can buy my CDs in local stores.

Q *Your Web site is really cool. Did you do that all yourself? How does your site work to promote you and your MP3 music?*

A: Yes, I did the entire site myself. I do all my own HTML and CGI scripts. The graphics are done with Photoshop. I also do a lot of 3D stuff. I work with NewTek's Lightwave 3D-Modeler, as well as Softimage 3D. My "Need For Speed" video was produced using those tools.

The site is the best way to get direct feedback from the public to me and from the public to the public. CLUB Digital is about that. [This can be found at **www.ireal.com/lucas/ltclub/**.]

The goal of CLUB Digital is to be a free point of unity between people who like techno/digital music and rave culture. In the future I would like to include a serial number on each CD that would give fans special access privileges to the club where they could download remixes, videos, and other special content.

Q *Do you think we'll see the day when musicians only release their work digitally?*

A: That day is today. For example, some of my songs are available only in the digital domain (no vinyls, no CDs), but we need better international laws (not Internet laws) and support from the major labels to make digital only work better for artists. The major labels fear this new technology because it is not under [their] control. In fact, though, if they [do] not support MP3 technology, then MP3 technology won't support them.

Q *Do you have any other favorite MP3 musicians?*

A: Yes, the Beastie Boys.

Q *What words of advice do you have for other DJs, musicians, and bands that want to take advantage of the MP3 revolution?*

A: MP3 is the first truly digital art revolution, a one-way revolution. Basically all the multimedia artists out there have to take a position in this digital revolution. A positive position—a position in favor of the public and the new media. In one word, legal. We need to make sure MP3s stay legal and we need to make more legal MP3s!

The big associations and corporations are trying to convince...the mass media and public that MP3[s] are illegal and negative, but artist[s] like [the] Beastie Boys or Underworld have turned MP3 in[to] something legal because they made legal MP3s files.

Q *You did your own video. Do you think we'll see more videos online too?*

A: Yes, at the beginning I did them with Flash from Macromedia and the related plug-in, but finally I just did one with full MPEG garage videos. I used to work as an animator and editor, so I used those skills and created my own video using Lightwave, 3D Studio MAX, and Softimage. All of that was then put together in Adobe Premiere with Adobe After Effects. It took two entire weeks to do the video. I don't have any idea about how many downloads it's had, but I have received a lot of emails talking about the video. I definitely think online videos are the next step in this digital revolution.

Q *Since you produce club/rave/techno/house music, do you think that online distribution and MP3 are actually a better way to reach that audience? It's such a worldwide audience and one very enthused about technology.*

A: Absolutely. I think that techno music is by definition pro-technology, pro-change, and pro-revolution and I like exploiting technology as a positive force. I receive daily emails, from ravers and others tribes around the world, and a lot of people that have begun to listen [to] techno music thanks to my work—and, of course, the MP3 format.

Q *How many people do you think have downloaded your songs?*

A: According to the MP3.com stats and other smaller sites I support, there have been 1.8 million downloads between both of my online projects "LUCAS" and "NEO-GEN."

Part III Digitizing Audio

Q *Have any major labels expressed interest in you due to your popularity online?*

A: Yes, two majors are interested in my works for a two-disc contract. I'm thinking about signing with a major label but...I might sign with an indie label. I'm also trying to start my own e-label with GIGAVIBE. [This can be found at **www.ireal.com/lucas/ltclub/under construction**.] The label will support hybrid CDs with e-label promos, videos, and an electronic serial number to provide access to MP3 online music remixes and additional content.

Q *Have you tried Nullsoft's SHOUTcast Radio? Might you do live shows via SHOUTcast?*

A: Yes, I know the SHOUTcast system, also I received proposals to Webcasting with RealAudio, but I think that Nullsoft's SHOUTcast Radio is more friendly and practical.

Part IV
MP3 Radio and More

12

Creating Your Own MP3 Radio Station: SHOUTcast and Beyond

One of the coolest things you can do with your MP3 files and content is use them to develop a personal Internet radio station. With the creation of SHOUTcast Radio, Nullsoft has created a simple system that lets you take any song you're listening to via Winamp and send it out over the Internet. If you've ever dreamed of running your own radio station, here's your chance.

In this chapter, you will learn about how to install the SHOUTcast plug-ins and server software you need to create your own station. You'll also learn some tricks about promoting your own station and how to be compliant with potential copyright and licensing issues.

The Creation of SHOUTcast

The creation of SHOUTcast came about after Justin Frankel decided he wanted to build a way for people to run their own personal radio stations. His motivation was sparked by his interest in having someone stream to him the show, *Love Lines* from its LA home base to Phoenix. The show, while syndicated, isn't carried by local stations in Phoenix. With a little help from Tom Pepper, Nullsoft's network engineer, the two developed SHOUTcast in a matter of weeks.

Developing Your Own SHOUTcast Station

To develop your own SHOUTcast station all you need is some special software, a bunch of cool MP3s, a little ingenuity to create a cool playlist, and a connection capable of supporting enough upstream to send your broadcast out onto the Net. To make a successful station you should also throw in some simple work to promote your station and experiment with some of the SHOUTcast DJ tools made available by MP3Spy.com and others. With everything installed, you'll be actively broadcasting (**Figure 12.1**).

Figure 12.1
The Winamp program, the SHOUTcast Server, MP3Spy with its DJ plug-in, and more.

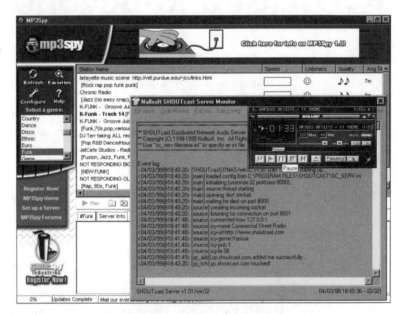

Step 1: Acquire the Necessary Software for SHOUTcast

The first step is to fill up your SHOUTcast toolbox. That means acquiring the necessary software you need. This includes two major Winamp plug-ins, MP3 CODECs (available from Microsoft), and the SHOUTcast Server program found at **SHOUTcast.com**. You might also want to download MP3Spy from **mp3spy.com** and get the DJ plug-in for it.

Step 2: If Needed, Install the NetShow MP3 CODECs

In order to create the MP3 stream that goes to users via SHOUTcast, Winamp needs to have a set of encoding plug-ins that will create the specific bit stream of MP3 content. Instead of supplying these CODECs, you need to get them from another route. The best place to get them is by installing the NetShow Server Tools, which includes a set of MP3 CODECs that work perfectly for the SHOUTcast system. The NetShow Server is actually an NT-only product, but the server toolset can be installed without consequence on any Windows 95/98/NT system.

There is a link on the SHOUTcast download page (**http://www.SHOUTcast.com/download.html**) from which you can acquire the NetShow Server Tools. You can also visit the NetShow Services: Server, Tools, SDK page at **http://www.microsoft.com/ntserver/ nts/downloads/recommended/mediaserv/default.asp**. You need to register with Microsoft in order to get to the page and download the tools. The download is 4MB.

Once downloaded, double-click on the NSTOOLS icon; the program will extract and run the Setup program (**Figure 12.2**). The first option for setup is to install either the complete tools package or just the PowerPoint tools. Complete setup is the choice to make, followed by inputting (or accepting) the choice of where to store the programs. The CODECs needed for SHOUTcast will be installed as part of the installation process. You needn't do anything more after the install is done.

Figure 12.2
Installing the Microsoft NetShow Server Tools is a critical step in enabling SHOUTcast Radio.

The CODECs included with the NetShow Server Tools don't allow you to broadcast at any better quality than 56Kbps. That and lower bit rates are fine for almost every broadcaster. If you want to broadcast at higher bit rates, you need to install another set of CODECs. Those, however, will have to be purchased directly from Opticom (**www.opticom.de**).

Step 3: Install the SHOUTcast DSP Plug-In Into Winamp

SHOUTcast needs to receive a stream of audio from your Winamp player in order to play. The server can then broadcast over the Internet. This stream is created by the combination of the SHOUTcast DSP plug-in and the aforementioned MP3 CODECs supplied via the Netshow Tools. You can download the SHOUTcast DSP plug-in from the SHOUTcast download page (**www.shoutcast.com/download.html**).

After downloading it, unzip, and store it in your Winamp Plugins directory.

There is also a Live Input plug-in to install if you want to be able to DJ and talk during your SHOUTcast sessions; more on that later.

Step 4: Install the SHOUTcast Server System

While Winamp itself is a Windows application, the SHOUTcast broadcasting server can be run on a number of platforms: Windows, FreeBSD, BSDi 4.0+, Linux, Irix 6.2, Irix 5.3, Solaris 2.6, and AIX 4.1x.

Windows users should download the file from the Windows server link found at **http://www.shoutcast.com/download.html**. Open the Zip file and extract it to a folder on your hard drive.

Those of you on the Unix platform should download the version appropriate for your operating system, unzip the distribution, and un-tar the archive. Use a text editor to configure the sc_serv.conf file. It doesn't matter what the user runs the server at, save that the user has read access to the config file as well as write access for the files you define for file storage and log storage.

Step 5: Configure Winamp to Send Content to the SHOUTcast Server

With the server installed, the CODECs downloaded, and the SHOUTcast DSP plug-in ready for action, you can begin creating the connections and settings that let you broadcast your MP3 files to the world.

Start by configuring the SHOUTcast DSP plug-in in Winamp. Go to the DSP/Effect Purpose settings in the Plug-ins Preferences section of Winamp. There you should see a listing for the SHOUTcast Source for Winamp (dsp_sc.dll) as shown in **Figure 12.3a**. Select that DSP/Effect plug-in and press Configure to bring up the SHOUTcast for Winamp Configuration dialog box (**Figure 12.3b**).

Figure 12.3a
Choosing the SHOUTcast Source plug-in from Winamp Preferences.

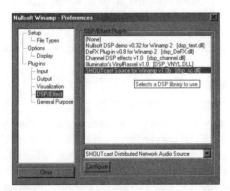

Figure 12.3b
The SHOUTcast Source
Plug-in Preferences
dialog box.

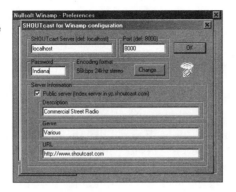

This dialog box has five major items to consider when configuring your
SHOUTcast station:

▶ **SHOUTcast Server** (def: localhost)—Specify the IP hostname or
address for the SHOUTcast Server. Use localhost if you're running
the SHOUTcast Server on the same machine.

▶ **Port** (def: 8000)—Define the port number listeners connect to and the
password. Select the bit rate you wish to use and click OK. From this
point forward, until you deselect the SHOUTcast Source plug-in,
everything you play in Winamp is sent to the SHOUTcast Server.

▶ **Password**—This is the password for the configuration settings. It
should match the password in the server definition file (more on this
later). For now, choose a password that should be used for remote
login.

▶ **Encoding format**—The encoding format lets you set the quality and
bit rate of the resulting SHOUTcast MP3 stream. Press Change to
bring up the Format selection (MPEG Layer-3 only) dialog box
(**Figure 12.4**). This dialog box lets you choose from all installed
MPEG Layer-3 CODECs. If you've installed the CODECs properly (as
outlined in the following section), you should have over 40 specific
choices you can employ. (Only 20 or so of those selections are of the
stereo variety.)

Figure 12.4
Choosing the MP3
format you want to
stream out at with
SHOUTcast.

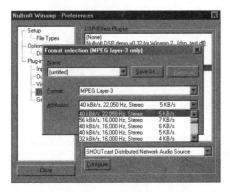

You can choose Save As to create a named setting for your choices. This lets you choose from the Name list to set the quality attributes for your SHOUTcast station.

Choosing the exact attributes requires a little bit of planning. Your Internet connection can only support so many simultaneous users at certain bit rates. See the "Selecting Bit Rates and Maximum Users" sidebar later in this chapter.

▶ **Server information**—If you'd like the server to be listed in the public SHOUTcast Server directory in real time, check the Public Server checkbox and fill in a description of the content you'll be serving. You can set the station description (essentially its title), the genre and a home page URL for the station. These are the settings SHOUTcast.com and the MP3Spy program use to list your station publicly. Table 12.1 shows the genres that are used by SHOUTcast.com and MP3Spy.com to categorize stations.

Table 12.1–
The Genres

SHOUTcast.com	MP3Spy	Supported in Both
R&B	Alt	Talk
Various	Ambient	Comedy
Mixed	Blues	Techno
80s	Christian	Dance/House
70s	Disco	Rock/Alternative
	Ethnic	Metal
	Euro	Rap
	Game	Pop
	Gospel	Funk
	Industrial	Jazz
	Oldies	Classical
	Punk	
	Reggae	
	Ska	
	Soul	
	Soundtrack	
	Trance	

> **TIP**
>
> Passive plug-ins (line input and CD audio, for instance) will not work with the SHOUTcast source plug-in. If you wish to serve these types of audio, use the live input plug-in for Winamp (Winamp, Open Location, URL=linerec://) with a sound card that is capable of recording its own output.

Step 6: Configure the SHOUTcast Server System

Your SHOUTcast Server is configured by editing the sc_serv.ini file found in the directory where you stored the SHOUTcast Server. Edit this file by using any standard text editor (**Figure 12.5**). Most of the file is full of **commented** text (text preceded by a semicolon is commented). Just type in the values you want to use for each of these variables that are in the file.

With SHOUTcast 1.1, Nullsoft has introduced a whole range of new features especially for the configuration and management of servers. While the majority of configuration still takes place in the SCSERV file, you can also administrate the server from a Web browser for some things.

Figure 12.5
To configure your SHOUTcast Server, you need to edit the sc_serv.ini file using your favorite text editor.

```
+ NoteTab Light - C:\Program Files\shoutcast\SC_SERV.INI        _ 8 X
File  Edit  Search  View  Modify  Document  Favorites  Tools  Help
SC_SERV.INI

; SHOUTcast Distributed Network Audio Server/win32 1.01 configuration file
; Copyright (C) 1998-1999 Nullsoft, Inc.
; All Rights Reserved.
; Last modified 15.1.1999

; If you want to manage multiple configurations, just copy
; this file to another name, and run sc_serv with that name
; such as:
; sc_serv.exe C:\shoutcast\sc_leet.ini
; or
; sc_serv.exe myconf.ini
; (where myconf.ini is in the same directory as sc_serv.exe)

; Config section
[Config]

; PortBase. this is the port listeners use to listen.
; The default is 8000.
PortBase=8000

; MaxUser. Maximum number of simultaneous users allowed.
; The default is 32. More users means more bandwidth.
MaxUser=32

; Password. The password the stream source must use to connect.
; Also used by the telnet LOG command (LOG <password> to read the
; log). Case sensitive. Default: 'changeme'
Password=indiana

; File to use for logging. Can be '/dev/null' or 'none'
; or empty to turn off logging. The default is sc_serv.log
; (in the same directory as sc_serv.exe)
```

▶ **PortBase**—The port on your server that SHOUTcast should use for sending audio. The default is 8000 and unless you know better, leave it as is. Unix users should be aware that they cannot use a port below 1024 unless they run the server as root.

▶ **MaxUser**—The maximum allowable listeners at any one time. Make sure you set this to a realistic number depending on your bandwidth and operating system.

Maximum bandwidth used for serving is equal to the bit rate at which you are serving multiplied by MaxUser + 1.

▶ **Password**—The password to use for streaming content and administration. Remember that this must match the password you entered in the Winamp SHOUTcast DSP plug-in.

▶ **Logfile**—The file in which to store the console log. Use /dev/null or leave empty to disable file-based logging. The default file is /tmp/sc_serv.log/.

▶ **RealTime**—On Unix hosts, a value of 1 will display a realtime indicator on the console.

▶ **ScreenLog**—Another Unix-only feature that will display the event log to the console as well as writing it to the log file. Default is 1 (on).

▶ **NameLookups**—Placing a value of 1 in this option asks the server to do a reverse DNS lookup on users connecting to your server and place the results in the log file. While this will make it more time-consuming for users to connect to your server, it adds more information about who is listening to your server log file. The default is 0 (off).

▶ **RelayPort**—This is optional. It is one of the main configuration options if you want to make yourself a relay server for another broadcast. If that's the case, then you set the RelayServer option to the URL for the server and place the port number (usually 8000) here. If you don't want to relay another broadcast, just leave this option and the RelayServer option commented out.

▶ **RelayServer**—Works with RelayPort as described above.

▶ **RelayPublic**—This lets you decide whether or not your server is publicly available (for others) to connect to. This is optional and is initially commented out in the file. When running a relay server, use Always to make the server public all the time (regardless of whether the source server is public), or Never to make the server public none of the time. Anything else makes the server the same as the source server.

▶ **BackupFile**—Sometimes for whatever reasons the source stream you are broadcasting to from Winamp (or relaying to from another server) goes down. At that point, you still want to be on the air perhaps with a simple song, or maybe a "we are experiencing technical difficulties…please stand by" message. You can store a single MP3 file on the server to be broadcast if the source stream goes down. The server then switches to this backup file and plays it.

The drawback is that this file must be encoded at the exact same bit rate and sample rate as defined by the broadcast or it'll not play properly. Use the BackupFile setting to type in the path to the file to use.

▶ **IntroFile**—If you want to control the first file someone hears before queuing up the broadcast, you can specify a file to use. You can use it for station ID or an advertisement (remember commercial use of SHOUTcast requires a license). As with the BackupFile, this file must match the sample rate and bit rate for the broadcast characteristics of your server or suffer the consequences.

TIP

For both the IntroFile and BackupFile settings, you can use a wildcard to denote a range of files to use. This is useful if you plan to vary the bit rate and sample rate from time-to-time for your broadcasts. For example, if during the day you broadcast at 24kbps but at night you broadcast at 56kbps, you could use the file name entries of intro%d.mp3 and backup%d.mp3. When the server went to play those files, it would look for the files intro24.mp3/intro56.mp3 and backup24.mp3/backup56.mp3, depending on what the stream was playing at. Make sure that if you do this, you have files encoded at all the variable settings you plan to broadcast with.

▶ **HistoryLog**—If you create a history log by defining a file for this log type, the SHOUTcast Server will place the number of listeners at specific intervals (defined by HistoryTime) to a text file. This can be useful to see over a period of time how many connections you served for usage patterns. Place the name and path of the file you'd like to generate if you want a history log.

▶ **HistoryTime**—The value placed here determines the number of minutes the server takes before adding an entry to the HistoryLog file.

▶ **CurrentLogOut**—The HistoryLog file and the vanilla log file are useful for basic stats about your server, but if you want to get really fancy you can create a custom log file which actually generates HTML files that you or your users can view from your server. The CurrentLogOut function indicates where in your system this file should be stored. (You'll need to put it in your servers public Web directory.)

▶ **CurrentLogIn**—This file determines the template used for the formatting of the CurrentLogOut file. The template uses tags that are formatted within an HTML file like comments <!—TAG HERE —>. This way you can dress up the page using HTML and insert the SHOUTcast log tags throughout the HTML document as you see fit. **Table 12.2** shows the CurrentLog tags supported.

Table 12.2–Template tags for the log file specified in CurrentLogOut.

<— LISTENERS —>	Shows the current active number of connections at the interval
<— MAXLISTENERS —>	Shows current maximum listeners setting at the interval
<— LISTENERTABLE —>	Displays all current listeners, their source IP, and time spent online at the interval
<— PRELISTENERTABLE —>	Same as above but doesn't generate an HTML table, but instead uses HTML <PRE>…</PRE> tag.
<— GENRE —>	Genre listing set by current source at interval
<— DESCRIPTION —>	Description listing provided by current source at interval
<— URL —>	The URL of the current source at interval
<— HITS —>	Total listeners since start of server

▶ **CurrentTime**—This determines in seconds the interval to use to generate a new current log file.

▶ **SrcIP**—Use this to set one and only one acceptable IP interface that the server will accept a source stream from. This is useful if you have multiple Ethernet/Nic cards configured on the server. Use ANY if it should accept any source that sends it a stream.

▶ **DestIP**—Use this to specify exactly what IP interface on the server it should listen to clients on (and for what it uses to connect to yp.shoutcast.com). Like SrcIP, it can also be set to ANY.

SELECTING BIT RATES AND MAXIMUM USERS

When selecting a bit rate to stream at and setting an appropriate number for maxusers, keep the following in mind:

▶ **You cannot serve more users than you have available bandwidth.** If you're running the SHOUTcast Server over a modem link at any speed, the most you can muster is one user at 24kbps or 32kbps. Attempting to serve more users than you have bandwidth only causes skippage.

▶ **Shell sysadmins will be unhappy if you consume their available bandwidth and server processes without their consent.** SHOUTcast is a highly demanding program of both software processes and bandwidth. A T1 line can only theoretically support about 60 listeners if no other traffic is on that T1. Additionally, each listener takes up a system process on the server operating system, which can crash some operating systems if allowed to expand beyond the limits of the system. If you throw up a SHOUTcast Server to the sysadmin without his or her knowledge with 50+ maximum users, you had better be prepared to face the consequences.

▶ **Pick a smart number of maxusers for your server.** Calculate by taking the available bandwidth you have, multiplying by 0.9 to account for overhead, and dividing by the bit rate you want to serve at. An ADSL connection, for example:

@ 768kbps upstream $\times$ 0.9 / 24kbps ~= 29 maximum users

Again, set this number too high, and when you reach the limit of bandwidth, ALL the streams will start to skip.

Using a Microphone with SHOUTcast

All DJs like to speak on radio at some point. Whether running a talk show or talking up a record, offering live talk for your station is a cool feature. Thankfully, the SHOUTcast system supports the ability to talk live via microphone.

The following is a step-by-step process for using a microphone with SHOUTcast Radio.

Step 1: Understand Your Sound Card's Capabilities

There are two ways to do voice input with SHOUTcast: Parallel to other sounds and music and in between the music. Which road you follow hinges on whether you have a full duplex sound card. Only full duplex sound cards allow you to broadcast voice simultaneously with music; if you don't have such a card, you have to stop the music to greet your public. (Full duplex card owners have the option to go either way.) Most modern cards are full duplex, but consult your hardware manual if you're unsure.

Step 2: Purchase a Microphone

No microphone, no talk. While the microphone that ships with many PCs and sound systems may seem good enough on a practical scale, they are pretty poor overall. You can get a decent microphone for as little as $25–$30 at your local Radio Shack or music store. A standard mike used by many semi-professionals is a Shure SM-58 (**http://www.shure.com/ sm58.html**). This mike runs around $100 and is a standard vocal mike for live performance in the industry. It works pretty well for home recording as well.

Step 3: Tweak Your Volume Setting

Double-click the speaker icon in your system tray; alternatively, you can open your settings and click on the Sounds option. This opens your volume control panel (**Figure 12.6**). You are looking at the playback controls, which essentially control the volume levels of all the audio types your computer supports (CD, computer audio, MIDI, and so on).

Figure 12.6
The volume controls on your computer are accessed through the system tray.

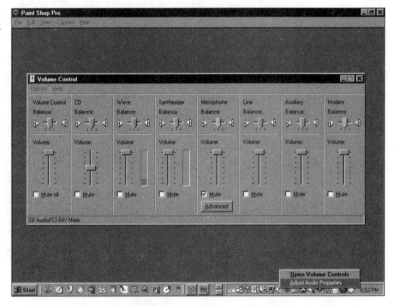

You can adjust the volume of all the sound that comes back to you. Check the microphone control here; you won't be able to hear your voice if the volume is very low or the Mute checkbox is selected. This doesn't mean that your listeners can't hear you, however. Playback affects what you hear, not what they hear. If you don't have a microphone control, select Options, Properties and scroll down in the list box until you see Microphone. Click the checkbox next to it; this will enable your microphone.

Part IV MP3 Radio and More

Click on the Properties choice on the Options menu to switch the volume controls so that you can access the recording controls. Select Recording; click OK. This switches you to the volume controls for recording levels. These levels control the volume of recordings your card generates (how loud the microphone level is).

In many cases, these controls are muted or set to 0. This is so that you can shut off access to additional noise coming from other audio sources and have only sound coming from one. You will want to "un-mute" the microphone and line inputs so that people can hear you (**Figure 12.7**).

Figure 12.7
Set the recording levels to enable the microphone to work after switching to the recording controls.

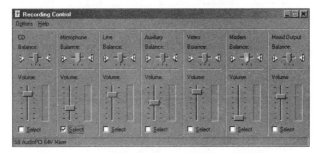

SPECIAL NOTE FOR SOUNDBLASTER LIVE OWNERS

SoundBlaster Live is a special case and doesn't work exactly as other cards do in terms of handling the recording controls. Instead of selecting each individual device in recording controls, SoundBlaster Live only allows you to select one. They have, however, added a control called What U Hear. When selected, this control allows you to record or broadcast everything that you hear through your PC speakers. Instead of selecting only the sources you want in the recording controls, go back to playback controls and mute the devices you don't want broadcasted. Everything that is not muted will be broadcast. Needless to say, you should be careful. All of your miscellaneous system beeps and ICQ incoming message warnings can be broadcast all over the Net!

Another way to disable this is to lower to zero the number of simultaneous .WAV files it will play. You can do this from the device controls panel found in the SoundBlaster Live Audio HQ folder.

Step 4: Configure and Use the Line Input Plug-In for SHOUTcast

The Line Input plug-in is built into Winamp. It takes input from the sound card and plays it, including input from the microphone or CD tracks. There is no need to set up the Line Input plug-in itself, but there are two ways to use it, depending on your sound card's capabilities.

Cutting In—Transmitting Voice In Between Songs

Setting up live input in Winamp is easy, and you won't need a full duplex card to do it. All you have to do is add an entry to your playlist by selecting the +URL option (or pressing Ctrl+L). When you get the open Location dialog box, type **linerec://**. Now click Open and press the Play button in Winamp.

That's it! Assuming your server is set up correctly, your voice is going out over the Internet! When you're done, just click on another item in the playlist to disable the microphone. If you're shuffling through your playlist randomly, I'd remove the linerec:// entry at this point. Otherwise, Winamp may randomly shuffle to the microphone when you're not ready, and who knows what fun things your users will be hearing at that point?

Cutting in is the simplest way to do live voice on SHOUTcast, and it might be all you need. For a little more polish, though, you can set it up so that you can talk over the music.

Parallel Voice Transmission—Talking Over the Music

Here's where it gets a bit complicated, but it's worth the effort. In order to broadcast simultaneous voice and music, you need to open multiple instances of Winamp.

Step A: Set Winamp to Allow Multiple Instances

In order work with two copies of Winamp simultaneously, you need to open the Preferences menu and choose the Options tab. Click the checkbox next to Allow Multiple Instances as shown in **Figure 12.8**. With this checked, Winamp will open a new version of Winamp, all of which can send information to the SHOUTcast Server. You can now also launch a second instance of Winamp.

Figure 12.8
Setting Winamp to work in multiple instances mode.

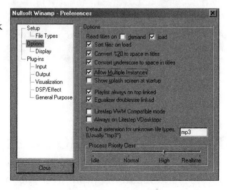

Step B: Set Up Two Streams to Mix Voice and Music

You should run the first instance of Winamp just as you have before. This time, however, make sure that Sound Processing in the Miscellaneous Plug-Ins tab in this version of Winamp is set to None. Queue any music you would like to hear to this playlist.

Set up the other instance of SHOUTcast to use the Linerec plug-in. That means configuring a playlist with linerec://. Just add an URL to the playlist and type in **linerec://**.

Now that everything's set up, here's how it works: Click Play on your first instance of Winamp (the Linerec-Only one); your voice will be broadcasting. When you click Play in the second instance, music from your playlist will go out at the same time. You can turn the microphone on and off during your broadcast by selecting and deselecting the microphone control. Meanwhile, in the other open version of Winamp, you can keep the music rolling at all times.

> **TIP**
> Always make sure that you mute the microphone when you're done with it.

Administering SHOUTcast

There are several ways to administer your SHOUTcast Server when it is running. First, if you're running Unix, you can use telnet in to the server and change configurations and so on as you would other programs. With Windows 95/NT you might use remote control software such as Symantec's PC Anywhere to access the system and control the server running on the system.

The key reason for remote control of the software is that in some cases you will need to kill the SHOUTcast Server program and restart it in order for new settings to take effect. However, with version 1.1 of the software, some log file and administrative functions can be administered from the Web. This makes the need for direct access to the server less of an issue.

Administering your server remotely involves making changes to the SCServ settings file, killing the SHOUTcast Server and restarting it and the connection. It also involves making changes to the configuration and examining various log files.

To administer a server via the Web simply connect to the IP address of the broadcasting server including the port. For example, if your server was at 129.255.255.255, and it used port 8000, the URL for the administration page would be **http://129.255.255.255:8000**. The default administration page is shown on **Figure 12.9**. Simply type in the password used for the server and then hit ok. You will be logged into the administration section of the server.

Figure 12.9
Shows the administration log-in page.

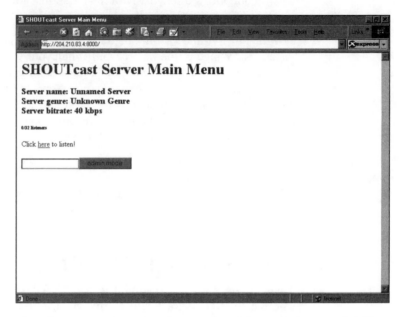

The administration section (**Figure 12.10**) lets you do several different things:

▶ **Disconnect Source**—Click this button to disconnect the source stream from the server. You will need to re-connect the source to the server once this is done.

Figure 12.10
The main
administration page.

SHOUTcast Administration Menu

SOURCE STATUS: connected from localhost at 40kbps -- [disconnect source]
SOURCE STATUS: name: Unnamed Server -- genre: Unknown Genre -- url: http://www.shoutcast.com
LISTENER STATUS: 1/32 listeners - Listener table:

1. host: dt0b6n9b.maine.rr.com - connect time: 35m 46s - 0 underruns - kick

SERVER CONFIGURATION STATUS:

Log file: \sc_serv.log
Configuration file: C:\WINDOWS\PROFILES\BEN SAWYER\DESKTOP\SSERVER\SC_SERV.ini
History file: C:\WEBSHARE\WWWROOT\sc_history.log (2s interval)
System is little endian
Name lookups are on
Intro file is disabled
Auto client disconnects are disabled
Source idle timeouts are 30s
Incoming interface: ANY:8001 - Outgoing interface: ANY:8000

view logfile / tail logfile
Usage Graph

Maximum listeners: 32   set

▶ **Kick Users Off**—Next to each user who is connected to your server is
a kick link that will disconnect them from your server. This is useful
if you need to remove some users from your server because it skips
due to the weight of too many users.

▶ **Check Server Configuration Settings**—Displayed on the administrative
page is also the basic SC_SERV configuration files settings.

▶ **View Entire Log File**—This link will let you view the entire log file
as currently compiled.

▶ **View Tail of Log File**—Many times your log file will be huge but all
you want to do is look at the last few lines of the file to see what the
latest information is. In that case, View Tail is a useful tool.

▶ **Usage Graph**—This link will generate a character-based graph
showing the number of users and server usage.

▶ **Set Maximum Listeners**—Type in a value here to set a new
maximum listeners setting. If, at the time, you have more listeners
than the new maximum listeners setting, the server won't disconnect
people—it just won't allow new users on the server. Consequently, if
you want to reduce the number of listeners down to below or at the
new maximum listeners setting, you'll need to use the Kick Users
option to remove listeners yourself.

Troubleshooting SHOUTcast

Like with any software, things can go wrong. SHOUTcast also relies on a number of various parts to be installed properly and configured to work together. Thus, problems occur. Here are some of the most common problems that Nullsoft has encountered along with some solutions to these problems:

Winamp says "Error creating ACM stream" when you try to use SHOUTcast.

This error is displayed if you don't have an MPEG Layer-3 ACM CODEC installed on your computer. Go back to the beginning of this chapter and make sure you have the NetShow Server Tools and installed them properly. You should have the MP3 Layer-3 ACM CODECs installed.

Once installed, restart Winamp and try playing a stream to your SHOUTcast Server. If you already have the NetShow encoding software installed and this isn't working, try restarting Winamp. If it still doesn't work, try reinstalling the NetShow encoder.

Winamp says "Error connecting to server" when you try to SHOUTcast.

This happens if your SHOUTcast Server is not running, or is not listening on the port on which you are trying to connect. If you have edited sc_serv.ini so that the PortBase=8000 line has changed, the URL must reflect that change. If it says "PortBase=31337" in this sc_serv.ini file, then the URL is **http://server:31337**. If you have not altered sc_serv.ini, the URL should be **http://[server address]:8000**.

Listeners on the Internet are getting "Error connecting to server" when they attempt to connect.

It is likely a problem with your connection or ISP. The two common problems in this case are that another program using the port is running. If another program is using that port on the server, you have to change in sc_serv.ini and in the Winamp DSP plug-in configuration, as well use a different port. This also brings about the "Error connecting to host" message.

My ISP has a firewall that prevents users from connecting to your host. What do you do now?

You need to contact your ISP (Internet Service Provider) and ask if he or she will let you run a SHOUTcast Server through the firewall. Good luck.

Winamp says "Invalid password on server" when you try to SHOUTcast.

The password set in the server in sc_serv.ini and the password you configured in the Winamp SHOUTcast DSP plug-in are not the same. They must be the same. By default, they are both changeme when things start. As stated earlier, you really should change that to avoid people streaming with your server when you do not want them to. To stop this error, make sure the passwords are the same in both the server .INI file and in the DSP configuration.

You get an error having to do with HTTP and mms URLs when you try to use linerec:// in the Open URL box.

This error occurs if you don't have the linerec:// plug-in installed. Get the Live Input plug-in from the SHOUTcast download page, unzip it to your Winamp\Plugins folder, then restart Winamp. You should now be able to access linerec:// without any errors.

The stream stops at 8K when prebuffering.

This has nothing to do with your Internet connection or your copy of Winamp—this happens when Winamp sends data to the SHOUTcast Server (and is still connected to it), but is no longer sending any data. Get the stream owner to play something in Winamp and the SHOUTcast Server should resume sending data to clients.

Winamp says "ICY 401 service not available" when you try to connect.

This error happens when the stream owner isn't connected to his or her server. If you are the owner, run through the following checklist. If you aren't the owner, track him down and have him run through this checklist.

> **TIP**
>
> The ICY acronym is a holdover from I CAN YELL—the original working title for SHOUTcast.

✔ Do you have the SHOUTcast DSP plug-in installed and selected inside Winamp? If not, get it from **http://www.SHOUTcast.com**.

✔ Do you have the SHOUTcast DSP plug-in configured properly for your SHOUTcast Server's settings?

✔ Are you playing anything in Winamp? You have to play something in order to send it to your listeners.

✔ Are you getting error messages when you first play something in Winamp? If so, check your SHOUTcast DSP plug-in settings.

✔ Try restarting Winamp, ensuring that the DSP plug-in is selected, and playing something.

Your listeners get "Error connecting to host" when they try to connect.

This happens if your SHOUTcast Server is not running or is not listening on the port on which you are trying to connect. If you have edited sc_serv.ini so that the PortBase=8000 line has changed, the port in the

DSP configuration must reflect that change. If PortBase=31337, then the port in the DSP configuration must be 31337. If you have not altered sc_serv.ini, leave the port as 8000 in both.

If you continue to get this problem, it is possible that another program is using the port you have selected. This is probably the case if you see errors similar to "[main] error opening dest socket! FATAL ERROR!" in the SHOUTcast Server's error log. Try changing the port number in the SHOUTcast Server and in the DSP plug-in configuration. (Remember, they must be the same.)

Listeners say the audio coming from the SHOUTcast Server is choppy.

This happens when your listeners are not receiving a continuous stream of data. This occurs for one of several reasons:

▶ **Your Internet connection**—If your Internet link cannot sustain the number of users connected to your server, all listeners will experience broken audio. Follow the guidelines outlined in the "Selecting Bit Rate and Maximum Users" sidebar, which explains how many users your Internet connection can safely serve a stream to. If you are on low-speed connection (such as a modem), you may want to consider relaying your SHOUTcast stream with a server on a faster connection.

▶ **Your processor speed**—If your computer is not fast enough to decode in Winamp, encode the stream, and broadcast it out to users, not only will you notice that your computer is slow, but your listeners will too. You can try lowering the decoding quality in Winamp to give the encoder/server more processor time, but this isn't a very good solution. Try running SHOUTcast on a faster processor.

▶ **Your listener's Internet connection**—Not everyone will be on a fast ISP and this may result in the stream getting broken up. First, make sure you are broadcasting at a speed your listeners can hear. If you are targeting modem users, broadcast at 24kbps and under; for ISDN users, 56k and under. Second, if one listener is getting broken audio but no other listeners are, tell him to increase his buffer (in the Nitrane preferences) and then restart the stream (by stopping and then playing).

▶ **Your listener's processor speed**—If he can't play MP3s without them breaking up, chances are he won't be able to play SHOUTcast streams either. (This user would have to own a very slow processor [below a 90MHz Pentium I] in order for this to occur.)

Licensing SHOUTcast for Commercial Use

SHOUTcast is free for general non-profit use. Commercial users must obtain a license from Nullsoft. Licenses are $299 per server, per machine. These licenses include free upgrades to all SHOUTcast 1.x servers, as well as the upcoming SHOUTcast Advanced Server. If you want to obtain a commercial license for SHOUTcast, contact Nullsoft sales at **sales@SHOUTcast.com**.

Licensed users receive limited technical support. Emails sent to **support@SHOUTcast.com** by registered users usually receive responses shortly from technical support. Nullsoft also runs a SHOUTcast listserver, and there is support available on IRC on the #SHOUTcast channel.

Making the Most of SHOUTcast

Assuming you've gotten SHOUTcast up and running, let's move our discussion to making the most of this exciting technology. Just slapping together a playlist and sticking your server out is probably what most people do at first. Let's face it: Life would be easy if that's all it took to have a cool SHOUTcast station. Like everything else on the Net, you need to take things the extra mile if you want to truly stand out. Here's how the better SHOUTcasters stand out from the crowd.

Developing Good SHOUTcast Playlists

Just throwing up any old playlist for people to hear isn't necessarily the best way to develop a SHOUTcast station. Make use of the following tips:

1. Stick to your labeled genre.

    If you're doing country, don't drop in the odd techno song. Make sure your station either sticks to its format or puts it in the mixed or various category. People want your content to match the advertised format.

2. Use the SHOUTcast promos. They're cool and they promote the technology.

    Nullsoft hired JJ McKay Productions to create wicked cool SHOUTcast plug-ins. These plug-ins promote SHOUTcast Radio to your listeners, and provide nice professional sounding bumpers between your songs.

Part IV MP3 Radio and More

3. Intersperse cool bumpers and sound bites.

    Create cool bumpers that talk up songs or your station ID; intersperse cool quotes and sound effects to give your station an attitude.

    If you want to hire the same JJ McKay Productions that Nullsoft did, you can find them on the Web at **www.jjmckay.com**. We emailed JJ and asked him to give us the ballpark cost of a 6–10-second station ID. He said it's about $15 **dry** (no effects) and $30 fully produced. JJ McKay Productions accepts American Express, Visa, and MasterCard. You can order the promos directly from their site, and they even will deliver them in MP3 format. Their pages even include some suggested phrases to use (**Figure 12.11**).

Figure 12.11
Not the type to come up with your own cool station ID tagline? Check out JJ McKay Productions' list of suggested promos.

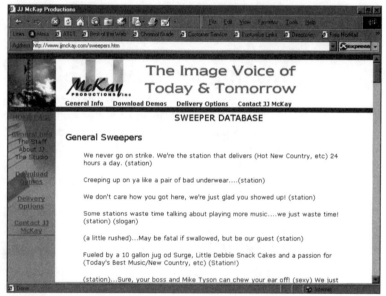

4. Follow the Statutory License playlist guidelines for Webcasters. Too legit or quit?

    There are some established rules you will want to follow in order to stay legit in the emerging world of Webcasting. You might otherwise get a nasty letter in the mail from any of the various organizations trying to keep Webcasters legitimate. At the same time, some of the rules actually try to force you to promote some variety in what you Webcast, which brings us to the next tip.

5. Mix up your playlists to keep repeat visitors listening.

    One playlist 3–4 hours long isn't going to cut it after a month. If you want a loyal following, vary that playlist. Give people new stuff to keep coming back to. The biggest complaint about regular radio (which, face it, sucks) is that they keep repeating way too many songs.

6. Listen to a full playing first and tweak the flow. Listen through your list.

Don't just dump your playlist in. Hit Random and Broadcast. Just like the best mix tapes you made before, spend the time to tweak your playlist. Find those rough transitions and look for opportunities to put in bumpers and station IDs. Make sure you have a playlist that sounds good from beginning to end.

7. Spice things up.

This is a more biased tip, but we find that some interspersed comedy is a nice addition to a lot of stations. Even if it's a one-liner, hearing a joke or two in an hour-long set is a nice way to give your station some attitude.

Promoting Your SHOUTcast Station

It's up, it's running, and you're doing all the right things. Yet you have two listeners. Other stations seem to be raking in the users. What's the difference? It may be your station promotion efforts. As the number of SHOUTcast stations expands, it will become more important that you get the word out about your station. Unless you want a small station for you and your friends, take some time to put in a little promotion legwork.

1. Create a Web page for your station.

It's easier to promote a Web site than it is your SHOUTcast Server. For example, Yahoo! might list the URL to your home page but doesn't necessarily let you have a direct listing that points to your SHOUTcast station. Thus, if you want to promote your station, do so first by creating a Web site, linking from that site to your SHOUTcast Server. (You can even use a free site like those found on GeoCities.) Add some basic content (or go all out) and then promote that address.

A successful Web site with lots of traffic will do wonders for the popularity of your SHOUTcast show.

2. Send MP3Spy.com a banner for your station.

The MP3Spy folks have created a great tool to help you find cool SHOUTcast stations. There is a banner ad at the top of MP3Spy. (It's how they make their money.) As a SHOUTcast station operator, you can submit a banner ad for free.

Your ad needs to measure 468✕60 and be in the .GIF file format. Your banner must be less than 13K. It can be an animated GIF, but animation it isn't a requirement. Worried that you're not much of an artist or have the graphic skills of a person who can neither cut nor paste? You can always hire someone to make a banner. Use some of the simple programs such as Jasc's Paint Shop Pro (**www.jasc.com**) or Metacreations Headline Studio (**www.metacreations.com**).

MP3Spy reserves the right to reject any banner—especially if uses unacceptable words or pictures. MP3Spy also asks if your SHOUTcast Server operates at certain times. It places that information into the banner; if your ad airs at an earlier time, people will then understand that the server exists but may be down when they see it. Finally, non-commercial banners are the only ones accepted in this complementary program.

Once you have your completed banner, send it to MP3Spy.com. Include the URL of a Web page that contains information about your server and the graphic and email it to **promo@mp3spy.com**.

3.   Hit the books.

There are two excellent books that help with promoting stuff (be they sites, products, services, or your SHOUTcast station) on the Net. If you want more help promoting your radio site on the Web, check them out:

—*Getting Hits* by Don Sellers (Peachpit Press, ISBN: 0201688158).

—*Publicity on the Internet* by Steve O'Keefe (John Wiley & Sons, ISBN: 0471161756).

4.   Tell your friends.

SHOUTcast stations tend to support small audiences. What better audience than friends and family? Be prepared to help them acquire Winamp and set it up to work with your station.

5.   Set up relay servers.

Relay servers not only let you broadcast to more people, but they give you partners that will work to promote the station.

The MP3Spy DJ Plug-In for SHOUTcast

In Chapter 5, we covered MP3Spy, a tool you can use to find SHOUTcast stations. That chapter covered the product from the user's perspective. For DJs however, MP3Spy offers a set of features that can be a crucial part of operating a station. These features are contained in the MP3Spy DJ plug-in [dsp_mp3spy.dll] that you should install in your DSP Plugins directory. To use this plug-in, simply select it from your DSP/Effect Plug-ins list in your Winamp preferences. When you select this plug-in, it will initiate the SHOUTcast Source for Winamp plug-in as well as the DJ plug-in. Assuming you've configured the SHOUTcast Source plug-in, you can concentrate on the DJ plug-in.

The DJ plug-in (**Figure 12.12**) is pretty simple. It contains a main chat window with three tabs and a chat participant window on the right. Note that the icons separating the windows, which control chat functions, are the exact same as those found on the main MP3Spy program (also explained in Chapter 5). The bottom two icons, however, are new. The hands icons are used to ban users from the chat room who may be causing trouble.

Figure 12.12
The MP3Spy DJ plug-in.

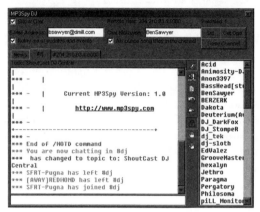

At the top of the plug-in are several checkboxes, buttons, and pieces of information:

▶ **Show Chat**—Shows or hides the chat stream that is taking place.

▶ **Remote Host**—Shows the IP address of the server you are broadcasting from.

▶ **Validated**—Shows the number of users currently validated as listening to your SHOUTcast.

▶ **E-Mail Address**—If you want people to be able to get your email address in the chat room, type it in here.

▶ **Chat Nickname**—Type in your chat room nickname.

▶ **Set**—Press this button to acknowledge the change in chat-room nickname.

▶ **Get Ops**—This lets you get operations on your chat channel (if it's available). It lets you set the channel topic and kick out or ban troublemakers.

▶ **Notify Me of Updates and Events**—Check this option if you want automatic updates and MP3Spy events to be sent to you when the plug-in is initiated.

▶ **Announce Song Titles in the Channel**—This is the most important feature of the plug-in. By checking this box, the song title contained in the ID3 tag of the MP3 file will be broadcast out to the MP3Spy client. Users can then see what the currently playing track is on your SHOUTcast station. This is not only a useful tool for your station, but it brings you more in compliance with the copyright act covering Internet radio broadcasting. See the section, "Making Your SHOUTcast Station Compliant with Current Webcasting Law" later in this chapter for more information on compliance.

▶ **Home Channel**—If you've left the home channel for your server, click this button to have it brought back up.

Overall, the MP3Spy DJ plug-in is a useful tool for you to use with your station. Not only does it help you broadcast additional station information to your users, it gives you a tool that lets you chat and interact with users. One of the great things about Internet radio broadcasting is the ability to build a community and close communication with your listeners. Using the DJ plug-in lets you do just that.

TIP
If you want to see a graph of recent SHOUTcast activity as mapped by MP3Spy, check out **http://search.gamespynetwork.com/graph/shoutcast.php3** (**Figure 12.13**). This site maps the number of servers and listeners using SHOUTcast on a daily basis.

Figure 12.13
The folks behind MP3Spy compile a graph that shows the amount of SHOUTcast Server and listener activity.

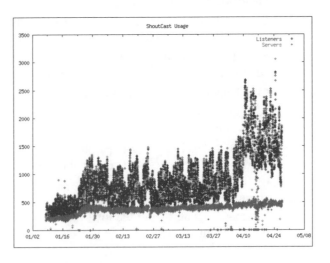

Creating Cool Web Site Track Listings with MusicTicker

The MusicTicker plug-in by Atul Varma lets you output information about your current playlist to an HTML page that you might display on your server (**Figure 12.14**). The idea is to make it easy for people to see the current file playing on your station and some of the past files that have been played.

Figure 12.14
MusicTicker in Action on the Amish Web Posse's Station Site.

MusicTicker can also monitor Winamp's playlist for better compliance with the statutory license rules for operating an Internet radio station. While it isn't perfectly compliant with all the rules, it will check tracks so that different songs by the same artist are not played consecutively and the same song isn't played twice in the same hour.

To use the MusicTicker plug-in, do the following:

1. Place the gen_mticker.dll file and the mt_subs.inf file into the Plugins directory of your Winamp directory.
2. Copy the mticker_pow.gif file to the directory to which you will output the mticker HTML file.
3. Restart Winamp to begin to use the plug-in.

The most current version of MusicTicker can be found on Varma's site at **http://www2.kenyon.edu/People/varmaa/mticker** or in the General Plug-Ins section of the Winamp Web site.

The MusicTicker Plug-In dialog box (**Figure 12.15**) lets you set the various features of the program. Click the Enable Music Ticker checkbox to make MusicTicker active.

Figure 12.15
The Music Ticker Plug-In dialog box.

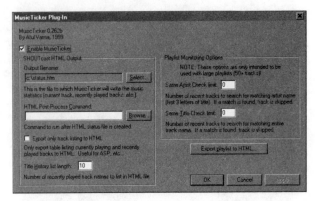

In the Output Filename field, place the file name and path where you want the HTML file to output. (Click the Select button to use a file dialog box to accomplish this task.)

Use the HTML Post-Process Command option to have another program or process run after the new HTML file is created. For example, you might launch an FTP process that will upload the new file to your remote Web site for your station.

Type in the name of the file to execute and any parameters to pass along with it. Selecting Browse will let you pick the executable or batch file using a standard file open dialog box.

In the parameters section, you can also use some special symbols to pass parameters (**Table 12.3**) to a program about the currently playing song, and recently played songs.

Table 12.3–Special parameters to pass to via MusicTicker's post-process command

Parameter	Function
%f	Inserts the name of the HTML output file name you created as a parameter.
%0	Uses the name of currently playing song as a parameter.
%1, %2 ... %n	Passes the name of the song played n times ago (for example, %2 equals two songs prior) as a parameter.
%%	Use two % characters to insert a single % if needed as a parameter.

Part IV MP3 Radio and More

TIP

If a path or program name has a space as part of its file names (for example, c:\Program Files) you must put quotes around the path\filename before the Parameters section.

The Export Only Track Listing to HTML option is for advanced users who might want to export just a stripped down version of the track listing so it can be used with ASP or other HTML application systems like Allaire's Cold Fusion. Essentially it'll give you a raw output you can use to meld with another HTML file using a program you've created. See the Readme file that comes with the MusicTicker distribution for more information.

The Title History List Length setting lets you limit the number of recently played files that MusicTicker will output. Most people tend to pick a number between 5 and 10. Note that this doesn't include the currently playing song.

The Playlist Monitoring options can monitor your song lists to prevent certain songs from repeating, such as songs from the same artist or a song played within the same hour. Disable this if you don't want MusicTicker changing your playlist.

NOTE

One thing that is annoying about this feature (however interesting) is that the song must be played for a few seconds before MusicTicker can analyze the playlist and the song's information and skip to the next song. The author claims to be working on fixing this problem.

Use the Same Artist Check Limit to set the number of songs that MusicTicker reviews when checking to see if the current song is from an artist just recently played.

TIP

MusicTicker checks the title of the MP3 as outputted by Winamp. This usually is the default setting of "Artist name - Title name". If songs aren't being output this way (because they are devoid of the information or you changed the settings in the Nitrane Preferences), then it won't work.

Use the Same Title Check Limit option to place the number of songs back that MusicTicker will go to see if a currently playing song title matches one of the previously played titles. Make sure to keep this number lower than the total number of songs in your playlist.

MusicTicker will include settings found in Winamp's master Plugin.ini file (found in your Winamp\Plugins directory) where you can set options that are in the dialog box but also a few additional ones not found in the current dialog box. **Table 12.4** covers the major settings for the [MusicTicker] section of Plugin.ini file.

Table 12.4– Variables and their explanations found in the [MusicTicker] section of Winamp's Plugin.ini file

Variable	Explanation
EnableHTMLOutput	When set to 0 means MusicTicker won't output an HTML file. If set to 0, the HTMLPostProcessCmd will not execute either.
HTMLTitle	The text which will be placed between the <TITLE>…</TITLE> HTML tags in the file MusicTicker outputs.
HTMLBodyProperties	Text that goes inside the <BODY> tag of MusicTicker's HTML output file. Not between the tag, just inside it. Use this to introduce attributes to the <BODY> tag, such as a background image, link colors, text colors, etc. See an HTML guide for more information.
HTMLFont	Base font for the entire HTML document created by MusicTicker.
HTMLHeader	This is what is at the beginning of the HTML output page, before MusicTicker writes the table about the currently playing/recently played songs.
HTMLListColor1	Background color of the table cell for track listing of current song. Use '#000000 BACKGROUND=" picture.gif"' to specify an image instead of color for background. Note that not all browsers support this feature.
HTMLListColor2	Same as above except used for all past tracks played.
HTMLServerOfflineMsg	Text to display instead of current track if server source (i.e. Winamp) is not running.
HTMLFooterImage	File name with path of the "Powered by MusicTicker" image. You may use a different image for the footer but this image is always linked to the MusicTicker home page.
HTMLRefreshTimeout	Value used for the META REFRESH tag in MusicTicker's output HTML file. The number is set in seconds and is used to generate the amount of time before the page displaying MusicTicker information checks for a new version of the HTML page.
EnablePlaylistMonitoring	Set to 0 to disable MusicTicker's playlist monitoring.
TitleCheckCount	Increase the variable amount here only if your HTML output is giving you garbage track names.

Part IV   MP3 Radio and More

> **TIP**
>
> Advanced MusicTicker users can also use a substitution system that will substitute words found in artist's names and track listings with other text, such as changing
>
> Lincolnville
>
> to
>
> <A HREF="http://www.lincolnville.com">Lincolnville</A>)
>
> This feature allows you to accomplish even more robust ticker outputs. See the file titled mt_subs.txt that comes with MusicTicker for more information about this powerful advanced feature.

Posting MusicTicker's Output to Your Site

There are two ways—one easy and one harder—to post the outputted ticker HTML file to your Web site. The less complicated way is if the machine playing Winamp is the same or on the same network as your Web server. If so, all you need to do is set the correct path name to where the program should output the HTML file and you're done.

If however, the Web server that users connect to is remotely hosted (via Tripod, GeoCities, or your own hosting provider), then you'll need to use the HTML Post Process command to initiate an FTP program and pass to it the server connection information and the file to upload. That isn't something done easily by novices. If you need to do this, the author recommends using WS_FTP and includes instructions in the Readme file for executing it using the HTML Post Process command.

Making Your SHOUTcast Station Compliant with Current Webcasting Law

Just because you have the ability to broadcast any MP3 (or other kind of audio files) out on to the Internet doesn't mean you legally can do it. Broadcasters of all shapes and sizes must respect copyright rules. In the broadcasting area that means paying licensing fees that inevitably find their way back to the artists and copyright holders of the music you broadcast.

WARNING

We've researched this issue diligently, but the authors are not lawyers and thus this is not legal advice. When in doubt, always consult a lawyer before acting on matters that may involve legal implications. This information is constantly changing due to the nature of the Internet, of technology, and of the law.

When the Web started and when Webcasting followed, the government didn't do much to cover how Internet-based broadcasters should be compliant with the law. In an attempt to clear matters up, Congress passed the Digital Millennium Copyright Act (DMCA) in October of 1998. The act amended U.S. copyright law to cover Internet licensing of radio stations. In addition, it brought the United States to join two new World Intellectual Property Organization (WIPO) treaties that cover international copyright issues in respect to the Internet.

While larger stations and other Webcasting entities may have to enter into many specific agreements with various rights organizations, the act does outline a type of license known as a statutory license. A **statutory license** guarantees Webcasters a license to broadcast sound recordings as long as those stations and their broadcasts are maintained as outlined in the statutory license rules.

Technically speaking, the law provides a statutory license, as opposed to one that is specifically granted by individual copyright owners. This process not only makes it easy for Webcasters to qualify for Internet broadcasting, but it is an efficient way for rights holders to have their rights protected and managed. The licensing agencies won't be overwhelmed by the inevitably hundreds of thousands of Internet radio stations that will exist on the Web in due time with the help of statutory licensing.

A station must meet conditions to be eligible for a statutory license.

▶ A Webcaster may not play in any three-hour period:

—More than three songs from a particular album, including no more than two consecutively.

—Four songs by a particular artist or from a boxed set, including no more than three consecutively.

—Prior announcements of songs that will be played are not permitted. You cannot provide advance song or artist playlists. A Webcaster can name one or two artists that are featured as a means of illustrating the type of music played.

▶ DJ teaser announcements using artists' names are also permitted, but these promos can't name a specific time they will be played.

▶ Stations that play a set list of songs in an archived format cannot play those fewer than five hours in duration. Playlists that are five hours or more can reside on a Web site for no more than a total of two weeks, and you can't change one or two songs every now and then to create a new playlist.

TIP

SHOUTcast Radio is not an archived on-demand system, so this condition should be moot for you.

▶ Many SHOUTcast stations are made up of looped playlists. The statutory license requires that **looped** or continuous programs be longer than three hours. As with the previously mentioned condition on archived sets, changing one or two songs does not change this requirement.

▶ Special programs under one hour and are performed at scheduled times can't be broadcast more than three times in any two-week period. This limit rises to four times if the program is one hour or more in duration.

▶ Webcasters are obligated to identify the song, artist, and album they are playing if service receivers are capable of displaying this information. This requirement takes effect October 28 of 1999. SHOUTcast 1.1 now broadcasts song titles to listening Winamp players, which gives it good compliance for this feature.

TIP

There are tools—including the MP3Spy DJ plug-in and SHOUTpager (**http://www.gcs.co.za/mbs/shoutpager/**)—that let you broadcast this information to users via the Web or MP3Spy.

▶ Webcasters are prohibited from falsely suggesting a link between recordings or artists and advertisements for products or services. For example, you can't tie the broadcast of a song to a particular product you're trying to sell or an ad the person should see.

▶ Webcasters are obligated to take steps to defeat copying of their streams by recipient, but only if they have the particular means to do so. This includes the need by Webcasters to accommodate any measures widely used by sound recording copyright owners to identify or protect copyrighted works. This applies only if it is feasible for them to do so without hurting the Webcasters ability to transmit their shows.

▶ Webcasters are obligated to cooperate in defeating scanning by services or people so that people can specifically tune into particular artists or recordings.

▶ The transmission of bootleg recordings is not covered by the license. The statutory license is limited to transmissions made from lawful copies of sound recordings. This doesn't give you implicit permission to broadcast bootleg or pre-released records, unless you otherwise get permission specifically from the rights holder to do so.

▶ Webcasters must not automatically and intentionally cause a device receiving their transmission to switch from one program they offer to another.

▶ If feasible, Webcasters must transmit **copyright management information**. This is the information encoded in the sound recording by the copyright owner, and it identifies the title of the song, the featured artist, and other related information (if any).

Getting the License

If you think you are running a station that meets all of the conditions of a statutory license, you need to file an initial notice with the Copyright Office in Washington D.C. This includes your full legal name, mailing address, phone and fax numbers, and the date of the first transmission qualifying for the statutory license.

Send this initial notice with a $20 filing fee to the following address:

Library of Congress, Copyright Office
Licensing Division
101 Independence Avenue, S.E.
Washington, D.C. 20557-6400

Files You Create for Webcasting

Copies are sometimes referred to as **ephemeral recordings**. The new law grants an exemption for ephemeral recordings if it meets two requirements: The Webcasting service making those ephemeral recordings is licensed to transmit them (it has a statutory license to transmit the recordings), and it meets the conditions of the exemption.

The following conditions apply to the exemption for ephemeral recordings:

▶ The copy of the recording must be used only by the Webcaster.

▶ The copy must be destroyed within six months, unless preserved exclusively for archival purposes.

▶ Only one ephemeral copy of the recording may be made, and no further copies of the recording can be made from that ephemeral copy.

▶ The copy must be used only for transmissions in the Webcaster's local service area.

A statutory license is available for Webcasters who wish to make more than one copy. (An example would be doing so in order to transmit sound recordings at different bit rates for different listeners.) Such Webcasters are disqualified from the ephemeral recording exemption. The statutory license for ephemeral recordings operates like the one for public performances. The royalty rate is set through negotiation or, if necessary, arbitration, and is effective for two years. The conditions of the ephemeral recordings statutory license are similar to those for the exemption. However, the terms of the statutory license may allow a Webcaster to make more than one copy of a recording.

Royalty Payments

Royalty payments for the statutory license are a bit sketchy at this point. The DMCA law doesn't set a royalty rate for the statutory license. Instead, sound recording copyright owners may negotiate with Webcasters to set that rate during the six-month negotiation period that started in December 1998. The law requires that the rates be what a "willing buyer and willing seller would agree to in a marketplace." If Webcasters and sound recording copyright owners do not agree on a rate, an arbitration proceeding takes place to determine rates.

Once the statutory license royalty rate is set, it applies to all Webcasting that took place since the new law became effective (October 28, 1998). Therefore, Webcasters who qualify for the statutory license must pay royalties for all transmissions made since October 28, 1998. The royalty rate will remain in effect until December 31, 2000.

If a Webcaster does not qualify for the statutory license, she must obtain licenses from each of the copyright owners of the sound recordings she wishes to transmit. Unfortunately, there is no group or organization that grants licenses on behalf of copyright owners to Webcasting services that do not qualify for the statutory license. Therefore, the Webcaster must contact each copyright owner individually. Those who do not qualify for the statutory license or obtain licenses directly from sound recording copyright owners risk infringement liability.

Part IV MP3 Radio and More

Dealing with Licensing Agencies

Compliance with the guidelines outlined in the statutory license doesn't guarantee you the right to broadcast whatever you want on your station. You must also potentially pay license fees to ASCAP, BMI, and SESAC, the major licensing authorities for music. These authorities are the means that artists and publishers use to get compensation for broadcasting their work.

You may also have to pay a fee to the RIAA. There is some dispute, however, about whether this is absolutely necessary; RIAA hasn't posted pricing on contract info on its site. You may also have to pay individuals or other smaller rights groups, although you're widely covered with the big three. Conversely, you don't need to pay licensing fees if you use work that isn't covered by these agencies, is out of the range of copyright, or is music for which you have some direct form of permission (it's your own music, for instance).

Some people might abhor the idea of paying a licensing fee to be able to non-commercially offer what looks like awesome publicity for an artist. Surprisingly, the licensing fees aren't too steep. If you're a small-time, non-commercial SHOUTcaster (and most SHOUTcast stations are), then you most likely qualify for the lowest rate yearly license from each of the big three firms. These minimum rates are outlined in **Table 12.5**.

Table 12.5–The minimum rates

Licensing Agency	Minimum Fee	URL for Licensing Page/Contract
ASCAP	$250/yr	Contract: **http://www.ascap.com/weblicense/webintro.html** More info: **http://www.ascap.com/weblicense/ascap.pdf**
BMI	$500/yr	Contract: **http://www.bmi.com/licensing/website98.pdf** More info: **http://www.bmi.com/home_li.html**
SESAC	$100/yr	Contract: **http://www.sesac.com/SESACNetLic.pdf** More info: **http://www.sesac.com/web.htm**

The licensing fees currently being charged by the major licensing organizations are considered experimental, which means they're subject to change at any moment. The agencies are experimenting with various licensing schemes under a trial period that will run through October of 1999.

To obtain these licenses, simply go to the information pages and read the details. (They're sometimes confusing, but there are FAQs and other documentation on almost all the info pages.) Obtain the contract, fill it out, and mail it in with your check. In terms of determining your fee, most of the licensing agencies have interactive spreadsheets or rate calculators you can use (**Figure 12.16**). Many also have representatives reachable via email or phone to answer questions.

Figure 12.16
ASCAP has an interactive rate calculator on its Web site. Just answer the questions and click Calculate to see your potential fee.

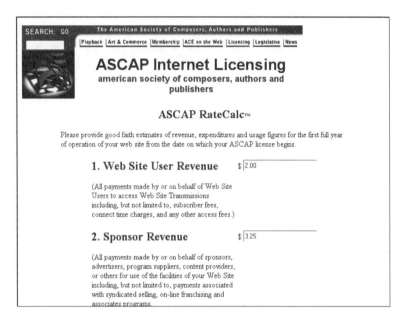

Get Legit?

The question you may be asking yourself right now is whether you should get legit at all. Why should you pay to broadcast music until one of these groups eventually sends you a nasty note or actually sues you? That would be like saying you're going to drive around without auto insurance until after you have an accident. It's a little late then, isn't it?

Truth be told, there is a good chance you might be able to get away without paying fees to Webcast. The law is new, enforcement is an issue that hasn't been worked out very well, and you can hide your broadcasts (and more) to deter getting snared by the lawyers. That doesn't make it right.

The solution for now is twofold. First: You should pay for the right to broadcast music or develop content for your station that doesn't require you to pay a fee. Second: Small-time Webcasters need to put the pressure on all the rights organizations and the governments. Such action will force the governments and organizations to create law and licensing agreements that make it easy for legitimate people to Webcast their music and create their own stations at a cost that isn't prohibitive. This pressure isn't created by not paying, but by paying and pushing on lawmakers and rights givers to make it easier and cheaper. Imagine a world where there are 10 million small broadcasters each paying $100 a year—less than $10 a month—to broadcast music on the Net. You think the people who grant rights would risk raising rates too much if it meant losing a billion dollars in revenue?

With some effort, the laws and the fees will become a no-brainer in the future and we can all groove together in a world where everyone is both a listener and broadcaster! This is why it's important for smaller broadcasters to get legit—there's a lot of leverage in your pocket when you're a paying customer.

More Rights Questions? What to Do?

You probably still have more questions, even as much as we've boiled down a lot of the information concerning the legal issues and rights in running your own Webcast. The rest of this section discusses issues you should check out if you want to double check things concerning your own situation or get even more information on Webcasting rights issues.

If you're very serious about being compliant, we strongly suggest you consult with a lawyer. While all the information in this chapter is relevant, the rules for Webcasting are changing daily. In addition, not all songs and material are licensed by ASCAP, BMI, SESAC, and the RIAA. There may be smaller and more local organizations to deal with. Having an attorney to help with your compliance can keep you up-to-date and better prepared for compliance.

Additionally, you might want to check out books by Bob Kohn (CEO of Goodnoise.com) on music licensing. Those books and his companion site (**www.kohnmusic.com**) are an amazing source of good information from an expert in the field written for the non-lawyer.

> *Kohn on Music Licensing*, 2nd Edition, by Bob Kohn (Aspen Law & Business, ISBN: 156706289X).

> *Kohn on Music Licensing 1998 Supplement* by Bob Kohn (Aspen Law & Business, ISBN: 1567068081).

Both are extremely comprehensive and a bit pricey for the small user. Thankfully, you can find lots of Webcast-specific information on the site. There is even a section where you can ask questions.

The RIAA is not mentioned in the table because it doesn't have a standard rate calculation or contract on its site. It's also not clear under certain laws whether smaller, non-interactive, non-commercial Webcasters have to pay RIAA fees (although it is certain they have to pay to publishers and other rights holders). This may eventually change, so consult experts about this and watch the various MP3 and music news sites (as well as **kohnmusic.com**) to see if this ambiguity about licensing clears up.

Radio Doesn't Have to Suck Anymore

Travel around from place to place and it's hard to find any city that has great radio stations across the board. With SHOUTcast, anyone can be his or her own program director. In addition, by focusing on smaller, more focused genres you can better tailor a station to closely appeal to a certain style of musical taste.

Both of these things and others mean an end to radio as we know it. We can now be put out of our misery. Instead of shouting at the radio stations that have been giving us top 40 hits, one-hit wonders, awful announcers, or the same Led Zeppelin songs every other day, we can now shout in a whole new way. The result: Radio won't suck anymore—at least when you're near a computer.

Interview:

Tom Higgins (aka TomWhore) SHOUTcaster Extraordinaire

As a founding member of his band, the Media Whores, he has long been known as simply TomWhore. In actuality he is Tom Higgins, a 34-year-old New Yorker who moved to Portland, Oregon, nearly two years ago. By trade Tom is a self-described "information wrangler." He creates and works with database systems, information servers, client-end interfaces, and "abstract methods of having all these things talk to and grow with each other—and make time for good lunches."

Tom is one of the most active users of SHOUTcast. Active on the SHOUTcast mailing list (see **shoutcast.com** for information on how to join), Tom is one of the earliest users of the product. His WSMF radio program broadcasts an eclectic mix of vintage radio and spoken word content (**www.wsmf.org**). Check out his Web site for more information, including playlist and show schedules (**Figure 12.17**).

Figure 12.17
wsmf.org is the home site of WSMF SHOUTcast Radio.

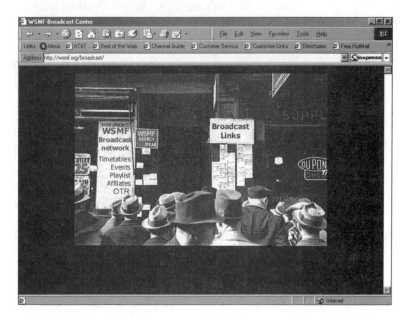

Q *Tell us more about you.*

A: I've always been aware of computers, always just waiting to get my hands on them. As the 70s and 80s unfurled as the years of the personalization of computers, I was trying my best to keep my aims and goals using the best tech I could understand. I had used several computers at school, but my first computer I owned was a Sinclair ZX81. From there it was a trail of Apples, Ataris, Commodores, an Eagle, Macs, and then the onslaught of Intel-based boxes.

I got the name TomWhore when I was trying to keep a real life band together in the late 80s. We were the Media Whores. There was Ed Whore, Viki Whore, Mukesh Whore and me...TomWhore. Over time the rest of the band did something called having a life. The name stuck and to this day I still keep the Media Whore idea going in some form or another. I still firmly believe I will have my shirt ripped off by lust-crazed fans in Bonn. I may be in my late 60s when this happens, but if you don't have that stick-to-it attitude, you'll get nowhere in life.

Q *When did you first learn about SHOUTcast?*

A: It was December of 1998. There were some folks who were given the beta...from the crew at Nullsoft. I saw mention of it on IRC and tracked down someone who was running a server; it was Hickboy.

I listened to his broadcast for a long time, talking to him on IRC about the ease of the server, the cool features it had, and how the quality was so far superior to RealAudio. It was amazing: With RealAudio you can tell right off that it's RealAudio, with SHOUTcast—even the beta—it was like hearing a whole different dimension to the sound of streaming on the Net.

During those days of the closed beta, a community sprang up, as it is likely to do on the Net when something truly great is happening. People were listening to the few servers that SHOUTcasted and the mantra of the month was "So when is this going to be out for general consumption?" Whenever it was going to be, a community was born.

Q *When did you get your server up? Tell us about your station. What's the format? Why did you choose the content you have?*

A: New Year's Eve, 1998. Nullsoft put the software out and I jumped on it fast. I only had a 56k dial-up at the time, so I found a bud who was happy to let me bounce my stream through a relay server he set up on a T1. It was the TomWhore WSMF Rocking New Year's Eve party coming from the Bountiful Bandwidth From the House of Ben. I stayed up for 16 hours. As the night went on we picked up listeners, set up the IRC channel, and started playing with formats. It was an amazing stretch of hours. It was a time for fast and hard decision.

First was [that] I needed my own bandwidth. A day or so later I called U.S. west and my ISP [Internet Service Provider] and got on the DSL train. I also started working out what type of content I wanted to play on the stream. I realized that just playing music was not going to hold my interest or the interest of the audience I wanted to have.

That first night I was on the idea of words, of the power of the spoken word and how little of it gets out to the ears these days. We have music galore, sound bites, slanted news shows...but precious few sources of words to make our minds question themselves and spur on the creative process.

As a kid I remember my mom and dad telling me about and playing old-time radio shows, records of Shakespeare being done by Burton, Taylor, Olivier, et cetera. I also remember them reading to me all the time, nights before sleep were filled with my parents passing on to me the story of the Hobbit, Lord of the Rings, and science fiction.

Something in all that stuck with me all these years. I've always been into the spoken word, into passing on an aural tradition of our times. With SHOUTcast, things finally clicked into place.

In the weeks between ordering DSL and getting it up and going on Jan 19th, I scoured the Net for all such manner of words. When I went on the air I had a few shows, but not enough to fill the stream 24/7. So I mixed it in with music that I wasn't hearing out there on the other servers. The response to the Spoken Word stuff was amazing. I went back out on the Net and searched harder for more. If there is one thing I am sure of in this life, it's that the Great Material Stream provides for those who know how to navigate it.

I found it here and there, stuck between other pages and in FTP sites. In a month I was up to 600 shows, ranging from *Fiber Mcgee and Molly* to *Amos and Andy* to *Johnny Dollar* to Orson Welles's production, to news reports from the front (of WW II, that is), to some of the best sci-fi I have ever heard. I hooked up with the OTR Link Society Web ring (**http://www.pkenny.com/webring.html**) and from there was able to keep the supply fresh; the number of folks trading this material is not large, but they are amazing in their capacity to share. Much thanks to the people who make these shows available.

I have also started working on my own creations for content. If you listen to the stream, you can hear some bumpers that were made for WSMF by myself and a long-time WSMF member Sin-naps. Sin-naps has the ability to speak into a microphone and make people listening laugh so hard they lose all control of their bodily functions. He is going to be one of the principles in the upcoming WSMF Sci-Fi and Fiction shows.

Another idea we are working with along with other people we know is a political round table. Most of the ones I've heard are so one-sided that it's not of any worth. I'm trying to do something more like the McLaughlin Group, where you get a good mix of ideas all ready to explode in informative ways.

Q *Why is SHOUTcast best suited for you?*

A: Simply put, it's the best-sounding, easiest-to-use, most cost-effective [it's free] and slickest-streaming server ever. It doesn't force me to retool my entire machine or to futz with stuff like the RealAudio server does. The sound difference between the two is the real test, though. Listen to an RA stream and a SHOUTcast stream at the same bit rates and be prepared to weep with joy.

Nullsoft has also proven to be a top-notch development team. These folks put a ton of sweat and late nights in this tech and then let it spread throughout the land. They are very responsive to new ideas and bug reports. Getting JJ McKay to do the SHOUTcast bumpers was an amazingly cool little aside. Things like that make Nullsoft and SHOUTcast the way to go.

Then there is the community of SHOUTcasters to take into account. On the SHOUTcasters mailing list and the IRC channels, there are always folks to help out in times of tech need and voices to be heard on all the issues that impact us. We may not all agree on the same things, but at our best we are there for each other in times of trouble. Never, ever underestimate the power of a group bound by a purpose and who are given the tools needed to go forth and do by the creators. Nullsoft are masters and [have] strong communities grow around their products.

Q *How do you promote your station?*

A: I'm not into the heavy advert phase yet. I don't know if I ever will. I only have nine streams open, [that] being what my DSL will handle. I have hit Old-Time Radio- and Spoken Word-related Usenet groups, pimped it on IRC to folks that might be interested, and had the good fortune to have some good friends who are also online take up the WSMF name and spread it about. There is no substitute for good friends with big mouths in getting the word out.

Q *Your station is like an entire community thanks to your kick-ass Web site. Tell us more about how the site supports the SHOUTcast station.*

A: The Web site is a growing beast, as all good Web sites are. It is by no means where I want it yet, but it is moving to address the needs of the folks who are using it. To make it easier on the listener, I'm making available lists of what has played in the last few hours, a page that shows what I have cued up for the day. I also have a BBS set up for folks to talk about what's on the stream, on their minds, or just to talk in general. I try to keep things fluid enough to let the users of the system move it where they want it to go, as well as where I see it going. The really great Web sites that are user-based need to do that, to grow with and by the users as well as by central planning.

One thing I am proud of is the Word Bank, which is now the home of the WSMF EMonks text collection. In this collection, all indexed and available at any time, are thousands of works of the written word. My partner on the project, WhoreNoir, and I started with the amazing *Project Gutenberg* and kept digging around the Net for more and more works of the written word. The WSMF Word Bank is our way to let users quickly get to these great works and to explore further. It ties in with the Spoken Word and Old-Time radio show nicely. For instance, a user can be listening to a *Tarzan* radio show and go grab the Edgar Rice Burroughs text files.

I hope that folks roam through it for hours and hours at a stretch. Keep browsing folks; it's all text and I got DSL.

The Web site also is beginning to grow areas [in which] to read up on its history, Web and SHOUTcast stats, plans, mission statement, and occasionally pictures of your humble narrator in various stages of blondness. Yes, I've gone West coast native and my hair is now blonde...and yes, we do have more fun; I have the stats to prove it.

Q *How did you sign up your affiliates that rebroadcast your streams?*

A: Good friends and connections.

Q *What's the design of your station (hardware, connection, max users, bit rate)?*

A: Right now WSMF is running off of a K6 266MHz CPU open-faced box with a DSL connection of 256k up and down supporting nine listeners on the port 8000 server and three listeners on the port 23 server. I run the port 23 server to relay the stream to a port that poor saps, like myself (at work), who are behind oppressive firewalls can still get the show without having to perform lewd acts on their system admins.

This is also the box I play games on, serve the WSMF Web site from, Net from, write on, create new sound content on, and occasionally order myself expensive items on. I am working on getting a second box to move my other activities to and leave the k6 266 for just SHOUTcasting and Web serving.

Q *What sort of advice do you have for SHOUTcast users?*

A: *[In regards to technical setup]*

Get a good sound card that can do duplex sound operations. I didn't and am now scrambling to make up for this error. With a good duplex sound card you can get much more creative.

Having an eight-track mixing board is a great help. I have various old studio gear from back when I was trying to make Media Whore a going concern. Finally, after ten years, this equipment is getting used. It's all old and dated and you can probably pick it up for cheap, but it makes that difference when you need it.

[In regards to maintaining your station]

In your mind set a tone for the station. Everything you play needs to somehow complement that tone. Playing something just to get ratings or to show off usually works out badly. A vision of what the station is, who your audience is, and what you *want* to do is key.

Go out! Leave your station running on a 12-hour playlist and go walk around, get a date, hit a movie, hang with friends. As with all things that deal with sitting on your ass in front of a computer, it is imperative to get away from it. Burn out is not pretty.

[In regards to promoting your station]

Friends are golden. Spread the word of your station, but don't beat people over the head with it. Let the word draw in folks, but let the station and its content make the sale. Getting listeners is not the tough part. Keeping a steady base of die-hard listeners is.

[In regards to legal issues]

As Sammy Davis sings, "Don't do the crime if you can't do the time."

You have to do some homework on this. I know that's not what most folks want to hear, but to really do this right you need to be aware of the laws, the stuff you're playing, the implications of the two, and the balance you are willing to teeter on.

If you want to be a clean bean with no fear of the RIAA coming in and suing you, go check out FABCA (**http://www.audiorealm.net/fabca/**). The Free Access BroadCasters Association [is] where you can get tons of great content.

Another thing: Never forget [that] you can make your own content. One of the things that really makes me excited about this whole notion of SHOUTcast is that people might make their own content, step up to the plate, and begin to say *no* to oppressive associations and legal-based bulldogs.

Q *What do you think is the future for WSMF and Webcasting with SHOUTcast?*

A: As long as I can get the bandwidth, WSMF will always have something going on. For the foreseeable future, WSMF will be moving on with the spoken word. I think this is where my interest and skills can really get a workout, where folks can enjoy the process as well as the outcome, and where we can look back and say, "Hey we did something creative and good."

Look for more content, and if you don't see much, yell at us to get off our lazy asses and get back to the mixing boards.

Q *SHOUTcasting in general?*

A: It is like a coin being flipped, tumbling in mid-air. It can either land on the side of the individual, being able to get creative, spread the waves, share the wealth of each others' knowing, and create a whole new way of hearing and being heard. Or we can find ourselves being regulated by FCC-style tactics, legal actions knocking streams off the Net, a few select hands controlling the path's progress, and very little creativity.

You want an example of my nightmare situation for Webcasting? Turn on your FM radio and spin around the dial. Welcome to my hell.

You want an example of my heart's desire? Tune in to SHOUTcast streams, turn on to creativity and individualism, and drop out of the bland regulated waves that pass for most broadcast.

Q *By the way, what's WSMF stand for?*

A: What should meaning find? Words streamed moving forward. Why say, manufacture fiction. WSMF seeks multiple futures. In short, "We ain't saying, more fun."

13

Alternative Formats to MP3

MP3 is not the end-all be-all of digitized audio on the Internet. It was neither the first format nor will it be the last format we all use to listen to our favorite songs or other audio content. There are already a number of interesting alternatives to the MP3 format.

While we expect MP3 to remain a dominant format for some time, understanding the alternatives is important. This is not only because at some point one of these formats may overtake MP3, but because you can already listen to some of these formats with the same player most people use to listen to MP3 files. This is possibly due to the modular format of the Winamp player.

Major Alternatives

There are ten major alternative files formats worth knowing about in relation to the MP3 format. Some are older technologies, others are peer technologies, and the rest are more advanced formats attempting to become the successor to the MP3 phenomenon.

These formats include:

▶ **VQF**—A format developed in Japan that offers higher quality sound and compression.

▶ **AAC**—An MPEG-2 and MPEG-4 standard that is being positioned as the successor to MP3.

▶ **AC2/AC3**—Created by Dolby and often confused with the AAC format. This format is not part of the MPEG standard and is a proprietary technology licensed by Dolby.

▶ **MP2**—A format that predates the MP3 format. Some older MPEG files on the Internet are still in the MP2 format, which is supported fully by Winamp.

▶ **MP4**—Part mythical format in that it isn't really happening yet, and part logical successor to MP3 because it will happen. MP4 files will refer to audio files created using the available standards of the MPEG-4 file format. This should mostly mean a superset format of the AAC technology already made part of the MPEG-2 standard. MPEG-4 is also set to include VQF technology.

▶ **ASFS**—A secure format created by AudioSoft that is going to be supported by Winamp 2.11.

VQF

The **VQF (Vector Quantization File)** format was created originally at Japan's NTT Corporation. Yamaha, Texas Instruments, and other companies have licensed the technology for use in creating digital audio tools and software. Of the licensees, Yamaha has moved forward with working players and encoders on the Internet.

As a format, VQF takes an uncompressed audio file and compresses it. In fact, the compression is better than what MP3 technology offers. On average, VQF files are one third smaller than the same file compressed into the MP3 format. Proponents also claim that sound quality is better. With its higher compression ratio, VQF files can provide the equivalent of a 128kbps MP3 file at 80kbps.

However, a higher compression ratio and other format issues mean that VQF files are slower to encode and require higher-end systems to decode in order to do so without taxing your machine. The result, according to format users, is that a VQF file takes up almost twice as many system resources as would the same MP3 file. This fact, coupled with the limited release of software that supports the format, explains why VQF remains on the fringe of the entire MP3 scene.

Using VQF Files with Winamp

With its support for various input plug-ins, Winamp can support playback of VQF files. To do so, you need to install the system that enables playback. This takes a bit of trickery, but when done properly it expands the types of compressed music files your Winamp player will support.

1. Go to the unofficial home of support for the VQF format: **VQF.com.** From the site's Download page, click on the Winamp VQF plug-in offering. This is a .ZIP file that you will download and open.

2. The .ZIP file (**Figure 13.1**) contains two files: In_vqf.dll and Readme.txt. The Readme.txt file covers installation issues. The In_vqf.dll file needs to be placed in the Plugins directory of your Winamp directory. (If you choose the default directory, this is c:\Program files\Winamp\Plugins.)

Figure 13.1
Opening the VQF plug-in .ZIP file for installation.

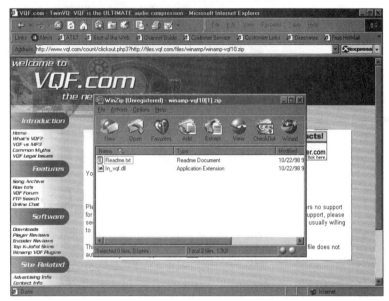

3. Once the In_vqf.dll file is extracted and installed in the Winamp Plugins directory, your next step is to install the additional files you need for VQF playback. These files are provided by Yamaha's own VQF player.

4. You must download Yamaha's VQF player. Start by accepting the license agreement located on the Web at **http://www.cyber-bp.or.jp/yamaha/SoundVQ/Pagreement_e.html**.

5. The next page displays three download sites from which you can get the player (**Figure 13.2**). Choose one; either save the file to your desktop or open it for immediate installation.

Figure 13.2
Obtaining Yamaha's
SoundVQ program is a
key part of installing
support for .VQF files in
Winamp.

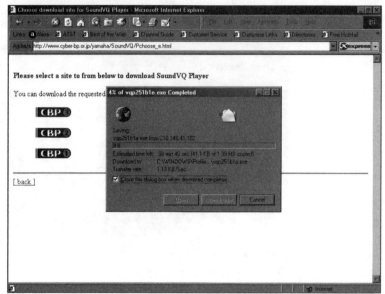

6. Follow the installation program instructions. Yamaha's SoundVQ player program is installed (**Figure 13.3**). You can use this simple client to play .VQF files. Here you make it work in Winamp so you can listen to playlists composed of both .MP3 and .VQF files.

Figure 13.3
The SoundVQ player
application from
Yamaha.

7. Once the program is installed, you need to copy two files from the SoundVQ program directory. The files are decode32.dll and twinvq2.cdb; you might find it easier to use the Find Files program included with Windows (**Figure 13.4**). Once you've located the programs, copy and paste them into Winamp's Plugins directory.

Figure 13.4
Using Find Files to find the decode32.dll and twinvq2.cdb files once they are installed with the SoundVQ player.

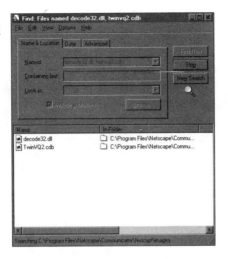

Part IV MP3 Radio and More

8. Three new files should be in Winamp's Plugins directory: In_vqf.dll, decode32.dll, and twinvq2.cdb.

9. Make sure the VQF Input plug-in is in your Input Plug-Ins listing. The listing can be found in the Nullsoft Winamp—Preferences dialog box in the Input System section of the Plug-Ins Preferences (**Figure 13.5**).

Figure 13.5
Check to make sure you installed the plug-in correctly by looking for it in the plug-in preferences section of Winamp.

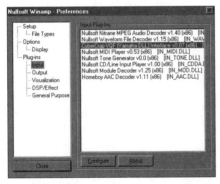

10. Download a .VQF file from **VQF.com** and then use Winamp to listen to it!

Encoder Software

There are two major encoders for the VQF format. One is made by Yamaha and the other is made by NTT. In a separate evaluation by VQF.com, the Yamaha encoder version 2.51b1 beat out the NTT 2.11 encoder by just a hair. Still—and to point out the reason MP3 is so popular—it took a machine running a fairly speedy K6-233 CPU nearly 12 minutes to encode a .VQF file with either encoder. You can download either encoder from VQF.com's software page.

Finding VQF Files

The best place to find VQF songs is on VQF.com's songs archive (**Figure 13.6**).

Figure 13.6
VQF.com is home to the format boosters, and thus, is a good place to find legally produced .VQF files.

AAC

The **AAC** (**Advanced Audio Coding**) format was developed as part of the MPEG-2 standardization process. As part of that, it is the child of several companies technologies, including IIS, AT&T, Dolby, Sony, and more. Dolby has been given the rights to license the technology on behalf of its backers, while Fraunhofer IIS (creators of the Layer 3 format) has been named the party in charge of integrating all the member contributions.

AAC is also known as an **NBC system** (non-backward compatible), and thus, no MPEG-3 playback engine can decode AAC files. AAC is, however, included in the new MPEG-4 specification; thus, any MPEG-4–compatible playback engine should be able to handle playing back AAC files. There will be a superset of features added to MPEG-4 on top of the MPEG-2 AAC scheme; those features will further enhance the AAC format.

AAC should not be confused with Dolby's own AC3 format. AAC is a more advanced format and is part of the MPEG-2 standard, while AC3 is a Dolby-specific technology.

AAC is format superior to MP3, but like the aforementioned VQF format, AAC requires more power from a user's computer, and the tools required to reach the mass market aren't as plentiful as are MP3's. In terms of specific differences, this, according to the AAC FAQ on Fraunhofer's site:

"AAC uses a different type of transform and incorporates a lot of additional features to enhance coding efficiency like Temporal Noise Shaping and Prediction. Additionally, AAC uses a very flexible entropy coding kernel to transmit coded spectral data. All these enhancements plus the careful tuning done by Fraunhofer IIS provide you with the best audio coding scheme you can get today."

In short, more advanced technology and algorithms mean better-sounding files with higher compression. AAC-encoded files are currently 40% smaller than the same song encoded in the MP3 format, which means that you can get the same song quality at a bit rate of 70% of a normal MP3 file.

AAC Software

At this time playing AAC content with Winamp is a "beta experience" as the software plug-ins for playing AAC content using Winamp are very early in their development. There is a plug-in from Homeboy Software on Nullsoft's Web site. Download the plug-in and store it in your Winamp Plugins directory. When installed properly, it will show up in the Input System listing of the Winamp Preferences dialog box (**Figure 13.7**).

Figure 13.7
Check Winamp Preferences to find out if the AAC plug-in for Winamp by Homeboy Software is installed properly.

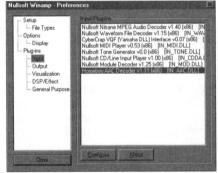

There are several companies on the Web developing AAC encoders. Check out Psytel's MPEG-4 Studio 1.0—an early AAC encoder product (www.psytel.com). As MPEG-4 and AAC become more popular, you can expect to see major MP3 encoder products such as AudioCatalyst incorporate support for AAC encoding.

MOD FILES

As discussed earlier in this book, Winamp includes support for a number of file types beyond MP3. One of these formats is the .MOD file format. MOD is a format that got its start on the Amiga platform back in the 1980s. The Amiga was one of the first computers to have good support for digital audio. However, less RAM and a small hard drive limited it when compared to today's heftier machines.

To get around these limitations, musicians and software developers created MOD. MOD files use digital samples as instruments that are then scored like MIDI files. Think of it as MIDI but you bring your own instruments (instead of relying on your sound cards built-in instruments). The samples can be of anything, an instrument, a vocal, even an entire chorus of a song. The samples are arranged in a way to create songs. Many of the samples are actually looping patterns (for example, a simple five second drum track endlessly looped). By varying the loops, adding various effects, and changing the pitch, .MOD files can create very interesting digital music.

The MOD format started with only four tracks available to it. As it moved from the Amiga to the PC, newer derivative formats (like .XM, .S3M and .IT) were spawned that supported more simultaneous tracks and effects. Sample sizes got bigger, and the format flourished in the PC game and graphic demo scene.

With MP3 and other digital audio formats, the need for .MOD files has somewhat faded but the format still lives on. There is a certain challenge about creating a good MOD song that fans of the format appreciate—and the format can still spawn incredible music in less than a megabyte of space.

.MOD files are written using a program called a **Tracker**. Trackers allow you to arrange samples into patterns and music—a technique itself called tracking. Once arranged the tracker writes all the samples and instructions about how to play them back to the .MOD file.

Depending on the amount of tracks you have, the effects you use, and the formats supported by your tracker of choice. Many people use the Impulse Tracker (**http://www.noisemusic.org/it/**). You can find much more information about MODs and tracking at United Trackers located on the Web at **http://www.united-trackers.org/**.

ASFS

The **ASFS (AudioSoft File Structure)** is a proprietary format that enables secure distribution of music. AudioSoft, found at **www.audiosoft.com**, makes the encoder and player available on its site. In 1998, however, AudioSoft also entered into an agreement with Nullsoft to make ASFS files playable using Winamp. The company operates a secure music distribution site and label known as CityMusic, where users can select from available tracks (**Figure 13.8**) in the ASFS format and download them (**www.citymusic.com**). At the time of this writing, Winamp hadn't yet supported the ASFS format. Nullsoft hopes to support it in a future release sometime in 1999.

Figure 13.8
The ASFS format by AudioSoft powers its own digital music label, CityMusic.

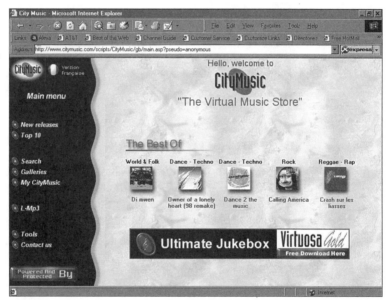

AT&T's A2B System

The first application was AT&T's downloadable music service, which is based on a modified version of MPEG-2 AAC. Unlike open MPEG files, however, A2B files are encrypted in order to protect copyrights. Thus, the final AAC stream is not MPEG-2–compliant.

Due to its proprietary nature, any music in the A2B format must be played using the A2B 2.0 player (**Figure 13.9**). The player is available on the A2B Web site (**www.a2bmusic.com**). The player lets you download and order songs secured in the A2B format.

Figure 13.9
The A2B 2.0 player is the only way to listen to audio tracks stored in A2B's secure AAC format.

Liquid Audio

Like A2B, Liquid Audio (**www.liquidaudio.com**) combines a known CODEC (also an AAC-based format) with a encryption system. The system prevents copying in order to create a secure format for distributing downloadable music over the Internet.

Also like A2B, you must have a proprietary player—the Liquid Music Player 4.0—to listen to the music (**Figure 13.10**). One cool thing about the program is that it lets you record the files to your recordable CD drive.

Figure 13.10
The Liquid Audio 4.0 player is the only way to listen to audio tracks stored in Liquid Audio's secure AAC format.

SDMI

SDMI (Secure Digital Music Initiative) is more of a movement than a format (**www.sdmi.org**). In response to the growing MP3 revolution, which much of the music industry is up in arms over, a group of labels and technology companies got together in February of 1999 to develop a standardized secure format for distributing digital music.

SDMI currently focuses on developing an initial framework for the initiative. The group has yet to even adopt any technology, although companies are proposing technologies to be used. The founding companies appointed Dr. Leonardo Chiariglione, a leading MPEG standards developer, as SDMI Executive Director. Meanwhile, companies such as Sony and IBM (which have been independently developing their own secure digital music distribution systems) are proposing that their technologies be considered as answers to the SDMI initiative.

The initiative's ultimate goal is to enable consumers to access music, but to make it difficult to easily copy or move the music into new forms or devices.

MSAudio 4.0

www.microsoft.com

At the time of this writing details were quickly forthcoming. MSAudio 4.0 is a proprietary compression system for digital music that has an optional security system for it enabled by Microsoft. In articles detailing the plans, Microsoft is building a backend system into Windows 2000 (the next version of Windows NT) that will be able to encrypt, manage, and track digital files. Part of the technology will come from Reciprocal, a company that Microsoft invested in during 1999. Reciprocal has developed a digital rights management system for copyright protection of digital content—including digital music.

The format is being built into an upcoming version of the Windows Media Player, which already supports MP3 (and will continue to despite this new format). The new player was released to the public in a beta form on April 14. The format creates files that are about half as big as that of a typical MP3 file. This is because the CODEC can encode 44.1KHz audio (CD Quality) at a bit rate of 64bps (MP3 requires 128bps for this level of sampling quality).

> **TIP**
>
> As of this writing, Winamp 2.11 includes support for playing back files encoded in the MSAudio 4.0 format.

To encode files into the format you can use Microsoft's free On Demand Producer or its Windows Media Encoder, which are both available at **http://www.microsoft.com/windows/windowsmedia/create.asp**. However, other leading edge sound editor/digitizer programs, such as Sonic Foundry's Sound Forge, are expected to offer support for the new CODEC soon.

If you want to encrypt and offer various sign-up fees or processes (instead of a fee you could solicit an email or demographic information), then you should check out the tools by Reciprocal (**www.reciprocal**) for rights management. Microsoft is also developing development wizards that will make it easy for you to set up the templates and other Web site pages needed to support the process.

While it's hard to tell whether this will be a replacement for MP3, most think that this is a technology Microsoft is trying to establish as its answer to the SDMI platform the record companies are working on. As pointed out, Sony, IBM, and AT&T are all trying to get their hardware and software to be part of the system. Microsoft has butted heads with the record companies before, most recently by including MP3 support in the Windows Media Player.

What About RealAudio?

No chapter about alternative formats would be complete without talking a bit about RealAudio and how it compares to MP3. RealAudio is the dominating force as a format for music and sound on the Internet. The format has pioneered streaming Internet media and beaten back other forms of streaming audio, including some MPEG variants and Microsoft's own ASF (Active Streaming Format). RealAudio can be quite clear and high fidelity in very high-end encoding situations, but this isn't its purpose—and MP3 remains superior for high fidelity playback.

TIP

If you're very interested in the CODEC options offered by RealAudio, check out the tables on Real's site that outline all the RealAudio CODEC in various versions of Real's player. This documentation is available at:

http://service.real.com/help/library/guides/production/htmfiles/audio.htm#12311

Of course, RealAudio excels in streaming and compression. The RealAudio CODEC is built to focus on degrading the sound file and arranging it in a way that maximizes quality while enabling high-end sound streaming. Like everything else on the Internet, it's a compromise meant to do one particular thing very well. While SHOUTcast has brought streaming to MP3 files, the ability to scale MP3 streams is not

Part IV   MP3 Radio and More

nearly as possible as it is with RealAudio. This is provided you are using Real's server systems. While you can stream Real files without using its backend server systems, the ability to have many simultaneous users, or offering content that matches the speed of each user's Internet connection, is limited. At the same time, there is the quality of the streaming. One article (see tip below) points out that at very low bit rates, RealAudio excels but others, particularly MP3 and Winamp fans, feel MP3 at 24bps and higher still has a better sound. Of course, while many feel that a streaming MP3 file is of superior sound quality to a RealAudio stream, you can only go through so many streams at one time on comparable hardware.

TIP

Read MP3 vs. VQF vs. RA-G2 by Panos Stokas available at **http://www.math.auth.gr/~axonis/studies/audio.htm** for an excellent background on the differences between MP3 and RealAudio.

Meanwhile, RealPlayer has morphed well beyond just supporting RealAudio and now includes video, MPEG formats, and as of this writing it had announced intention to support MP3. If you don't want to wait for Real to add MP3 playback to its RealPlayer, there is an easy way to do this now. Bitcasting.com has created an MP3 playback plug-in for the RealPlayer. Simply go to **www.bitcasting.com** and click on one of its MP3 demo files. The file will automatically force the RealPlayer G2 program to download the Bitcasting MP3 plug-in and then the demo file. Once it is downloaded you can play an MP3 file with RealPlayer. Just drag and drop an MP3 file onto the RealPlayer and it will begin playing.

Despite the addition of MP3 to the RealPlayer, true, MP3 fans will continue to use Winamp. This is because with its visualization and DSP plug-ins, Winamp rocks for the hardcore MP3 fan. However, RealPlayer, like that of Windows Media Player, should help expand the MP3 format to a wider audience.

Real isn't stopping with MP3 either. It recently announced plans to support IBM's new EMMS (Electronic Music Management System) initiative. This is IBM's encrypted music system that is similar in scope to the SDMI initiative and is slated to debut this fall with support from several major music labels.

To MP3 or Not to MP3.
Is That Even a Question?

It can be easily argued that the momentum behind the MP3 format should carry it past some superior-sounding formats or those featuring better compression. Standards, whether they are agreed upon or are adopted de facto because of their popularity, are not always the best technology. However, these standards are usually adopted because they are "good enough." As "good enough," these technologies tend to offer the best tradeoffs in terms of what is needed to make them popular. For example, MP3 is neither the best sounding format, nor is it the one with the best compression. It does, however, have the most available tools, runs on a wider range of hardware than do other formats. MP3 also doesn't tax your hardware as much and has the most content stored in its format. Those are important issues that will keep the MP3 format popular for years to come. As it becomes more popular, that popularity will feed upon itself, as they say success breeds success..

Yes, the MP3 format will fade in popularity at some point. The MP4/AAC format will most likely take over or perhaps MSAudio 4.0 will. As faster machines and the software that supports it grows, MP4's or MSAudio's benefits will be better accessible by the people who made the MP3 format a success. By all accounts, however, that time is far off, and with its modular support for various formats, your Winamp investment means you won't miss a beat.

14

MP3 and Winamp Programming Information

You've read almost everything there is about finding, using, making, and broadcasting MP3 files and using the Winamp application. What could possibly be left? How about programming? This chapter holds information for programmers who have an interest in programming. For those of you who aren't programmers, it might provide some interesting insight into the tools and software that are making MP3 tick.

Only after legions of programmers brought forth the many players, Winamp plug-ins, and encoding tools did even one major company—Microsoft—implement support for the MP3 format. It took Real Networks until early 1999 to support a format that had been widely jumped on by independent programmers as early as 1996.

In some ways this chapter is a homage to the hacker culture that has been critical to the rise of the MP3 format. You may have little interest in programming, but this chapter is interesting—you never know who might use this information to create your next favorite plug-in or add MP3 support to your favorite application.

Types of MP3 Programming

As it pertains to MP3 programming, there are five main areas programmers can concentrate on:

▶ **Creating Winamp plug-ins**—The Winamp player lets people construct all kinds of exciting plug-ins. These include **Visualization** plug-ins, which match graphical effects to the music; **DSP** plug-ins, which let you change the shape and sound of the digital waveform; **General** plug-ins, which let you extend the application itself; and **Input** plug-ins, which let you add support for new audio formats and control how the digital audio stream is sent out on the other end. Each plug-in has a mini SDK that Nullsoft has published.

▶ **Creating encoders**—To create an encoding program, you must learn how to convert a .WAV (or other format) into the MP3 format using the techniques developed by Fraunhofer. Be warned, though: Fraunhofer enforces its encoding patents. If you plan to make a commercial product, you will have to enter into a licensing agreement with Fraunhofer for your program.

▶ **Creating playback programs**—One would think Winamp would be enough, but it seems that someone creates a new player every week or so. Developing your own MP3 playback program can be a great process for the would-be programmer interested in learning more about MP3 and digital audio. There are several SDKs and free source programs available.

▶ **Using MP3 within applications**—Not every application that uses MP3 files needs to be a player. From games, to multimedia CD-ROM products, to sound editors, and more, there are many other programs that can benefit from using MP3 technology. Several SDKs for digital audio already support the MP3 format, so that programmers can utilize the format in a range of new applications.

▶ **Other MP3 utilities**—Not every MP3-focused application is one that plays music. Many programmers are creating interesting utilities for hard-core MP3 users. From the myriad of MP3-organizing programs, to programs that scour the Web for MP3 files, to ID3-editing tools, there is a wide range of interesting support utilities being contributed daily to the MP3 scene.

Constructing a Winamp Plug-In

There are four major plug-in types you can create for the Winamp player: Visualization, DSP, General purpose, and Input. You will find mini SDKs for each type on the Winamp site (**http://www.winamp.com/plugins/dev.html**).

All of the mini SDKs are constructed for use with Microsoft Visual C++ 4.0 or later. The project files included are for version 4.2, but with minor changes, they should work with 4.0 and later versions of Visual C++.

All Winamp plug-ins are 32-bit Windows .DLL files. They are to have one exported function, which varies with the type of plug-in. Visualization plug-ins export the symbol 'winampVisGetHeader'. DSP, General, and Input plug-ins all export similar functions. Plug-ins are named according to what type they are, such as vis_*.dll, dsp_*.dll, gen_*.dll, and in_*.dll.

Sample Code Available

There is quite a bit of source code out there for those interested in MP3 programming. There are code packages to suit any kind of programmer, from the publicly available code provided for education or open source purposes, to commercial quality SDKs. It's hard to imagine how many more MP3 players are needed, but being such a hot item, there are many programmers who want to mess around with things and learn more about the technology. In addition, MP3 playback is becoming a feature provided with many types of software from multimedia players, to portable playback devices, to other interesting applications of MP3 (such as Carrot Software's Virtual Turntables, a DJ-like mixing program).

Publicly Available Code

You might find many people out there floating various code snippets for MP3 decoding and playback, but two popular starting places are the original demonstration code provided by Fraunhofer and the open source Freeamp project.

Fraunhofer Example Code

Fraunhofer (**ftp://ftp.iis.fhg.de/pub/layer3/public_c/**) has made available some source code located on its FTP site. The disclaimer on the link that leads to this directory says: "This code has been written mainly for explanation purposes, so do not expect too much performance." For the beginner, this basic, from the roots, code should prove interesting.

Freeamp

The Freeamp project (**www.freeamp.org**) is an effort to make an open source player that has a medium set of features (as opposed to Winamp's more robust feature set). As an open source player, all the code is available to the public for modifying and extending the Freeamp code base as long as developed code is then given back to the community. The Freeamp Web site has code for both the Windows 32-bit and Linux versions of the project. The site also has documentation set up, with more coming online every month.

X11 Amp

X11 Amp is another Linux player (**http://www.x11amp.org/**). This one, however, isn't being developed under the open source model. It does provide source code for the player, which is an attempt by the programmers to create a Linux MP3 player modeled after an earlier version of Winamp.

mp3asm

Developed by Oliver Fromme, this Linux program is designed to analyze MP3 audio files, as well as find and fix errors that can occur in them (**http://dorifer.heim3.tu-clausthal.de/~olli/mpg123/mp3asm.html**). It can also cut and reassemble MP3 files. While the program is not full featured and is in its alpha stage at the time of this writing, there is code here to play around with.

mpg123

mpg123 is a popular MPEG-decoding engine that supports Layers 1, 2, and 3. The source is available and there is wide porting to multiple platforms including Linux, FreeBSD, NetBSD, SunOS, Solaris, IRIX, and HP-UX. Check these pages to find out more: **http://www-ti.informatik. uni-tuebingen.de/~hippm/mpg123.html** and **http://dorifer.heim3. tu-clausthal.de/~olli/mpg123/**.

MP3 for Applications

Commercially oriented programs have a couple of strong choices to use for including MP3 support in their applications. There is not only a complete SDK and sample code in both cases, but both companies have developed licensing programs that make sure you're legally compliant with all the patents and licensing issues for utilizing MP3 technology in your application.

Miles Sound System

Game and other multimedia programmers looking to use MP3 files in their software can now turn to Rad Game Tools Miles Sound System, whose version 5.0 has support for MP3 playback (**www.radgametools.com**).

With Miles 5.0, Rad has arranged through Fraunhofer and Thomson multimedia to provide a legally redistributable MP3 decoder for no extra cost to developers. Developers still have to sign an extra MPEG license addendum. This, among other minor things, requires you to add a credit to Fraunhofer and Thomson in your game.

MP3 support is also used by Rad for the .DLS format, which stores various instruments in a digital format for mixing and playback within programs. The Miles Sound System 5.0 SDK lets you compress specific instruments within a .DLS file using the MP3 compression method. This makes .DLS files even smaller, and that means more music on a single CD.

While faster processors mean fewer problems decompressing an MP3 file, Miles tries to alleviate trouble as much as possible. The SDK allows you to pre-decompress MP3 data, for example. This avoids tying up the CPU when performance issues are critical. If, however, memory is critical and CPU performance isn't important, you can decompress all of the MP3 files on the fly.

Xaudio MP3 SDKs

For professional purposes, Xaudio is perhaps the leading company for a broad range of MP3 playback engines (**www.xaudio.com**). They have ported its Xaudio SDK engine to numerous platforms (**Table 14.1**), which makes it a good choice for developers working on applications that will run across numerous platforms. Xaudio's toolset has been used to drive MP3 applications for Diamond's Rio, Carrot's Virtual Turntables, and MP3CD (a hardware system for playing back MP3s as part of a stereo system).

The SDKs are free to use for personal purposes, but commercially oriented products require a licensing fee to MPEGtv, the creators of the Xaudio SDK. Licenses can be negotiated directly with the company.

Table 14.1–Details on the Xaudio MP3 Playback Engine SDKs

Platform	Languages	Other Notes
Windows 95/98/NT	C/C++, Delphi, Visual Basic	N/A
Windows CE	C/C++	Sources for MIPS, SH3, ARM, and x86em
Linux	Glibc, libc5	Glibc is for Redhat 5.X and later, Denian 2.X and later. libc5 is for Redhat 4.X and later that do not use Glibc. Versions available for x86, PowerPC, Alpha, ARM, and Sparc
FreeBSD	C/C++	x86 platform
Solaris	2.5/2.6	Available for x86 and Sparc versions
IRIX	6.X	Separate version for Irix 5.3 or earlier
SCO Openserver	C/C++	X86 platform
IBM AIX	C/C++	PowerPC platform
Digital Unix	C/C++	Alpha platform

Part IV MP3 Radio and More

Fraunhofer Commercial Tools

Fraunhofer does make commercial tools for MP3 technology, but they are only available from marketing partner Opticom (**www.opticom.de**). No set package is available from its site; you must contact Opticom directly for information regarding its Fraunhofer OEM software kits for Developers and Manufacturers.

Testing Your Software

Fraunhofer developed and posted some sample files designed to help verify that your MPEG decoder works. These **conformance bitstreams** are those used as official test bitstreams by the MPEG committee. You can find these streams at **ftp://ftp.fhg.de/pub/layer3/**.

ID3 Tags: File Managers and Editors

As related in Chapter 2, "Inside the MP3 Format and Players," MP3 files accompany meta-information that is attached to the MP3 file (which includes information about the MP3 file such as artist, genre type, etc.). This information is known more commonly as **ID3 tags**. ID3 tags are supported widely in the 1.1 format. That format, however, is still pretty limiting. Martin Nilsson is developing an ID3v2 proposed standard. It is getting off to a good start, but support for ID3v2 is not widespread.

Programmers have created, with ID3 tags, a number of tools that help users organize, edit, and track their collections of MP3 files. Many even support features such as creating Winamp playlists and more. To program your own special MP3 file manager, you must need to know how to work with ID3 tags.

The overall structure of the ID3v1.1 tag is exactly 128 bytes and is located at the very end of the audio data. All you have to do is read the last 128 bytes of any compliant MP3 file. The byte order is shown in Table 14.2.

With that information, you can do any number of things to create databases, file managers, and other utilities for handling, organizing, and labeling MP3 files.

Byte Position	Total Byte Length	Tag Field
(0–2)	3	Tag identification. Must contain text 'TAG' to notify that a compliant ID3v1.1 tag
(3–32)	30	Title
(33–62)	30	Artist
(63–92)	30	Album
(93–96)	4	Year
(97–126)	30	Comments
(127)	1	Genre

Table 14.2–ID3v1.1–Byte Order

Part IV MP3 Radio and More

Null characters (ASCII 0) are used as placeholders for bytes not used within the tag. However, not all applications use the null character. Winamp uses a space character to pad its ID3v1.1 tags.

There is a complete specification published on the **www.id3.org** Web site for ID3v2. This includes the informal 2.0 standard, a development document, and ID3 Library with source code and documentation. Contributors have so far created versions for Windows (both Borland and Microsoft compiler implementations), Macintosh, and Linux. You can also find example tags.

Info on Patents and Licensing Issues

Remember that while MP3 is a standard adopted by the MPEG committee, it is not completely free and open. Fraunhofer has the right to patent and then license the work, which it has done with partners Thomson and Opticom. In fact, Fraunhofer recently sent a letter to many developers regarding free encoders that they had developed based on the ISO source that Fraunhofer had made available, which demanded royalties for various software products based on its patents.

According to available licensing information, developers currently using the ISO source code can do so at no charge as long as it is not compiled and distributed in binary form. Fraunhofer is not yet going after any decoder tools provided free of charge, although it's unclear whether its patents cover decoding issues.

The letter sent to developers sets a price of $1.00 per commercial unit sold of decoding software; this would apply if the patents are covered. Fraunhofer is asking for a reported royalty of $2.00 per unit for hardware decoders. Encoders definitely require a payment, although it's unclear what the cost is. While pricing starts at $25 per encoder, it drops based on volume.

Licensing has been through three main entities with Fraunhofer; its partner, Opticom, handles most of the software-oriented licenses. Addresses are as follows:

Fraunhofer IIS
layer3@iis.fhg.de

Am Weichselgarten 3
D-91058 Erlangen
Germany

Opticom GmbH
info@opticom.de
Am Weichselgarten 7
D-91058 Erlangen
Germany

Thomson Multimedia has made available a ten-page .PDF document (**http://www.mpeg.org/MPEG/mp3-licensing-faq.pdf**), which includes additional information on the entire situation. Pricing seems a bit high given that many professional encoders and other tools sell for less. It's clear that volumes and negotiated pricing can result in a lower price per unit.

In addition to its claims on patents and royalty pricing for software that encodes and decodes MP3 files, Fraunhofer is also trying to charge a royalty on any MP3-formatted files that are sold. The price is .01, or 1% of the file's cost.

The entire licensing issue for MP3 software and files is unclear. The law, while perhaps favoring Fraunhofer, isn't necessarily enforceable. Even if they can enforce its rightful patents, it's hard to say if its pricing is very smart for the business because content providers usually switch to other royalty-free formats if forced to pay royalties.

Thus while there are lots of numbers publicly being thrown around as MP3 spreads, we expect licensing arrangements and rules to become more inline with the overall prevalence of the technology. Despite this optimistic assessment, serious MP3 software developers will want to cover themselves and make sure they're working to comply with what are essentially fairly enforceable patents.

More MP3 Interesting Technology and Programming Resources

Looking for more MP3 technical information? Lots exist, but it's scattered throughout the Web. The following links should prove useful and interesting to those of you trying to get under the hood of MP3-related technologies.

MPEG.ORG

The unofficial home of the overall MPEG technology, run by MPEGtv (the creators of the Xaudio SDK and players), can be found at **http://www.mpeg.org/**. The site includes continuously updated links and technical information.

Good Information on MP3 Frame Header Information

Every MP3 file is composed of smaller sections known as frames. Each frame has its own information. To learn more about the precise structure and nature of MP3 frames, see **http://www.multimania.com/bouvigne/mp3tech/frame_header.html.**

Original Patents for MP3 Layer-3 Technology

IBM's patent server is an incredible resource. With these two links you can retrieve and read the original patent filings and documentation made by Fraunhofer concerning the MP3 format: **http://www.patents.ibm.com/cgi-bin/viewpat.cmd/5742735** and **http://www.patents.ibm.com/details/patent_number=5579430**.

Bring the Power

If it weren't for independent and inventive programmers, the MP3 format would not resemble what it is today. MP3 exists in as many shapes and sizes because a large community of programmers want the power of a strong digital audio format. Armed with the available free and commercial code, and many of the resources outlined in this chapter, you too can be a part of this revolution.

It's one thing to take in the power of MP3 by being a listener and user of the products and files. It's a totally different kind of power—power you bring to the legions of MP3 users—if you develop the next interesting tool or plug-in. Doing so will make MP3 just that much more amazing.

Jeff Myers, along with Tom Hubina, wrote Spectrum 3D Pro (**Figure 14.1**) a 3D plug-in that visualizes the audio spectrum produced by Winamp. You can find the plug-in and source on the CD-ROM that comes with this book. We talked to Jeff to get a deeper perspective on Winamp plug-in programming.

Figure 14.1
Spectrum 3D Pro
Visualization plug-in
(courtesy of Jeff Myers).

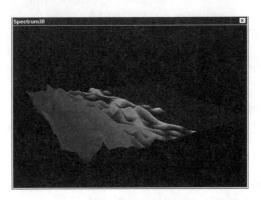

Interview:

Jeff Myers

Q *When did you discover Winamp and what motivated you to create a plug-in?*

A: I found Winamp one day a long time ago (at least a year ago) when our MIS guy showed us MPEGs and how we could play them on our PCs. I remember we were using some really early betas, before there was even plug-in support. When support for plug-ins was released, I was naturally interested in the Visualization plug-ins. We work for a software company making CAD/CAM software and had just done some initial research into OpenGL and 3D acceleration. I thought it would be really neat to see a "3D" visualization of music data.

Q *How did you create your first plug-in?*

A: While searching around one day I saw some Visualization plug-ins that did wireframe 3D visualizations of Winamp data. I showed these to my roommate, and we thought, "Hell, we can do better then that." So we got all the code on plug-ins we could find and busted one out.

Q How long did it take?

A: The first version took about three hours to make. It just did a basic 3D visualization. Over the next few weeks we just added different features that people requested.

Q Have you thought of creating other types of plug-ins?

A: We have thought of making the Vis plug-in into kind of a game where you control some kind of player or craft that interacts with the Vis data. I would also like to make a Winamp plug-in that allows control for Winamp over the Web, for SHOUTcast Servers.

Q What level of programmer does it take to create a cool Visualization plug-in?

A: Well, you should have some level of experience with C and Windows. The plug-in architecture that Winamp uses relies heavily on callbacks and the DLL features found in Windows 95/98 and Windows NT. If you're doing a 3D Visualization plug-in, I would also recommend having some knowledge of general 3D graphics programming, and whatever 3d API that you plan on using (OpenGL, Direct3D, Glide, etc.). The sample plug-ins will show you what is being done, but it helps to know why they are doing it.

Q What are the basic step-by-steps for creating a plug-in for Winamp?

A: [These steps are as follows:]

1. Figure out what you want the plug-in to do. I cannot stress how important planing is. Winamp will do the job of giving you the waveform and spectrum data for each visualization frame, but it's up to you to know what to do with it. Map out what you want everything to do, it really helps when you're in the middle of the development cycle to have something that shows the global direction of the project. I have seen way too many projects fail due to a lack of planing.

2. Create the basic functionality first. Get the visualization window set up the way you want it. Leave the other callbacks stubbed out initially until you have the main part of the plug-in stable. Then go back and add in the rest.

3. Create a configuration dialog box. People like to have settings, I don't know why, but they just do. Maybe it has to with being in control of your environment, or something. If there is even the remotest possibility that you could have the user set some preferences in your plug-in, let them do it. It will make your plug-in appeal to a much broader audience.

4. Test, test, test. Test your plug-in on as many different machines with as many different configurations as you can find. You will find bugs this way. Try different versions of Winamp; they do different things with plug-ins. If you find that there is a problem and can't fix it, be sure to document it.

Q *Do you have any tips for people thinking about creating their own plug-ins?*

A: Be aware that people will be running your plug-in on a wide variety of hardware configurations. One problem we had was that some people were complaining that the configuration dialog [box] had no "OK," "Cancel," and "Apply" buttons. I know that I put them in there, and we couldn't figure out why these people weren't getting it. It eventually turned out that they had their display size set to 640×480 and the dialog [box] was being clipped by the bottom of the screen. We run at much higher resolutions here, so we never saw the problem.

It also helps to look at other people's plug-in code. This will give you a basis for where to start, and an example of what works.

Q *What are some of your favorite plug-ins and why?*

A: Winamp Speakers v2.0 Beta 1: I just think they look cool, and found it a very original idea. SHOUTcast: Internet radio, ohhh yeah. We have one at work and we love it.

Q *What are some plug-ins you'd like to see?*

A: Internet control over playlists. I would like to see web controlled jukeboxes running over SHOUTcast Servers.

Q *Any other thoughts?*

A: Support Winamp by developing plug-ins, and registering your Winamp.

Part V
Appendices

Appendix A
All About Virtual Turntables

DJ can mean a lot of things, but in the case of this appendix, we're talking about DJs who mix it up in clubs with turntables. If you've ever dreamed of being the next Paul Oakenfeld, DJ Spooky, or DJ Red Alert, then you've come to the right place.

Many people in the MP3 movement are fans of electronica, hip hop, club, house, acid, and every other form of techno music. It's no wonder, then, that some of the programmers out there have created specific programs that might be of interest to those people who want to put MP3s into the mix. This appendix looks at two neat tools that exist for the professional DJ and wannabe DJ who want to use MP3-based music.

PitchFork

PitchFork (**Figure A.1**) by Leif Claesson is a Winamp plug-in that lets you **pitchshift** (that is, increase or decrease the speed, and pitch of the song to match that of another) and nudge a song position so you can sync up two different MP3 streams in real time for classic DJ beatmixing. You can download the plug-in from Winamp.com's Plug-Ins page or directly from **mp3stocker.tsx.org**.

Figure A.1
PitchFork is a Winamp plug-in that allows you to do classic DJ beatmixing with two MP3 streams being played back by Winamp.

To use PitchFork, Leif "Liket" Claesson, recommends having two sound cards and a mixer table. This will allow you to use it to its peak ability. Then set up two instances of Winamp, each feeding into the mixer that

Part V Appendices

lets you set the output to either card. PitchFork lets you adjust the feed of the MP3s coming out so that you can sync them up together to the same beat. This is accomplished by changing the pitch of one song to fit the pitch of another. Once one song is synced via its pitch, you can then use PitchFork's nudge controls to sync the actual set of beats. You can use the mixer from the two cards to shift between channels and generally cut it up.

According to PitchFork's documentation you need a somewhat speedy computer that can decompress two simultaneous streams. (Claesson says that he's had good results on a K6-2 300 or better machine.) You also have to configure Winamp specially. First you need to disable the buffering in Winamp. This is accomplished by going to the WaveOut plug-in configuration and setting the buffer length slider to 0. You should also set the thread priority to Maximum. On the Nullsoft Nitrane Preferences dialog box, make sure that Decode Thread Priority is set to Highest on the General tab. Claesson also recommends making sure you are using the best graphics drivers on your system. This reduces interference from display adapter issues, which can cause Winamp to skip.

PitchFork is fairly self-explanatory once you have the setup in place. The program lets you adjust a song's pitch by sliding it up or down using the pitch slider, which is on the left side of the program. A variety of buttons lets you also nudge the pitch into place for your liking. You have to do this by listening via headphones in one ear while the speakers blare the song currently fed to them. Press the equal sign (=) button when you have the pitch in place. That locks things into place. The documentation notes as a rule of thumb that the songs are incompatible if you have to slide the pitch higher than 8% or lower than -4%.

Once the beat is synced, you need to get the beats hitting together at the same time. They may be hitting at the same rate but not hitting at the same time. Using the nudge buttons located in the lower-left corner, you can eventually nudge the two beats together. As PitchFork's documentation says, "Doing that by ear is supposedly easy for an experienced DJ," but novices will need a good amount of practice to do it right.

PitchFork offers a cueing feature to help with this. The cueing feature in PitchFork lets you set the position of one song a second earlier and then pauses at just the right time. That allows you to wait until you hear the other song in place and then press the Cue button. This can help drastically reduce the time it takes to synchronize beats.

Complete documentation and explanations of how to set cues in memory and use the nudge controls can be found in the documentation file that comes with PitchFork.

NOTE

Check out AudioStocker Pro, another application by Claesson. This Winamp plug-in lets you control the volume of songs that are played by Winamp. The overall song-to-song volume is controlled, which avoids that nasty instance where the volume seems to jump up or down depending on the normalization of each MP3 file itself. AudioStocker Pro is compatible with SHOUTcast and PitchFork and is available on Claesson's Web site.

TIP

If you want to run more than one plug-in at a time in an effort to run the SHOUTcast DSP plug-in and PitchFork, you need the MuchFX^2 plug-in. This plug-in allows you to run multiple Winamp plug-ins at the same time.

Virtual Turntables

Unlike PitchFork, Virtual Turntables is not a plug-in for Winamp. Instead, Virtual Turntables is a complete standalone DJ mixing program that includes support for MP3 files (**Figure A.2**). It can be found at **http://carrot.prohosting.com/**.

Figure A.2
Virtual Turntables by Carrot Innovations is a completely self-contained MP3 DJ mixing console.

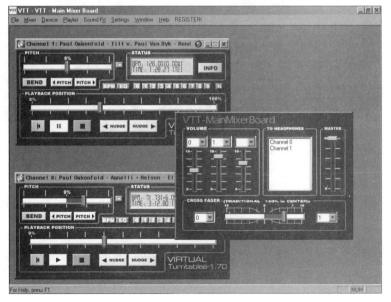

The program lets you set up two complete MP3 streams (or .WAV files) and allows you work with them to first pitch them into place and then to nudge the beats into place. With PitchFork you must have two sound cards and a mixer to be able to crossfade the streams together. Virtual Turntables includes a virtual mixer console that lets you control all the

Part V Appendices

mixing of the two streams within the computer. The means you can avoid the need for an outside mixer. The downside to this is that streams aren't separate; you can't listen in your headphones to one while the other goes out to speakers. You also don't have visualization and the other features Winamp offers while using PitchFork.

Virtual Turntables lets you sync the tempo of each song by calculating their beats per minute and then letting the program calculate the best BPM sync. You can save the BPM characteristics to a file so that doing so becomes even easier later on. BPM is set by bringing up a BPM calculator (**Figure A.3**) that lets you tap the beat on your keyboard; this determines its setting. You can also enter it manually. Finally, you can use the pitchshifters located on each playback console to set things in place.

Figure A.3

A nifty beats per minute calculator lets you figure out the BPM of any song and then calculate it to match another song's BPM.

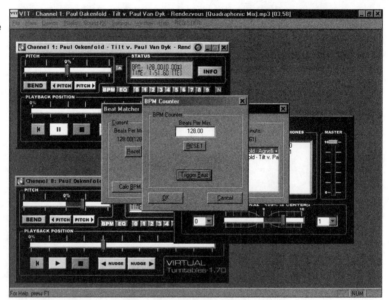

Once BPM is matched via pitch, use the forward and backward nudge keys to sync the beats to hit together. Then you're off to the races using the crossfader.

Virtual Turntables doesn't just stop at normal beatmixing. The program has a host of other features, including support for DSP effects, skins, an equalizer, and sound effects that can be mapped to keys.

The program also includes excellent documentation via its help file and Web site. The help file contains a complete step-by-step tutorial and the download includes sample tutorial files.

Virtual Turntables is shareware. If it is unregistered, it will stop working after 20 minutes of initial use. You can order the fully registered version for $32.00 from Carrot Innovations. If you want to order an optional specialized headphone jack for your sound card (to be used for queuing up the next song), it costs an additional $12.00.

Appendix B
Alternatives to SHOUTcast

While SHOUTcast is certainly becoming a favorite of MP3 fans for creating Internet radio stations, there are other alternatives worth knowing about. Some of these products offer some interesting features that may work for certain situations.

Fluid Streaming Server

Subside Radio, a Swedish-based upstart Internet record company, is offering an MP3 streaming server called Fluid, which is available for download at the Subside Web site (**www.subside.com**). The server is written in Pure Java, which allows it to run on any system that has a virtual machine installed. The server allows you to do the following:

▶ Transmit an MP3 stream from a predefined playlist.

▶ Relay a stream from another server, creating a network of servers.

▶ Relay and scale radio streams by setting the server to listen to a port for an incoming stream and broadcast that stream.

▶ Use telnet to connect to the server and get information about connected clients and current song playing.Subside uses the server on its own site to broadcast its own tunes. A separate applet lets you display the song title and other information on your server. However, Fluid requires you to re-encode your MP3s into the bit rate you intend to broadcast in. Configuration is handled through three text files that set port information, playlist information, and other server features. Upgrades call for a graphical administration interface and better log file support.

Part V   Appendices

Icecast

Icecast, created by three college students (Jack Moffit, Barath Raghavan, and Alexander Havãng) is an MP3 streaming server that is being developed as an open source project and distributed freely under the GNU General Public License. Icecast (**www.icecast.org**) allows transmission of MP3 streams that can be listened to with a standard MP3 player on almost any platform. The product runs on various flavors of Unix, but is being developed on Linux 2.2. A Java version and versions for OS/2 and BeOS are also reportedly under development. There are three main components to the server system:

▶ **Shout and LiveIce**—Shout is a program that provides streaming of MP3 files to Icecast. LiveIce is a live streaming program that allows input either from your sound card's line in or from MP3 files to be mixed, re-encoded, and streamed to an Icecast server. You can use LiveIce with a microphone to create live audio broadcasts. You can also use an MP3 playlist and the multi-channel support to adjust speed and volumes, mix between the two channels, and then re-encode the data at a lower bit rate to be sent out to an Icecast server.

▶ **Icedir**—Icedir is a directory service that provides a listing of Icecast servers and can maintain a list of current broadcasts. This allows other broadcasters to list their broadcasts through your Icedir directory server.

Icedir is designed for Apache-based servers running MySQL (**mysql.org**) for a database and PHP (**www.php.net**) for the scripting. These programs are freely available on their respective sites. Icedir can be installed with those two programs in place. There is complete documentation in the Icedir distribution.

To run the server you must download and compile Icecast on your system. You must then send to the server an audio stream from an encoder program. This can be pre-encoded files or audio streams from Winamp. There isn't an easy way to currently have an encoder that can re-encode files at a lower bit rate on the fly; SHOUTcast does this using Microsoft's MP3 CODECs and the SHOUTcast DSP plug-in for Winamp. The developers behind Icecast hope to overcome this drawback in time.

You can listen to Icecast streams with Winamp or any player that supports streaming MP3 files. According to its creators, Icecast is compatible with Nullsoft's SHOUTcast. You can use Icecast with Nullsoft's directory server, and you can use Iceplay to send streams to SHOUTcast servers.

LiveAudio

LiveAudio by Ipp-Soft (GmbH) is another MP3 server product that offers real-time MP3 encoding. There are two versions of the LiveAudio system—Advanced and Professional; they are found at **www.liveaudio.de/eng/**. The Advanced version allows a live encoding of a MPEG Layer-3 stream up to a 56bps bitrate, depending on your computing power. The Professional version of the software can stream 44kHz music using a 128bps bitrate.

Xing MP3 Server

Xing's MP3 Encoder, found at **www.xingtech.com**, is an outgrowth of its work constructing MPEG-based streaming servers. The StreamWorks MP3 Server streams MP3s like SHOUTcast, via a TCP/IP stream. The server is free for you to use and is available for Windows 95/NT and Linux. Xing Technology's server also has a live audio component—the MP3Live! Encoder—which lets you encode and broadcast a stream in real time.

What's Real Up To?

Real networks has been one of the pioneers of Internet broadcasting. Its RealServer product is used by thousands of customers world-wide to stream audio and video to millions of users. Real even makes a basic server available for free that can support up to 60 streams at a time.

However, Real hasn't done nearly as much to promote and promulgate the personal radio station revolution like SHOUTcast has. At the same time, Real hadn't been pushing the MP3 format much in its efforts. Its own RealAudio CODEC is good and popular, but clearly the MP3 format has caught fire.

In April of 1999, a new strategy seemed to emerge from Real: They purchased Xing, which has grown to become a key tool and server developer in the MP3 scene. Using Xing's tools and add support to its products for the creation and distribution of MP3, Real seems to be picking up steam.

Digital Bitcasting Corp. (**www.bitcasting.com**) has already shipped a MP3 plug-in for the RealPlayer G2. It also has server side software to add to the RealServer product to enable MP3 broadcasting. Still the ease of use for using RealServer as a substitute for SHOUTcast or Icecast isn't there.

It may be that this company does a better job orientating itself on the personal broadcasting revolution, but unless you have specific needs for high-end multi-user streaming, then SHOUTcast remains a better and easier alternative.

What About MSAudio 4.0 Streaming?

With MSAudio 4.0 you have a couple of options for streaming. One would be to use Winamp 2.11+ and the SHOUTcast DSP plug-in to covert any MSAudio 4.0 file to the MP3 format that SHOUTcast uses. In this capacity, Winamp does the same thing with SHOUTcast that it does with other file types you broadcast out using SHOUTcast. So for SHOUTcast operators, this isn't much of a big deal.

If you prefer to set up a radio station using Microsoft's offerings you're in a different ballpark. Microsoft's streaming server software for Windows is an NT-server based product that runs on top of Internet Information Server 4.0+. It's not much of an alternative to SHOUTcast unless you specifically want to work with the MSAudio 4.0 CODEC. Be sure to make use of some of the content-protection elements that the new MSAudio 4.0 server-system is offering (see Chapter 13, "Alternative Formats to MP3," for more information).

Appendix C
MP3 for Your Car

The spirit of MP3 fans is that of taking control of their music. While anyone can listen to MP3s on their computer and anyone with a spare $200.00 can go mobile with the Rio, not everyone can hit the highway with the top down and MP3's blasting. Not yet, anyway.

Empeg is hustling to become the first company to release an MP3 player for your vehicle, but many individuals and small groups aren't waiting— they're doing it themselves.

Empeg Car

With its Rio player, Diamond Multimedia has allowed MP3 users to wander away from their computers with MP3s in hand. The next step is moving the MP3 experience from the sidewalk to the freeway. Many individuals have equipped their vehicles with MP3 players of varying size and capability. Empeg is attempting to become the first company to ship an MP3 player for your car.

Empeg Car, which runs on the Linux operating system and is powered by a 200MHz StrongARM processor, was initially scheduled to ship by the end of January 1999. As of April, Empeg Car had yet to be released. When Empeg Car—complete with display, car mount, remote control, cables, and download software—finally reaches stores, it will carry a price tag of roughly $1,000.00. The removable unit includes an FM radio receiver. With a 2.1GB capacity to store up to 35 hours of music, it should be sufficient for even the longest of road trips. You can categorize tunes with the supplied PC-link software and play the music that you like whenever you want it.

To get sound out of the unit, you need to hook it up to an amp; either a dedicated car audio amp or the auxiliary input on another head unit will do. When linked to your PC, you can download music via the Empeg Car's serial port or USB port.

The Windows software allows you to view, add, delete, and categorize tracks. Once in the car, you control the player using a credit card-sized remote control. You can play your music using random playlists, year playlists, mood playlists, artist playlists, and so on.

Empeg says it expects the software to evolve from user suggestions. Upgrades will be free and downloadable from the Web site. As standards change, Empeg says it intends to support them using its hardware: CODECs for other compression methods such as MPEG AAC will be made available, although these may be chargeable upgrades dependent on licensing issues.

The PC software is Windows 95/98-based. (You'll need Windows 98 or NT 5.0 and a machine with a USB port to use the USB connection.) If you can't use USB, the serial link works with almost any machine, but you still need Windows 95 or NT.

For updates on Empeg Car, visit **www.empeg.com**.

GreenGroup's MP3Case

The MP3Case car player is a system fed with an overclocked Pentium 133 with 32MB of RAM and a SoundBlaster 16 sound card. It is commanded from a keypad and an infrared remote control. The audio signal is processed through technology from Alpine electronics. The performance and sound quality is improved by a "black box" allocated in the nearest position to the main musical source, an Alpine CTA-1505R.

For more information, visit **http://members.xoom.com/MPCASE/welcome.htm**.

Do It Yourselfers

MP3car.com (**www.mp3car.com**) is a Web site dedicated to MP3 devices, including complete units for your car. Many of the DIY crowd use Linux. Linux is often used by these people for several reasons (you don't want to stop your car to reboot all the time do you?). For one thing, it's a very crash-proof operating system. Second, many of the homebrew MP3 community are also fans of Linux, which itself is a key part of the homebrewed computer revolution. Finally Linux is a free to use operating system, while a new copy of Windows 98 or NT will set you back $125 or more. If you want to find out how different individuals have MP3-equipped their vehicles, visit **MP3Car.com** or the following sites:

► MPChevy—**http://afrosquad.com/mpchevy.html**—A relatively simple, $500.00 setup.

► Smilk's MP3Car site—**www.carplayer.com**—You can order the plans for this $325.00 player for $20.00. You can also order software and cases.

► Ryan's Car MP3—**http://www.ryanspc.com/carmp3/**—Ryan Veety's site gives you all the ingredients of his $375.00 player. He was able to keep the price down by using items he already had. Ryan was even featured in *Wired.com*.

LCD Output Interfaces

MP3 On Demand

MP3 On Demand is a wired remote control device that controls MP3 decoding software on any Pentium computer. Originally designed as a head unit for an automobile system, the small size ($8 \times 3 \times 1$ 3/8 inches) lends itself to home use. It costs $299.00.

Production units are made of black plastic with a gray lens and buttons. For $299.00 you get the control unit, cables, AC adapter, and software with free updates until the next full release.

For more information, visit **www.mp3ondemand.com**.

Interface Controllers

Irman

Produced by Evation.com, Irman is a small ($3 \times 2 \times 1$ inches), inexpensive ($35.00) device that allows you to control your PC with the remote from your TV, VCR, CD player, or stereo. It's specially used to control Winamp from anywhere in the room. The Winamp plug-in allows you to define exactly which keys on your remote you want to use for Winamp. Evation.com says this hardware has been successfully tested with more than 40 different brands of remotes.

Irman can receive the infrared signals transmitted by numerous types of remotes. It converts these signals to computer commands understood by software in your PC.

For more information, visit **www.evation.com/irman/**.

Appendix D
Winamp Shortcut Keys

Main Winamp Console Shortcuts Only

Shortcut Key	Action
F1	About box
Ctrl+A	Toggle always-on-top (all but Playlist Editor)
Ctrl+Alt+A	Toggle always-on-top (Playlist Editor)
Ctrl+D	Toggle Doublesize mode
Ctrl+E	Toggle Easymove
Ctrl+T	Toggle Time Display mode
Alt+W	Toggle main window
Alt+E	Toggle Playlist Editor
Alt+G	Toggle Graphical Equalizer
Alt+T	Toggle Minibrowser
Ctrl+Tab	Cycle through different Winamp windows
Alt+S	Go to Skin Selection dialog box
Ctrl+P	Go to Preferences
Alt+F	Jump to Main menu
Alt+K	Configure current Visualization plug-in
Ctrl+Shift+K	Start/stop current Visualization plug-in
Ctrl+K	Open Visualization tab of Preferences
Ctrl+J	Jump to time in current track
J or Keypad	Open Jump-to-file in Playlist dialog box

Main Winamp Console Shortcuts Only

Shortcut Key	Action
Ctrl+Alt+N	Spawn new Winamp instance
R	Toggle Repeat
S	Toggle Shuffle
Ctrl+W	Toggle Windowshade mode
Alt+3	Current File info box/ID3 Editor
X or Keypad 5	Play/Restart/Unpause
V	Stop
Shift+V	Stop with Fadeout
C	Pause/Unpause
B or Keypad 6	Next Track
Z or Keypad 4	Previous Track
Keypad 1	Jump ten songs back in playlist
Keypad 3	Jump ten songs forward in playlist
Left Arrow or Keypad 7	Rewind five seconds
Keypad 9 or Right Arrow	Fast-forward five seconds
L or Keypad 0	Open/Play File
Ctrl+L or Ctrl+Keypad 0	Open/Play Location
Shift+L or Insert	Open/Play Directory
Keypad 8 or Up Arrow	Volume up
Down Arrow or Keypad 2	Volume down

Playlist Editor Keyboard Shortcuts Only

Shortcut Key	Action
R	Toggle Repeat
S	Toggle Shuffle

File I/O-Related

Shortcut Key	Action
L or Keypad 0	Add file
Ctrl+L or Ctrl+Keypad 0	Add location
Shift+L or Insert	Add directory
Ctrl+N	New (Clear) playlist
Ctrl+O	Open (Load) playlist
Ctrl+S	Save playlist
Alt+3	View/Edit track info for selected track(s)
Ctrl+E	Edit selected track file name(s)

Playlist Manipulation-Related

Shortcut Key	Action
Ctrl+A	Select all
Ctrl+I	Invert selection
Delete	Remove selected files from playlist
Ctrl+Delete	Crop playlist
Ctrl+Shift+Delete	Clear playlist (same as Ctrl+O)
Alt+Down Arrow	Move selected files down
Alt+Up Arrow	Move selected files up
Down Arrow	Move cursor down
Up Arrow	Move cursor up
Enter	Play selected file
End	Jump to end of Playlist
Home	Jump to start of Playlist
Page Up	Move up by a fifth of a page

Page Down	Move down by a fifth of a page
Alt+Delete	Remove dead (non-existent) files

Playlist Sorting-Related

Ctrl+Shift+1	Sort playlist by title
Ctrl+Shift+2	Sort playlist by file name
Ctrl+Shift+3	Sort playlist by file path and name
Ctrl+R	Reverse playlist
Ctrl+Shift+R	Randomize playlist

Playback Controls on Playlist

X or Keypad 5	Play/Restart/Unpause
V	Stop
Shift+V	Stop with fadeout
C	Pause/Unpause
B or Keypad 6	Next track
Z or Keypad 4	Previous track
Keypad 1	Jump ten songs back
Keypad 3	Jump ten songs forward
Left Arrow or Keypad 7	Rewind five seconds
Keypad 9 or Right Arrow	Fast-forward five seconds
Ctrl+F4	Close (hide) Playlist Editor

Part V Appendices

Graphical Equalizer Keyboard Shortcuts Only

Shortcut Key	Action
1 - 0	Increase EQ bands
Q - P	Decrease EQ bands
`	Increase EQ preamp
Tab	Decrease EQ preamp
N	Toggle EQ
S	Open Presets menu
A	Toggle EQ auto-loading
Ctrl+F4	Close (hide) Graphical Equalizer

Minibrowser Keyboard Shortcuts Only

Shortcut Key	Action
Alt+Left	Go back one screen
Alt+Right	Go forward one screen
Ctrl+L	Open 'Go' menu
Ctrl+O	Open Internet Location dialog box
Ctrl+R	Refresh/reload page
Ctrl+Alt+R	Update Minibrowser link list
Ctrl+F4	Close (hide) Minibrowser

Part VI
Index

Part VI Index

Creating Paint Shop Pro
Web Graphics

1999 BENJAMIN FRANKLIN AWARD WINNER!

Price: $44.99
ISBN: 0-9662889-0-4
Pages: 384
Author: Andy Shafran

- Full Color
- Foreword by
  Chris Anderson,
  VP of Marketing,
  Jasc Software

Highlights:
- Sixteen focused
  chapters that teach
  you how to
  understand layers,
  special effects, plug-ins,
  and other important Paint Shop Pro features

- Integrates with a comprehensive Website that
  contains updated information, complete examples,
  and frequently asked questions

- Detailed Web specific topics such as transparency,
  animation, web art, digital photography, scanners,
  and more

Creating
GeoCities Websites

Price: $39.99
ISBN: 0-9662889-1-2
Pages: 352
Authors: Ben Sawyer,
Dave Greely

- Full-color
- Foreword by
  David Bohnnett
  & John Rezner,
  co-founders of
  GeoCities

Highlights:
- Complete coverage of
  the free Geocities tools, services,
  and programs

- Developed in conjunction with GeoCities' technical staff

- Full color guide with dozens of templates, tricks, and
  techniques

QuicKeys Solutions
for Windows and Mac

Price: $24.99
ISBN: 0-9662889-5-5
Pages: 240
Author: Don Crabb

- Solution-focused
  format
- CD-ROM with
  valuable software
- Includes $20
  coupon towards
  QuicKeys software

Highlights:
- Teaches you how to
  get around shortcomings
  in Windows and Mac OS using QuicKeys to
  automate repetitive and complicated procedures

- Shows how to turn common or complex sets of
  commands into a single keystroke, saving you
  significant time

- Comfortable book tone for novice and power users

eBay
Online Auctions

Price: $14.95
ISBN: 0-9662889-4-7
Pages: 240
Author: Neil J. Salkind

- Glossary
- Question and Answer
  format

Highlights:
- Explains the concepts
  behind how eBay works

- Fully explains the
  bidding, buying, and
  selling process for items,
  exchanging currency, and obtaining the
  auctioned items

- Describes the different types of auctions, options
  available for bidders and sellers, and limitations of
  each format

- Shows how businesses can use eBay to buy and sell
  items affordably

MUSKA & LIPMAN

Order Form

Postal Orders:
Muska & Lipman Publishing
2645 Erie Avenue, Suite 41
Cincinnati, Ohio 45208

On-Line Orders or for more information visit:
http://www.muskalipman.com
Fax Orders:
(513) 924-9333

Qty.	Title	ISBN	Price	Total Cost
_____	Creating Paint Shop Pro Web Graphics	0-9662889-0-4	$44.99	_____
_____	Creating GeoCities Websites	0-9662889-1-2	$39.99	_____
_____	eBay Online Auctions	0-9662889-4-7	$14.95	_____
_____	MP3 Power! with Winamp	0-9662889-3-9	$29.99	_____
_____	QuicKeys Solutions for Windows and Mac	0-9662889-5-5	$24.99	_____

Subtotal _____

Sales Tax _____
(please add 6% for books shipped to Ohio addresses)

Shipping _____
($4.00 for the first book, $2.00 each additional book)

TOTAL PAYMENT ENCLOSED _____

Ship to:

Company _____

Name _____

Address _____

City _____ State _____ Zip _____ Country _____

Educational facilities, companies, and organizations interested in multiple copies of these books should contact the publisher for quantity discount information. Training manuals, CD-ROMs, electronic versions, and portions of these books are also available individually or can be tailored for specific needs.

Thank you for your order.